THE PHOENICIANS

LOST CIVILIZATIONS

The books in this series explore the rise and fall of the great civilizations and peoples of the ancient world. Each book considers not only their history but their art, culture and lasting legacy and asks why they remain important and relevant in our world today.

Already published:

The Assyrians Paul Collins
The Aztecs Frances F. Berdan
The Barbarians Peter Bogucki
Egypt Christina Riggs
The Etruscans Lucy Shipley
The Goths David M. Gwynn
The Greeks Philip Matyszak
The Hittites Damien Stone
The Inca Kevin Lane
The Indus Andrew Robinson
The Maya Megan E. O'Neil
Nubia Sarah M. Schellinger
The Persians Geoffrey Parker and Brenda Parker
The Phoenicians Vadim S. Jigoulov
The Sumerians Paul Collins
The Three Kingdoms of Korea Richard D. McBride II

THE
PHOENICIANS
LOST CIVILIZATIONS

VADIM S. JIGOULOV

REAKTION BOOKS

To Maria, Aleksandra and Anastasia

Published by Reaktion Books Ltd
Unit 32, Waterside
44–48 Wharf Road
London N1 7UX, UK
www.reaktionbooks.co.uk

First published 2021
First published in paperback 2024
Copyright © Vadim S. Jigoulov 2021

Printed and bound in India by Replika Press Pvt. Ltd

A catalogue record for this book is available from the British Library

ISBN 978 1 78914 944 9

CONTENTS

CHRONOLOGY

c. 700,000 years ago	The earliest artefacts discovered in Borj Qinnarit, near Sidon
c. 3500 BCE	The founding of Sidon
c. 3300 BCE	The founding of Byblos
c. 3000 BCE	First contacts between Byblos and Egypt
2750 BCE	The founding of Tyre (traditional date)
c. 2600–2300 BCE	First writing appears in Byblos
c. 2181–2040 BCE	Egypt's First Intermediate Period
1437 BCE	Thutmose III's raid against the Levant and the establishment of Egypt as the undefeated power in the Ancient Near East
14th century BCE	The Amarna Letters, a collection of diplomatic correspondence between pharaohs of Egypt and various rulers of the Ancient Near East

14th century BCE	The founding of Kition in Cyprus
13th century BCE	Emergence of the Proto-Canaanite script
c. 1200 BCE	The destruction of Ugarit by the Sea Peoples at the beginning of the twelfth century BCE. The emergence of the Phoenician city-states; Tyre and Sidon replace Byblos as the most pre-eminent city-states
1114–1076 BCE	Reign of Tiglath Pileser I of Assyria; Phoenicia is defeated and made part of the Assyrian Empire
11th century BCE	The emergence of a 22-letter Phoenician consonantal alphabet
c. 1000–900 BCE	The beginning of Tyrian trade expansion into the western Mediterranean
814 BCE	The founding of Carthage (traditional date)
744–727 BCE	Reign of Tiglath-Pileser III
720S BCE	Phoenicians establish first settlements in Sicily
c. mid-8th century BCE	Homer's *Iliad* and *Odyssey*
662 BCE	Tyre's rebellion against Ashurbanipal
612 BCE	The fall of Nineveh, the capital of Assyria

605 BCE	The Battle of Carchemish, in which Nebuchadnezzar II, king of Babylon, defeats the joint forces of Assyria and Egypt
585 BCE	The beginning of Nebuchadnezzar's siege of Tyre
546 BCE	Cyrus II defeats King Croesus of Lydia
539 BCE	Cyrus II's capture of Babylon
525 BCE	Conquest of Egypt by Cambyses
513 BCE	Invasion of Asia Minor by Darius I
492 BCE	Invasion of Greece by Darius I
480 BCE	Defeat of Xerxes I at the hands of the Greeks in the Battle of Salamis
c. 450 BCE	The introduction of coinage in Phoenicia
c. 449 BCE	The purported peace treaty between the Greeks and the Persians
405 BCE	The revolt in Egypt against Persia
c. 359–355 BCE	King Abdashtart I's rebellion against the Achaemenids
351–347 BCE	King Tennes's rebellion against the Achaemenids

333 BCE	The conquest of Arwad, Byblos and Sidon by Alexander the Great
332 BCE	The conquest of Tyre by Alexander the Great
331 BCE	Alexander the Great's victory over the last Achaemenid king Darius III at Gaugamela
146 BCE	Rome crushes Carthage at the end of the Third Punic War
64 BCE	The collapse of Seleucid rule and the arrival of the Roman Empire to the Near East

PROLOGUE

This book explores the history and artistic heritage of the much mythologized Phoenicians, as well as the scope of their maritime and colonizing activities in the Mediterranean. Two aspects of the book will stand out from other studies of Phoenician history: the source-focused approach; and the attention paid to the various ways that biases, ancient and modern, have contributed to widespread misconceptions about who the 'Phoenicians' were.

We will describe and analyse various sources (epigraphic, numismatic, material remains) and consider how historians have derived information about a people with little surviving literary heritage. We will also consider how the term 'Phoenicians' was one attached by outsiders, arguing that the 'Phoenicians' did not see themselves as belonging to a single ethnic or cultural entity; rather, they maintained their distinct identities as inhabitants of individual city-states (Sidon, Tyre, Byblos) that happened to be in close proximity to one another.

The Phoenicians are frequently mentioned in the Hebrew Bible, and we explore ancient Jewish views on Phoenicia and its people. Finally, we consider the Mediterranean as a place of competing political and economic agendas, where we explore Phoenician colonial activities and their interaction and competition with the Greeks and others.

The book sets out to focus on aspects of Phoenicia and the Phoenicians that deserve deeper inquiry, including a critical look at the primary sources (classical, Near Eastern and biblical), the relationship between the Phoenician and Punic worlds, and the issue of cultural appropriation of the Phoenician heritage in modernity.

A few words should be said about technical matters. In consulting sources, preference was given to English-language materials, but sources in other languages have been employed as well. In transliterations, the most commonly used, simplified variants have been preferred, making it easier for the reader to look up names and places.

The argument will emerge that we should not consider the Phoenicians as a single people, nor Phoenicia as a single polity. Although the terms 'Phoenicians' and 'Phoenicia' are used throughout these pages for the sake of convenience and simplicity, when referring to Phoenicians and Phoenicia, no such unity is implied.

ONE

THE PHOENICIAN HOMELAND: HISTORY AND ARCHAEOLOGY

The Phoenicians are a clever branch of the human race and exceptional in regard to the obligations of war and peace, and they made Phoenicia famous. They devised the alphabet, literary pursuits, and other arts too; they figured out how to win access to the sea by ship, how to conduct battle with a navy, and how to rule over other peoples; and they developed the power of sovereignty and the art of battle.

S o wrote the Roman author Pomponius Mela in his *De situ orbis* (Description of the World) in the first century CE.[1] He, like many others in the ancient world, admired the Phoenicians for their contributions to human civilization. In this chapter, we will consider the history of Phoenicia by placing it in the context of the Ancient Near East and introduce the major events, themes and topics of both the Phoenician homeland and the broader Mediterranean. Our focus will be on the period from 1200 BCE to the end of the Persian period (332 BCE) – the scholarly consensus regards these centuries as the time when the Phoenicians were most visible on the international stage, although we will briefly venture into the Hellenistic and Roman periods as well. We will also address the material culture (mostly pottery, burials and building remains), either to derive missing information or to test the evidence drawn from written sources. We will focus mostly on homeland Phoenicia, understanding that Phoenician colonizers in the Mediterranean, once having established their bases, would

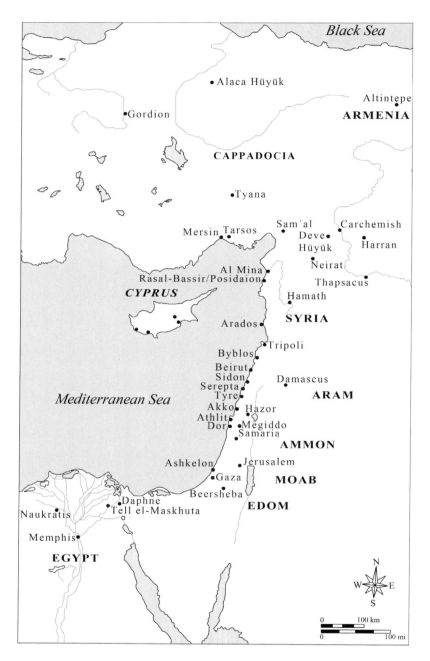

The Levant.

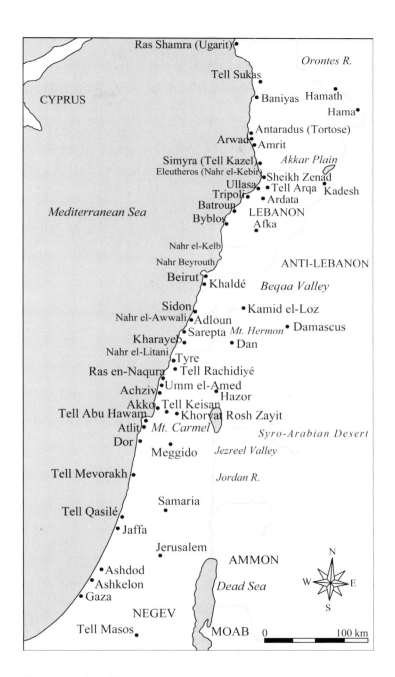

Phoenicia and neighbouring territories.

develop and sustain their new artistic and cultural traditions with only a tangential nod to the heritage of the Phoenician homeland.

Geography and climate of Phoenicia

Geography was crucial in the social, cultural and political life of Phoenicia, at least in the minds of the classical authors who envisioned and defined it. Although Graeco-Roman writers thought of Phoenicia as a land between the Gulf of Alexandretta (İskenderun, on the coast of modern Turkey) to the Gulf of Suez, in reality the Phoenician homeland occupied a relatively narrow strip of land (10 kilometres at its widest) stretching from southern Syria to northern Palestine between the Lebanon Mountains and the Mediterranean Sea. That land was further naturally divided by rivers and mountains, including the Anti-Lebanon Mountains, which run parallel to the Lebanon Mountains and which served as a natural border between Phoenicia and Syria. Protected from the east by the mountain range, the people inhabiting Phoenicia had an easier and more secure environment in which to set up and develop a system of urban settlements. The coastal location afforded additional opportunities for seafaring as the two largest polities, at least initially, Arwad and Tyre, were island city-states, providing an easy way to sail westward. Opportunities for agriculture were provided by the Beqaa Valley, rising about 1 kilometre above sea level and located 30 kilometres to the east of Beirut between the Lebanon and Anti-Lebanon mountain ranges.[2] Two rivers flowing through the valley, the Orontes and the Litani, kept it well irrigated for growing crops.

The climate of Phoenicia was more or less comparable to that of modern Lebanon, as palaeoenvironmental evidence based on the study of tree rings has suggested.[3] In essence, it was a Mediterranean climate with subtropical characteristics. In winter, storms from the Mediterranean moved eastward, bringing with them abundant precipitation (750–1,000 mm) and mild temperatures (around the low 10s Celsius), but summertime was usually hot and arid, with temperatures reaching the low 30s Celsius.[4] Temperatures and precipitation would vary depending on the location, higher altitudes receiving more rain (and snow in winter-time). Such a climate afforded the growth of many kinds of trees, including cedar. A valuable resource for shipbuilding and construction in ancient and medieval times, cedar is the symbol of Lebanon and is even prominently featured on its currency.

Phoenicia's earliest periods

The territory of what we consider Phoenicia was continuously occupied from the dawn of humanity. The earliest artefacts, sharp-ened splinters of flint dating to around 700,000 years ago, were discovered in Borj Qinnarit, near Sidon, and traces of human occupation in Lebanon have been discovered at dozens of Stone Age sites.[5] Josette Elayi points out that the three main habitat types from that period are caves, rock shelters and open-air settlements.[6] We have little concrete information about those earliest societies, but we can surmise that they were primarily hunter-gatherers. However, things started to change in the Chalcolithic period (also referred to as the Copper Age, *c.* 4500–3500 BCE). This period is best illustrated by the findings at Byblos, Sidon-Dakerman (near Sidon), Khalde II and Minet ed-Dalieh, on the Lebanese coast, and the inland sites of Mengez and Kfar Gerra.[7] From 1924 to 1975, Maurice Dunand, a French archaeologist, carried out thor-ough excavations at Byblos, the longest continuously occupied site in Lebanon. Our knowledge of the entire chronology of human occupation of the Lebanese coast is based primarily on his work there. Among the features of Byblos and other Chalcolithic sites is the emerging use of jar burials (besides plain and cave burials) accompanied by a great variety of burial goods. Another promi-nent feature of the Chalcolithic era is the organization of dwellings into private houses, silos and paved roads. Private houses were pri-marily single-room stone-walled constructions reaching a size of 6 × 9 metres and evolving either into circular or square dwellings by the end of the Chalcolithic period.[8]

Based on the close proximity of dwellings to burial sites, archaeologists conclude that the Chalcolithic societies in Lebanon were mostly sedentary, with no clear social hierarchy, as burial goods comprise symbols of power (weapons) as well as everyday goods.[9] Burial goods are indispensable for archaeologists, since valuable conclusions can be derived from even the most pedestrian objects. For Chalcolithic Phoenicia, these bone artefacts, pottery, ornaments and metal objects provide clues about human occupations, which included herding, agriculture, fishing, hunting and crafts. The grave goods also reveal that Chalcolithic pottery was rather plain and made without the use of a potter's wheel, suggesting that the pots were produced for everyday use in the shortest time possible. A gradual move away from bones to metals is characteristic of all Chalcolithic societies, and the burial goods in Phoenicia illustrate this process by the use of copper arrowheads for weapons and silver ornaments. Overall, the Chalcolithic period was a transitional time between the Neolithic period and the Bronze Age, and it introduced several technological developments that paved the way for societal progress in later eras.

Phoenicia in the Early Bronze Age

The Early Bronze Age (c. 3500–2000 BCE) is largely a mystery for the study of Phoenicia. There are 140 known sites that have not yet been excavated, and those that have been excavated have not yet been fully described.[10] The sites of Byblos and Sidon-Dakerman are again the ones that have provided most information. Jar burials are again attested, but there appear to be emerging signs of social stratification, as some burial goods include gold and silver jewellery whereas others have much more modest goods.[11] The earliest pottery from the period is still shaped by hands, but in Byblos we now encounter decorated jars and red and reddish-brown slip (a mixture of water, clay and a pigment used for decorating pottery). Stamp seals, used for marking the ownership of objects, appear on handles and shoulders of some burial jars.[12] Tools are mostly made of flint, although the use of copper and silver is present as well.

From an architectural point of view, residential dwellings mostly comprised several rooms, and the buildings themselves, constructed using either limestone or mud-brick, were arranged along narrow streets.[13] Burials shifted towards rock-cut tombs at a distance from the settlements. Such tombs were multi-use, possibly belonging to a single family or dynasty. With time, significant strides were made in pottery production in the Early Bronze Age, evidenced by the introduction of the potter's wheel and a proper kiln. These innovations in turn initiated the process of the standardization of pottery types throughout the entire region.[14] Hunting became less important because of the density of populated areas, and fishing and herding replaced it to become the major sources of food.

Egypt becomes a major player in Lebanon in the Early Bronze Age. Byblos was the main recipient of Egyptian interest from at least the beginning of the third millennium BCE, although Tyre and Sidon participated in trade with Egypt as well. The main attraction for Egypt was timber in the hinterland regions of Byblos along with resin used in mummification, although agricultural products such as wine and olive oil were also valuable imports.[15] It was not a one-way movement of goods, however, as the presence of imported materials in Byblos such as metals and obsidian hints at the wide-ranging commercial network in which the city was involved.

The end of the Early Bronze Age shows indications of instability in Byblos, and archaeological excavations reveal signs of a major calamity towards the end of the third millennium BCE (Egyptian stone vases, gifts from pharaohs to the royalty of Byblos, covered by a thick layer of ash).[16] Historians have traditionally explained that this instability was caused by raids by the Amorites, semi-nomadic tribes of Syrian origin. However, recent studies reject this proposition, since the destruction in Byblos is not present at other sites. Among the recent proposed explanations is a combination of climatic changes and intraregional competition for dwindling natural resources.[17] The tumult at Byblos did not result in its demise, however, as the city restructured and continued to exist and prosper.

Middle Bronze Age (2000–1550 BCE)

Many of the changes that started in the Early Bronze Age continued in the Middle Bronze Age. This was a generally peaceful time that witnessed developments in technology and trade among many

Phoenician sites, such as Arqa, Byblos and Sidon.[18] Byblos recovered from the destruction of the previous period and renewed its ties with Egypt, which were broken for a short time in the First Intermediate Period (c. 2150–2030 BCE).[19] The rise in population, observable even in the Early Bronze Age, intensified, leading to the emergence of new urban centres near sources of water, especially in the Akkar Plain and the Beqaa Valley. In an atmosphere of competition for natural resources, emerging mini-states controlled smaller settlements, the latter contributing agricultural products in exchange for protection from the former. The coastal sites, usually located near natural bays for the ease of anchoring ships, were situated 15–20 kilometres from each other, which most likely indicated the scope of their influence.

Much attention in this period was paid to fortifications, and the ramparts at Byblos, Kamid el-Loz, Arqa and Beirut hint at both the existing threats and the means of construction. Domestic architecture, characterized by comparatively sizeable houses with in-house ovens and basalt grinders, suggests a new level of prosperity. Religious architecture has been discovered mostly in Byblos, which boasts the largest number of Middle Bronze Age temples in Lebanon. The most famous of these is the Temple of the Obelisks, a well-preserved sanctuary built on a podium and surrounded by a courtyard. The obelisks are the central feature of the temple, and one of them bears a hieroglyphic inscription mentioning the Egyptian god Herishef-Rê, possibly the god to whom the sanctuary was dedicated. Burial customs evolved in the Middle Bronze Age, leading to the introduction of four new burial types: the shaft tomb, the pit burial, the cist burial and the built tomb.[20] Whereas adults were usually buried in these, infants and children were typically interred in storage jars, their remains within arranged in the foetal position. That and the fact that many burial goods included everyday pottery may suggest that the Middle Bronze Age saw the development of nascent beliefs in an afterlife.[21] Sometimes burial sites were reused, although jar burials were usually one-use vessels. Food offerings often accompanied burials, and they included both meat (mutton, goat, beef, pork) and bread and beer, as was the case in Byblos. Conceivably, burials were followed by funerary banquets, as burial locations in Sidon are accompanied by the remains of ovens.[22] It is not clear, though, whether the banquet was a feature among all Phoenician cities.

Pottery became diversified in the Middle Bronze Age, and decorative embellishments continued from the previous era. Pottery came in handy for exporting agricultural products, including olive oil and wine. Trade networks were busy, with goods imported from Cyprus (copper), Egypt (fish, agricultural products, gems, grave goods), Anatolia (silver) and the Aegean (bronze and its alloys and ceramics).[23] Egypt, however, traded with not only Byblos, its main partner, but Sidon. Advancements are clearly seen in metalworking, whereby weapons, domestic utensils and ornaments were fashioned using Egyptian, Syrian and Mesopotamian motifs and examples.

Late Bronze Age (1550–1200 BCE)

The political ambitions of Egypt, the Mitanni, the Hittites and Assyria of the Late Bronze Age had a sizeable impact on Phoenician cities. Thutmose III (r. 1479–1425 BCE), the sixth pharaoh of the Eighteenth Dynasty of Egypt, was determined to finally subjugate southern Lebanon, the coast of Lebanon and southern Syria, something that his grandfather Thutmose I (r. 1504–1492 BCE) had been partially successful in doing. In the 42nd year of Thutmose III's reign, a coalition of kings from the coastal cities in Palestine, Lebanon and Syria challenged Egyptian claims over their territory. In a decisive battle near the important city of Megiddo, Thutmose III was victorious, and after sixteen more campaigns he established Egypt as the undefeated power in the Ancient Near East, controlling important trade routes in the region. Egypt's power did not come unchallenged, however, and in the second half of the fifteenth century BCE, the newly minted state of Hurri-Mitanni laid claim to southern Syria. The two powers battled it out, coming to an agreement that apportioned northern Syria to the Mitanni and southern areas to Egypt. Another challenger, the Hittite Empire and its king Šuppiluliuma I (c. 1380–1346 BCE), sought to rein in Egyptian ambitions by ousting the Mitanni from northern

Syria and endangering Egypt's supremacy in Syria. The tension was resolved when the Hittites and the Egyptians divvied up their spheres of influence; the Hittites took over Ugarit and Qatna, an important trading centre of Syria, while Byblos, Damascus and the Beqaa Valley remained in Egyptian hands until the Nineteenth Dynasty (*c.* 1295–1186 BCE).

The Akkar Plain, the Beqaa Valley and the entire Mediterranean coast down to Tyre were the three major settlement areas during the Late Bronze Age. Most of the settlements transitioned to urban status, as excavations in Arqa, Beirut, Kamid el-Loz, Tyre, Sidon and Byblos demonstrate.[24] These urban centres existed in reciprocal relations with rural areas, providing administrative services in exchange for agricultural goods.[25] Given the power play of menacing empires in the region, it is unsurprising that most settlements were heavily fortified with stone city walls and towers, although these could not protect city dwellers from an overwhelming military force. In such conditions, all industrial activity had to be done close to the living quarters – excavations in Sarepta unearthed pottery kilns in the midst of dwellings.[26] The arrangements of buildings in the Late Bronze Age were determined not by their function but by their proximity to each other. Even the dead were placed close to the living, under floors and in courtyards, as excavations in Kamid el-Loz and Sarepta have indicated. As in previous eras, a variety of burial goods were placed along with the deceased, including ceramics, weapons and jewellery. As many of these objects were of everyday use, it is conceivable that they were meant to accompany the dead in the afterlife. Closely connected with belief in an afterlife are notions of eventual bodily resurrection; this concept may explain why no cremation burials have been found in Late Bronze Age Lebanon – the body had to be intact to come back from the dead.

The Egyptian influence can be observed throughout most Phoenician cities, especially in Byblos, Beirut and Tyre. In Byblos, archaeologists discovered stone blocks upon which the name Thutmose III was inscribed.[27] Similarly, a calcite vessel engraved with the name Ramesses III (r. 1184–1153 BCE) was discovered in Beirut.[28] Tyre's relations with Egypt are confirmed by the Amarna Letters, a collection of diplomatic correspondence between Egyptian pharaohs Amenhotep III (r. 1390–1352 BCE) and Akhenaten (r. 1349–1336 BCE) and various rulers of the Ancient Near East.[29] Besides Egypt, Phoenician cities also engaged in trade with the Mycenaeans and Cypriots, as suggested by pottery finds. However, Egyptian imports tend to be found in cultic and royal contexts, which suggests that they, unlike other imports, were prestige items, lifting the status of the owner by association with the powerful empire at the time. The exchange of goods between the elites of Egypt and those of the coastal cities in Lebanon was part and parcel of diplomatic gestures and international communication between royal elites.[30] In general, the interregional trade of the Levantine coastal cities with the outside world was an extension of the processes of global expansion that many polities in the ancient world engaged in during the Late Bronze Age. Levantine cities had much to offer to the outside world, including pottery, craft objects and, above all, cedar, which proved to be an enviable asset to the wood-deprived Egyptians. The desire to control these resources undoubtedly moved empires to seek control of the Lebanese territories.

Origins of the Phoenician city-states

Since 'Phoenicia' hardly existed, as the term was attached to the land by the Greeks, it is difficult, if not impossible, to speak about its origins. Instead, we can talk about the primarily coastal Levantine population that gradually organized into self-sufficient and self-governing Phoenician city-states. In general, such a population is thought by most historians to have emerged from the thirteenth-century BCE Canaanite populations indigenous to the area, as opposed to the testimony of classical sources that saw the Phoenicians as migrants into their own land. Another view, voiced by Susan Sherratt, proposes that the Phoenicians emerged from the economic collapse of 'old centralized politico-economic orders' (that is, international trade) and the arrival of a new 'decentralized economic system'.[31] Sherratt's model is similar to the theories that explain the emergence of Israel – out of the turmoil of the

Late Bronze Age there appeared a number of polities, and if we extend the same paradigm to the Phoenician city-states, it would make sense of how and why all the new polities in the Levant appeared at that juncture.[32] Ann Killebrew, noting the emergence of a distinct Phoenician material culture that combined indigenous Levantine elements with small infusions of non-Levantine elements, describes Phoenicia as 'a confederation of merchant communities of predominantly indigenous populations residing along the central and northern Levantine littoral, with a similar material culture and language, who likely self-identified in terms of their cities and family lineage'.[33]

The disruption of the Late Bronze Age is attested both in ancient texts and in the archaeological record. For the state of affairs before this, we can consult the Amarna Letters, which mention the Phoenician city-states already in existence. The evidence from the tablets from Ugarit, an important port on the northern coast of Syria, is also instructive. These tablets, addressing the events of the fourteenth to the twelfth centuries BCE, also mention the Phoenician cities of Beirut, Sidon, Tyre, Akko and Byblos. Although the texts from Ugarit are mostly records of commercial transactions, they nevertheless provide a wealth of historical information. Finally, the fictitious Report of Wenamun (also spelled as Wen-Amon), a priest from the Temple of Amun at Karnak, also sheds some light on the events at the end of the Late Bronze Age, and it touches upon the city-state of Byblos. The report tells of Wenamun's journey to Byblos to secure timber to build a ceremonial ship for Amun. However, Wenamun falls short of the finances needed to procure the wood, indicating the feeble and fractured nature of the state of Egypt.[34] Although the Report is dated to the tenth century BCE, it still accurately reflects the prevailing concerns of that period, with a declining Egypt playing a major role in the narrative.

The turmoil in the Near East around 1200 BCE is most often associated with the arrival of the 'Sea Peoples' who are mentioned in Egyptian records. Other factors, including natural ones, could have contributed to the upheaval as well. Whatever caused the disruption, the result was the weakened influence of Egypt on the

Levant, the collapse of the Hittite Empire and the destruction of many states in the Aegean. The coastal city-ports of the Levantine littoral weathered the storms rather well, which led to their expansion and rise in influence in trade and maritime exploits. Archaeology, although hampered by a lack of researchable sites, generally confirms the status of the Phoenician city-states. Tell Kazel (ancient Simyra) in the Akkar Plain, for example, shows continuity of material culture remains from the Late Bronze Age to the Iron Age, pointing to the absence of the destruction one would expect from the turmoil of the 1200s. The same continuity has been observed in Sarepta, Tyre and Akko as well.[35] As a result of surviving the turbulence of the Late Bronze Age, the Phoenician cities returned to their political, cultural and economic independence and self-sufficiency. Politically, the Phoenician cities rose in prominence in the broader regional structure. Also, finally being freed from Egyptian influence, the Phoenician city-states could now conduct their affairs independently. Additionally, the events of the Late Bronze Age led to a reshuffling of regional powers, some diminishing and others rising. All these factors led to the establishment of what we now refer to as the Phoenician city-states. The transition from the Late Bronze Age to the Iron Age also brought some structural changes in the broader Mediterranean, and they helped shape Phoenicia into a maritime superpower.

From the very beginning, the institution of kingship was the cornerstone of the administrative and religious set-up of the Phoenician city-states.[36] Phoenician kings and queens held their positions for life, and they made extraordinary efforts to keep royal dynasties from breaking up or being replaced by outsiders, including marrying within the same family and instituting co-regencies if the heir to the throne was too young to rule. One of the major roles that kings played was soliciting the assurance of divine protection through the building and upkeep of temples, and by acting as the link between humans and gods. At the same time, there was no implied understanding that royal status was imbued with divinity, as was believed by peoples in other regions of the Near East such as Persia and Egypt.[37] Another area of concern for the Phoenician kings and queens was international diplomacy, as they tried to navigate, often masterfully, the tumultuous political world of the Ancient Near East. Phoenician royalty were also closely engaged with the military affairs of their city-state, participating, when necessary, in action. Finally, royalty were responsible for the maintenance of state enterprise as part of a palace economy system. In the Iron Age, such systems gradually gave way to civic economic systems, where privatization was a much more manageable way for the royalty to avoid the burden of maintaining ownership and control of economic enterprises (mostly maritime), focusing instead on the much more convenient and pleasant task of deriving dividends and taxation revenues from the private sector.[38]

Phoenicia in the Iron Age (1200–586 BCE)

By the Iron Age, Phoenicia's 'cultural boundaries' extended from north to south to include the following polities: Arwad and the Akkar Plain, Tell Kazel, Beirut, Byblos, Sidon, Sarepta, Tyre, Tell Keisan and Akko.[39] Sometimes Dor, lying southwest of Mount Carmel, is included in this list because of the correspondence of its material culture to Phoenician archaeological finds, but such similarity ended in the ninth century BCE when Dor fell into the Israelite domain of influence. Furthermore, Assyrian written records indicate that Iron Age Phoenicia was thought to consist of two clusters. The northern cluster coalesced around the cities from Arwad to Byblos, and the southern group comprised Sidon and Tyre, stretching southward towards Akko.[40] In the southern group, it was the city of Tyre that held pre-eminence as the most economically powerful city-state, owing to its overseas expansion. Tyre may have formed a political and economic coalition with Sidon, since some iconographic representations and epigraphic materials from Assyria lump Tyrians and Sidonians together, and no kings of Sidon are mentioned before the seventh century BCE.[41] Further, some settlements in the Mediterranean have been traced not only to the usual Tyre but to Sidon as well.

Aside from occasional inscriptions that mention the names of the Tyrian and Byblian kings, the main sources of historical information are the records of empires that swept through the Ancient

Near East.[42] Of course, the ancient Near Eastern rulers mentioned competitors mainly in the context of gloating over their demise and celebrating their own victories, and such reports should be taken with a pinch of salt. However, when the ideological impulse is more subdued and the coverage concerns mainly economic and supply issues, there would have been little incentive for the writers (or whoever did the writing for them) to embellish reality.

Tiglath-Pileser I (r. 1115–1077 BCE) is the first Assyrian ruler to mention the Phoenician city-states. A report tells of how he went to Lebanon to 'cut timber of cedars for the temple of Anu and Adad'.[43] In the same document, it mentions that he received tribute from Byblos, Sidon and Arwad and went on a fishing trip off the coast of Arwad during which he killed a 'sea-horse', possibly a narwhal (or a hippopotamus).[44] Tiglath-Pileser I revitalized the Assyrian Empire, embodying the opposite of the complacent and ineffective kings who had come before him. He added to his empire through a series of military campaigns in the Ancient Near East. Another Assyrian king, Ashurnasirpal II (r. 883–859 BCE), also reports collecting tribute from Tyre, Sidon and Byblos, among other territories, consisting of 'gold, silver, tin, copper, copper containers, linen garments with multicoloured trimmings, large and small monkeys, ebony, boxwood, ivory from walrus tusk',[45] and, of course, the inhabitants of those cities embraced his feet in a gesture of compliance. Overall, the Assyrians were content with exacting tribute from the Levantine cities and receiving those subjects' continued loyalty, and representatives from Tyre and Sidon were even invited to Ashurnasirpal's coronation at his palace in Kalhu (Nimrud).[46]

Overall, the tenth and ninth centuries BCE saw the Phoenicians left to their own devices, and Assyrian kings such as Tiglath-Pileser I were mostly satisfied with collecting tribute from the newly flourishing Phoenician city-states (other Assyrian kings who reported receiving tribute are Shalmaneser III, r. 859–824 BCE, and Adad-nirari III, r. 810–783 BCE).

Assyrian sentiments changed in the middle of the eighth century BCE. Starting with Tiglath-Pileser III (r. 745–727 BCE), the Assyrian thirst for tighter control of its empire led to renewed attempts to subjugate more lands militarily. As a result, Phoenicia often fell victim to political games in the region. When several Levantine kings decided to form a coalition to repel Tiglath-Pileser III's expansion, Hiram II (r. 739–730 BCE) of Tyre joined it. The consequences were dire – many instigators paid a dear price for the revolt, and Tyre was besieged and obligated to pay a heavy tribute to Assyria. Sennacherib (r. 704–681 BCE) also received 'sumptuous gifts' from the kings of Sidon, Arwad and Byblos in his campaign in the Levant.[47] However, Luli, king of Sidon (r. 728–695 BCE), managed to flee to Cyprus and hide there, afraid of Sennacherib's 'terror-inspiring glamor'.[48] The Assyrian king installed Ethbaal (Tubalu) as Luli's replacement and imposed tribute on him. Sidon's wealth at that time troubled yet another Assyrian king, Esarhaddon (r. 680–669 BCE), who went on a Syro-Palestinian campaign of his own and destroyed Sidon, beheaded its king Abdimilkutte and deported many Sidonians to Assyria.[49] In the campaign's aftermath, Baal I (r. 680–660 BCE), king of Tyre, was obligated to pay heavy tribute, but Esarhaddon, possibly remunerating Tyre for its support against Sidon, granted Tyre the ports of Akko and Dor, the entire Philistine coast, Byblos, and mountain towns, in addition to the provinces of Simyra and Sidon.[50] Tyre's tribute to Assyria was very likely in the form of conscripted service rendered to the king, as it is reported that Baalu I of Tyre, Milki-ašapa of Byblos and Mattan-Baal of Arwad participated in the erection of Esarhaddon's palace in Nineveh.[51]

The last significant ruler of Assyria, Ashurbanipal (r. 668–627 BCE), continued the campaigns of his predecessors, securing all the lands on the way south to Egypt. He sought to build coalitions, but change was in the air. The empire was bursting at the seams, and numerous polities burdened by unmanageable tribute sought to rebel against the great king. This time it was Tyre that was the principal recipient of Ashurbanipal's wrath, when it rebelled against him in 662 BCE.[52] He marched against it, and Baalu I eventually submitted to the Assyrian king, 'kissed his feet', was forced to pay a heavy tribute, and gave up his own daughters and nieces to provide 'menial services' to the king.[53]

Assyrian power began quickly to unravel in the aftermath of Ashurbanipal's death in 627 BCE (or 631 BCE, according to other sources). A family feud over claims to the kingship left the empire vulnerable to the ever-present Egyptian danger. Regions started to break away, thus further incapacitating the once mighty empire. In 612 BCE, Nineveh, the capital of the Assyrian Empire, was sacked by the joint forces of Babylonians and Medes; the Battle of Carchemish in 605 BCE, when Nebuchadnezzar II, king of Babylon, defeated the joint forces of Assyria and Egypt, dealt the final blow to the dying empire.

Free from obligations to pay tribute, the Phoenician city-states could finally breathe and recuperate, at least for a little while, until they became subject to other empires' vociferous ambitions. Babylonian sources do not specifically mention what was transpiring in Phoenicia in the early days of Nebuchadnezzar II's reign, but Flavius Josephus, a Roman-Jewish historian from the first century CE, mentions deportations of 'the captive Jews, and Phoenicians, and Syrians' and their relocations to 'the most proper places in Babylonia'.[54] Josephus might be reflecting a common understanding that Nebuchadnezzar besieged Tyre for thirteen years starting in 585 BCE (although the date is disputed), which reportedly culminated in the deportation of Tyrian royal elite, including the king of Tyre Ittobaal III (also spelled Ithobaal), to Babylon; however, the city returned to its general autonomous status in subsequent years under the leadership of King Baal II (572–563 BCE), a sycophantic ruler installed by Nebuchadnezzar.

Overall, though, the Babylonian period was relatively quiet for Phoenicia, a time of prosperity and continued commercial activity. The Phoenicians engaged in lively trade with Babylon, and they were even employed as artisans at the royal court. Babylon did, however, appropriate Phoenicia's cedar trade, and timber from the Levantine cities was transported through the mountains to the capital of the empire, partially to be used in the construction of Nebuchadnezzar's own palace, with additional contributions by the kings of Tyre, Sidon and Arwad.[55]

Phoenician economy in the Iron Age

Economic competition, along with occasional cooperation, was the hallmark of relations between the Phoenician city-states, and the ebb and flow of Tyre's and Sidon's fortunes illustrates this very well. Sidon emerged the economic victor in the aftermath of the disruption of the Late Bronze Age, when it was the more powerful of the two in the late twelfth and eleventh centuries BCE, assisted by its geographic location at a distance from the weakened Egypt, with whom Tyre was enmeshed in increasingly burdensome trade relations. In the following few centuries (900–600 BCE), Tyre's fortunes improved as Tyrian trade expansion brought forth tangible economic benefits. A few important developments propelled Tyre's economic fortunes. The destruction of Ugarit by the Sea Peoples at the beginning of the twelfth century BCE shifted the centre of trade towards the south.[56] Additionally, Egypt's position left Tyre and other Phoenician city-states to carry out their affairs more independently. Finally, the lack of competitors left Tyre in the enviable position of being the supplier of valuable resources (copper, silver and tin) to the reigning empires in the region. However, in the mid-sixth century BCE, Tyre was recuperating from the wounds dealt by Nebuchadnezzar's siege of the city, while Sidon, unscathed by the Babylonian raids, was quietly building a navy that would go on to prove superbly useful to the Persian kings and contribute to its status as the most powerful economic and political city-state in the Levant.

Several proposals exist to explain why the Phoenicians ventured westward in the Assyrian period. Some of them look to the economic pressure on the Levantine polities from the Assyrian imperial authorities and the associated heavy tribute that made them seek new markets and resources.[57] Others see the temporary Assyrian decline of the late ninth century as providing a stimulus for not only the Phoenicians but other polities to seek engagement in the western Mediterranean.[58] With the renewal of Assyrian ambitions under Tiglath-Pileser III, trading opportunities in both the Levant and the Mediterranean increased, and so did chances to avoid paying tribute to the Assyrian authorities. Phoenician, mostly

Tyrian, overseas colonies enjoyed not being subject to Assyrian taxation, but it also led to the prosperity of the Levantine city-states.

Archaeology of the Iron Age

Archaeologists usually divide the Iron Age in the Levant into two distinct periods, Iron I (*c.* 1200–900 BCE) and Iron II (*c.* 900–600 BCE). The earliest Iron Age I strata in Lebanon are poorly excavated and scarcely described in scholarly literature. One of the best excavated sites is Sarepta Area II, and historians often extend their conclusions from the site to the entirety of Phoenicia, including that of its continuity, without major destruction, from the Late Bronze Age to Iron I.[59] In Iron II, significantly more cities (Tyre, Sarepta, Dor, Tell Abu Hawam and Tell Keisan) have yielded material culture remains, including pottery samples and architecture.[60]

During Iron I, most of the coastal areas (Tyre, Sarepta) were engaged in various forms of industrial activity, mostly pottery production, which became more sophisticated with the addition of new decorative styles.[61] Moreover, production of storage jars for the transportation of liquids and grains increased in response to burgeoning trade on the coast. Towards the beginning of Iron II, Tyre and Sidon transitioned primarily to the distribution of products and raw natural resources that originated outside Phoenicia, thus gaining the status of great merchants. Among the products that were produced in Tyre in Iron II were pottery and precious metals, as suggested by the archaeological discovery of a sizeable industrial quarter dating from the tenth and eighth centuries BCE.[62] Sarepta has also provided valuable archaeological information, including the introduction of the 'header-and-stretcher' building technique, the discovery of large quantities of Cypriot pottery, and the inauguration of an industrial zone with many kilns and olive presses. Excavations of Beirut revealed several cycles of destruction and abandonment in Iron II and a fortified citadel towering over a low-lying city. Inland sites in the Beqaa Valley (Kamid el-Loz, for example) do not appear to have had much going for them and are mostly represented by small rural settlements of very modest one-room houses.

Besides written sources, Tyre's hegemony in the Levant in Iron II is supported by several archaeological discoveries. In Tel Dor, archaeological strata dated to the tenth century BCE and later reveal a typical Tyrian technique of 'ashlar masonry with a fill of stones between the pillars'.[63] At the site of Tell Keisan, among the Tyrian markers dated to Iron II are bichrome pottery, ashlar masonry, and other artefacts similar to the material culture of Tyre. The same phenomenon has been observed at the site of Khorvat Rosh Zayit, which is thought to be the 'Cabul' mentioned in biblical sources. Besides Phoenician architectural elements and pottery, archaeologists at the site discovered weights, seals and stamps, which suggests that Khorvat Rosh Zayit was an administrative and processing centre concerned with producing, packaging and distributing agricultural products on behalf of Tyre.

Very little can be said of funerary practices as no tombs dated to Iron I have been discovered in Lebanon. The situation is different for Iron II, however, as a few necropolises from that period allow us to draw some conclusions regarding the social and religious dimensions of disposing of the dead. One of the largest burial grounds dating from the tenth to the seventh centuries BCE is the Al-Bass necropolis on the coast, about 2 kilometres to the east from the previously existing island of Tyre.[64] The cemetery was the principal burial ground for Tyre, which politically controlled a few settlements within a 15-kilometre radius (Tell Rachidiyé, Qrayeh, Qasmieh, Khirbet Silm, Joya and Qana),[65] along with several more remote cities (Achziv, Akko and, perhaps, Sidon).[66] About 500 square metres of the necropolis were excavated between 1997 and 2008, revealing more than three hundred cremation urns. The cemetery was used mostly for burying the remains of adults, and María Eugenia Aubet concludes that children 'were not entitled to full membership in the funerary community'.[67]

Archaeologists identified three major types of burials at the necropolis. The first, a single-urn grave, comprised an urn accompanied by considerable funerary offerings, which may signal the individual's high social status. The second type, a double-urn grave, consists of two jugs, one containing the ashes of the deceased and the other filled with their charred bones along with personal

Location of the Al-Bass cemetery in Tyre.

possessions. It is apparent that these burials were accompanied by a ritual whereby the ashes and bones would be separated after the cremation. In the third type, double-urn graves would be clustered, 'forming a horizontal development of the burial space'.[68] Such an arrangement hints at the existence of cemetery plots that were set aside for families. Based on the archaeological evidence, Aubet proposes the following sequence of burial practices at Al-Bass: 1) a cremation ceremony accompanied by a ritual banquet (*marzeaḥ*) around the grave and the sacrifice of domestic animals; 2) ceremonial placing of the remains in the urn(s) and burying them, representing a rite of passage from the world of the living to the abode of the dead; 3) performance of fire rituals after the tomb was covered with dirt; and 4) placement of a stone funerary stele to commemorate the place where the deceased was buried. The protruding stele would serve not only as a grave marker but as a sacred place for remembering and venerating the dead. Thus the funerary traditions and belief in an afterlife represented at the necropolis of Al-Bass demonstrate a clear development from previous eras.

Reliefs of Achaemenid warriors in Persepolis, *c.* 5th century BCE.

The Al-Bass necropolis joins other cemeteries found in Iron II Phoenicia in illustrating the various means of disposing of the dead, including rock-cut tombs, family chambers and sarcophagi. Also, we can observe clear social stratification at some of them, for example Sidon, where the elites were usually buried in rock-cut tombs and sarcophagi. There are hints of such stratification at Al-Bass as well, suggested by single-urn burials.

The Neo-Babylonian period, sandwiched between the Assyrian and Persian periods, is very difficult to define from an archaeological point of view. First, it is just a sliver of time in the grand scheme of things, lasting less than seventy years. Second, there would have to be a drastic change in material culture from the preceding period to trace any transformations that might have happened from 605 BCE to 539 BCE, but none have been detected.

One of the more remarkable events in the Neo-Babylonian period, the Siege of Tyre by Nebuchadnezzar II, which lasted from about 585 to 572 BCE, left no trace in the archaeological record. Among the undisputed remains of that period is a series of inscriptions left by Nebuchadnezzar in northern Lebanon. The decrease in pottery imports from Cyprus and Assyria and the increase in imports from Greece are also indicative of the region becoming an important player in the broader Mediterranean economic exchange, something that would become an important factor in Achaemenid Phoenicia.

Phoenicia in the Achaemenid period (539–332 BCE)

It can be argued that Cyrus II's capture of Babylon around 539 BCE ushered in the Persian Empire, although his reign actually started in 550 BCE, lasting until his death in 530 BCE.[69] Although we call the empire 'Achaemenid', the earliest mention of the family of the Achaemenes comes from the time of Darius I (r. 522–486 BCE), who traced his genealogy to them in the famous Behistun inscription. The sequence of the Great Kings (or Kings of Kings), as the Persians referred to them, includes Cyrus II, Cambyses II, Bardiya, Darius I, Xerxes I, Artaxerxes I, Xerxes II, Sogdianus, Darius II,

Behistun inscription of Darius I, r. 522–486 BCE.

Artaxerxes II, Artaxerxes III, Artaxerxes IV and Darius III. Major events that took place in the Persian period include the conquest of Egypt by Cambyses (525 BCE); the invasion of Asia Minor (513 BCE) and Greece (492 BCE) by Darius I; the defeat of Xerxes I at the hands of the Greeks in the Battle of Salamis (480 BCE); the purported peace treaty between the Greeks and the Persians around 449 BCE; the satrap revolts of the fourth century BCE; and, finally, Alexander the Great's victory over the last Achaemenid king, Darius III, in 331 BCE at Gaugamela. In various ways, these events served as a background for the history of Phoenicia and the entire Levantine coast in the Persian period.

Although the same paucity of material remains and epigraphic evidence characterizes Persian period Phoenicia, we get an additional boost from classical sources, which provide more colour and specificity compared to previous eras. They allow us to distinguish between the three unique periods in the history of Achaemenid Phoenicia. From the initial years of Cyrus II's reign to the early years of Darius (the period from about 559 to 522 BCE), not much happened in Phoenicia as it was a transitional stage from the previous Neo-Babylonian reign, and classical sources treat it as relatively smooth and uneventful. In the second distinct period, lasting from the early days of Darius's administration to the beginning of the reign of Xerxes – about 522 to 486 BCE – the Phoenician city-states found themselves grouped with cities on the island of Cyprus in the so-called Fifth Satrapy (or 'Transeuphrates' Satrapy). It was during this period that Sidon emerged as the most significant Phoenician city-state because of its assistance to Persia, including, among other events, in the suppression of the Ionian revolt in 499 BCE. Other Tyrian city-states assisted Persia as well; Herodotus reports that Tyre's fleet played an important role in supporting Cambyses's operation against Egypt in 525 BCE. After a few years, another distinct period (about 405 to 333 BCE) was ushered in by the increasing uneasiness of the Phoenician city-states at their association with once-dominant Persia. As formal control was dwindling and as new political and commercial opportunities opened in the west, the Phoenician city-states reoriented their kingdoms towards Greece. The Persian

Empire's dominance was challenged by several disturbances, including the revolt in Egypt of 405 BCE, which ended with the Upper Nile Delta coming under the leadership of Amyrtaeus, an Egyptian royal family member. The loss of Egypt encouraged other satrapies to rebel, which led to the satrapal revolt of the 360s BCE. Although the Phoenician city-states reportedly formed a coalition, only Sidon revolted against Persia. First it was King Abdashtart I, whose rebellion against the Achaemenids lasted a few years (r. 359–355 BCE) until it was quelled by Persia, with large numbers of Sidonians exiled to Susa and Babylon but the king allowed to remain on the throne. His replacement, Tennes (r. 351–347 BCE), although initially loyal to the Persians, also revolted, but his rebellion was short-lived as Artaxerxes III brutally eliminated it. This time, the Persians, undoubtedly exhausted by the treacherous Sidonians, installed a foreign-born king, possibly Evagoras II of Salamis. The scheme worked, and Sidon returned to its practice of assisting the Persians in their naval affairs. Gaining economic and political confidence, the Sidonians eventually drove out all foreign rulers from their city-state and once again installed a local king, Abdashtart II (r. 342–333 BCE), who was eventually deposed by Alexander the Great.

Phoenician economy under the Achaemenids

The transition from the Babylonian to the Persian period was relatively smooth for the Phoenician city-states as they could maintain their independent political and economic trajectories, albeit under the patronage and oversight of the Persian authorities. They also continued their age-old competition in the economic sphere, vying for lucrative contracts with imperial authorities and attempting to secure new economic venues. The two major polities that were visible during that period were Tyre and Sidon, with the latter emerging as an economic powerhouse that extended its reach along almost the entire Levantine coast.

One of the contributing factors for the rise of Sidon was its active help and participation in Persian naval confrontations with Greece. Sidon supplied ships and sailors, likely benefiting not only financially but politically. Their efforts were richly rewarded by Persian kings, who were said to maintain a *paradeisos* (an oasis, or park for relaxation; from which is derived the word 'paradise') in Sidon, as Diodorus Siculus reports in the first century BCE.[70] Sidonian support of the Persian campaigns followed from the conscious decision on the part of Sidonian royalty to carry out a policy of 'compliance and non-resistance' in relation to the rule of the Persian kings. Margaret Cool Root and others have noted the existence in the Achaemenid Empire of a deliberate artistic programme meant to extol and propagate Persian might through a series of meaningful artistic elements and images.[71] The Sidonians were able to capitalize on this by using the same iconography used in Achaemenid Persia to proclaim their compliance with imperial authorities and to establish themselves as loyal and committed subjects. One of the more visible means was via coinage, on which Sidonians deliberately adopted prestigious Persian symbols of power and divinely sanctioned rule.

Sidonian pre-eminence in the Persian period affected the region in several ways. The cult of its city-gods Astarte and Eshmun spread far and wide, not only among other Phoenician city-states but throughout the broader Levant as well. So pervasive was Sidonian political and economic power in the Levant that even biblical writers, operating mostly in the Persian period, voiced their discontent with it by casting Sidon in a mostly negative light.

Phoenician cities maintained a network of economic interests, and both Tyre and Sidon imported Greek pottery and Egyptian sarcophagi. Of the two, Tyre appears to have had stronger relations with Greece as Tyrian coinage frequently featured Greek iconographic motifs such as the owl and borrowed freely from Athenian numismatics.

Political organization of the Phoenician city-states in the Persian period

The Phoenician city-states were loosely organized by the preceding Neo-Babylonian Empire, but in the Persian period imperial authorities took steps to form a confederacy that lasted through the first quarter of the fifth century BCE. Around 482 BCE, the Phoenician city-states were united under a more structured unit headed by Sidon, undoubtedly to reflect its contribution to the Persian military campaigns. Diodorus Siculus even reports that the leaders of the three cities, Sidon, Tyre and Arwad, founded the city of Tripolis in the fourth century BCE, where they would hold their 'common council' on important matters.[72]

The hallmark of the administrative system of Phoenicia under the Persians was a state of semi-autonomy granted to individual city-states whereby they could carry out their political and economic affairs largely unhindered by imperial authorities – something that I have previously termed 'managed autonomy' in trying to convey the sense of uniqueness that characterized various Phoenician city-states.[73] There was no uniform monetary system, religious homogeneity or economic union among those cities – the Persians allowed them to conduct their business independently, without burdensome oversight. Any Achaemenid 'influence' took the form of spreading and maintaining the ideologically infused imperial iconography, which was most visible in Phoenicia through distinctly Persian architectural styles. In such a laissez-faire environment, there was unlikely to be any Persian administrative presence as there was no need to control the generally compliant royal houses, which were mainly concerned with maintaining and expanding their trade networks in the Mediterranean and managing the Persian fleet that was docked on the Phoenician coast. If troubles did take place, they were singular occurrences, as was the case with Tennes – an attempt by an individual king to stand up to the Persian authorities and to assert closer ties with Athens.

Archaeology of Persian Phoenicia

The same continuity of the material culture of the Phoenician city-states from the Assyrian to the Neo-Babylonian periods can be observed in the Persian period. The four major kingdoms that existed from the ninth century BCE (Arwad, Byblos, Sidon and Tyre) continued to exist in the Persian period, although the Phoenician territory expanded from Tell Sukas in northern Syria to the cities of Dor and Jaffa and the Plain of Sharon in the south.[74] Many Phoenician cities had a bipartite composition, comprising a fortified upper part and a lower city; such a two-part arrangement is present at the sites of Tell Arqa, Beirut, Tell el-Burak and Byblos.[75] There was a clear functional division between different parts of the city, some playing a more pronounced economic role, others serving as residential quarters; a separate, distant area was always reserved for a necropolis. A new construction method appears to emerge in the late Iron Age, referred to as a 'pier and rubble' technique – ashlar pillars with rubble filling in the gaps – and it was widely spread in Achaemenid Phoenicia. In burials, inhumation and cremation were used for both children and adults. The dead were often buried in vertical shafts, stone-lined pits or natural caves.[76] Burial goods often indicated the social status of the deceased person, with more elaborate objects accompanying more well-to-do persons. Social stratification can also be observed through elaborately decorated sarcophagi from the Persian period discovered in Sidon, including the Satrap Sarcophagus, the Lycian Sarcophagus, the Mourning Women Sarcophagus and the Sarcophagus of Abdalonymos (the so called 'Alexander Sarcophagus').[77] Also, new religious structures appeared in the Persian period, the two most prominent being the Temple of Eshmun at Bostan esh-Sheikh, near Sidon, and the Maabed complex at Amrit.

Besides this continuity, some distinct developments were under way in Persian Phoenicia, including increasing cultural influence on the Palestinian coast at the beginning of the fifth century BCE. Quite a few explanations for this process have been advanced, including trade monopolies granted to Tyre and Sidon by the Persian authorities to curtail Greek merchants from accessing inland markets.[78] Another emerging phenomenon in Achaemenid Phoenicia was the increasing atmosphere of 'syncretism, eclecticism and multiculturalism'.[79] Material remains strongly suggest that populations of the Phoenician city-states were remarkably open to borrowed elements, mostly Greek and Persian, in their architectural styles, iconography of coinage and preference for Greek pottery imports. Undoubtedly, the political situation in the region played a major role in such cultural flexibility. As Egyptian political

Alexander Sarcophagus of King Abdalonymos, late 4th century BCE.

influence declined, so did the adoption of indigenous Egyptian stylistic elements. Then, the newly emerged Persian Empire and its
artistic cache made an impact on its imperial subjects. As time went
on, Greek styles and products gained popularity, almost certainly
owing to high levels of Greek trade in the region and the orientation towards Athens as the Persian Empire was weakening in the
fourth century BCE. It was especially evident during the reign of
Abdashtart I of Sidon (also known by his Greek name, Straton;
c. 365–352 BCE) when the Athenians erected a stele in his honour on
the Acropolis with a decree granting him and his people whatever
they needed. Old animosities gave way to the new realities, and the
Sidonians quickly realigned themselves with Athens, sensing the
coming political demise of Persia.

Phoenicia in Hellenistic times and beyond

Alexander's victory over the Achaemenids can be dated either to
331 BCE, when he defeated Darius III, or to his march of 330 BCE

towards Persepolis, which resulted in the complete destruction of the city and the main royal palace. Whatever the date, in the aftermath of the Persian defeat the Phoenician city-states gradually disappeared; but their cultures continued to exist for centuries.[80] Historians frequently evoke the concept of 'Hellenization' to describe the process of instilling and adopting Greek language, culture and institutions, and one can argue that Phoenicia was subject to those developments as well. In recent years, however, the concept has received some criticism, with detractors arguing that we should instead concentrate more on cultural and economic exchange and networks rather than a one-way process of the imposition of Greek traits and customs on conquered populations.[81] Such an understanding, applied to Phoenicia, allows a more nuanced picture of the coastal Levantine city-states, where various aspects of continuity and change were organically at play.

Many of the processes that started in the Persian period and even earlier continued uninterrupted in the Phoenician city-states, but they could not remain unaffected by the changing geopolitical situation, new ideas and, in Corinne Bonnet's words, 'ways of being'.[82] Alexander's conquest of the Achaemenid Empire and the Near East encountered established and flourishing commercial networks, existing administrative polities and intercultural exchange. Even while under the aegis of the Persians, in the fourth century BCE, the Phoenicians established numerous ties with the Aegean. In some ways, it was a realignment towards the west conditioned by an increasingly chaotic Achaemenid Empire far from its prime. Unsurprisingly, the royal houses of many Phoenician city-states (Arwad, Byblos and Sidon) embraced Alexander's rule wholeheartedly, although some reshuffling had to be done. In Sidon, Alexander the Great replaced the king with a gardener by the name of Abdalonymos, who happened to have some royal blood in him. Tyre resisted, but Alexander's famed siege, described by Arrian,[83] put an end to that in 332 BCE. The story deserves a mention here. When approaching Tyre, Alexander expressed his wish to make a sacrifice to Heracles of Tyre (the Phoenician god Melqart). However, the Tyrians were not willing to let a Macedonian within their city, fearful that it would bring forth war. Alexander, of course, was displeased; he assembled his companions and commanders and made a speech before them, emphasizing the importance of conquering the entire Phoenician coast so that his march towards Egypt would not be deterred. That very night, according to Arrian, Alexander had a dream in which Heracles welcomed him to the city. That omen effectively sealed the fate of Tyre, although everyone understood that it would not be an easy feat since Tyre was an island, located approximately 800 metres off the coast, and was heavily fortified. Besides, the Tyrians still had plenty of ships at their disposal to combat any Greek incursion. Then the Macedonian ruler made the brilliant and bold decision to build a causeway from the mainland to the island, through which he finally overpowered Tyre. As a result, around 30,000 Tyrians were sold into slavery. Another author, Quintus Curtius Rufus, using earlier Greek sources, mentions that 6,000 Tyrian fighters were slaughtered in the fortifications and another 2,000 were crucified along the beach.[84]

Notwithstanding the Siege of Tyre, Alexander was not interested in imposing an iron rule over his conquered territories. He was respectful of the heritage of the Persians (his introduction of *proskynesis*, a Persian custom of bowing before a superior, comes to mind), and it was not in his character to bring humiliation and destruction to Persia's former domains. Moreover, he did not have to impose anything similar to a Greek *polis* in the Phoenician city-states because, even during the Persian period, Phoenician kings turned away from strict monarchy to include councils of members of the nobility and people's assemblies, inspired by the example of Carthage, which nurtured these institutions.[85] We should also note that in the Hellenistic period, Phoenician dynasties quickly faded into non-existence within several generations, and the Phoenician cities became integrated into first the Ptolemaic and then the Seleucid empires, thus losing the status of a 'city-state'.[86] With the erosion of the institution of royalty, nobility featured more prominently in Hellenistic Phoenicia. Because of the cosmopolitan atmosphere characteristic of that period, nobility was especially attuned to changing sentiments. Their approach was bifold, on the one hand embracing the dominant Greek 'winds of change' and seeking legitimacy in their traditional association with powerful Phoenician ancestors on the other.[87]

Coinage from Hellenistic Phoenicia shows how a fragile balance between local traditions and the larger Hellenistic world was maintained through the choice of iconography. Since coming to power, Alexander had seized all minting authority, and Phoenician workshops were producing coinage at the direction and under the supervision of imperial authorities. The first coins featured Alexander's name in Greek along with the traditional Greek symbols of Athena and Nike in gold, Heracles and Zeus in silver and Heracles alone in bronze. At the same time, the names of local kings, either in Greek or Phoenician (or both), were also found on those coins, symbolizing the hierarchy and balance of power.[88] Later Ptolemaic coins transitioned to the Egypt-inspired iconography of Ptolemy and deified Alexander to project an image of power and authority that extended over Phoenicia. The Seleucids had a different take on authority as they allowed greater autonomy to the Phoenician cities. So the Phoenician alphabet returned to Phoenician coinage to designate the date of production. The tutelary goddess Tyche (a generic patroness of the city) served as a bridge between Greek and Phoenician concepts of a city's power. Around the middle of the second century BCE, a few Phoenician cities launched an intraregional bronze coin, which featured Antiochus IV on the obverse and the name of the city of the reverse.[89] Through various means, the Phoenicians attempted to preserve their heritage in the changing political landscape.

In language and religion, the same combination of continuity and change was under way. The Greek language replaced Phoenician dialects, although inscriptions in Phoenician were still produced until at least the first century BCE.[90] Many Phoenicians adopted Greek names, although some continued to give their children traditional names. In the religious sphere, the Hellenistic period brought about a process through which Phoenicians willingly and tastefully rethought their traditional deities to attach new meanings to them. For example, Melqart, the traditional god of Tyre, was associated with Heracles even before Alexander's conquest. However, in its aftermath, he largely dissolved in the

Heraclean identity provided by the Greeks. A similar develop-ment took place in Sidon, where Eshmun, the god of healing, transformed into the Greek Asklepios, whose domain was also healing. Not much changed in the ritual sphere, though, where the collective dimension still remained central. Bonnet speaks of the 'de-barbarization' of local Phoenician deities, which aimed 'to break them out of local contexts and incorporate them into inter-national networks, and to read them through the polyvalent lens of *interpretatio*, as well as to exalt their power rooted in a given land'.[91] Overall, the Phoenician re-evaluation and rethinking of their traditional gods was yet another example of their cultural flexibility and of their enviable ability to morph and adjust to sur-vive and prosper in changing circumstances.

Most histories of Phoenicia end either with its conquest by Alexander the Great or with the collapse of the Seleucid rule and the arrival of the Roman Empire in 64 BCE.[92] This is not to say that the Phoenician cities ceased to exist – they continued to experience fluctuating fortunes, but now firmly under the aegis of another empire, with yet another language replacing the Phoenician (the last Phoenician inscription is dated to 25/24 BCE).[93] Some cities experienced a renaissance (Tyre, for example) and others came to prominence for the first time (Berytus/Beirut). Phoenician cults continued but new gods arrived on the scene and old gods gained new names and characteristics. However, the combination of fac-tors that made the inhabitants of Phoenician cities unique, that allowed the world to identify 'Phoenicia' and 'Phoenicians' and attribute a special meaning to them, was lost.

TWO

LOST IN TRANSLATION: PORTRAYALS OF PHOENICIANS IN GRAECO-ROMAN SOURCES

One reason we call the Phoenicians a 'lost civilization' is because very little information comes to us from Phoenician sources. At best, we have royal inscriptions, which do not allow us to discern a clear and convincing voice as to how the Phoenicians saw themselves and their place in the ancient world. For this reason, the testimony of classical, both Greek and Roman, sources cannot be overstated, as they mention the Phoenicians frequently and provide a slew of information that would not be available otherwise. For historians, these sources provide a dilemma: although they are informative, their bias is obvious, and the multiple layers of meaning must be analysed and dissected in the hope of revealing who the Phoenicians really were. In this chapter, we will overview the major classical sources in an attempt to do just that – uncover their biases and glean the most pertinent information. To address the entire corpus of classical literature concerning the Phoenicians would be a gargantuan task; therefore, we will focus on the most important texts.

The very first observation to make is that the entire enterprise of Phoenician and Punic studies is based on terminology invented by the Greeks. The major terms, 'Phoenicia' and 'Phoenicians', are constructs introduced by Greek writers. *Phoiniké* (Phoenicia) and *Phoinikēs* (Phoenicians) are derivatives of *phoinós* (blood-red, purple) and they present an outsider's view of the 'Other', as the term can refer both to the purple dye famously produced by the coastal people and to their skin colour. The terms reveal a collective identity assigned to the populations of the Phoenician city-states with apparent xenophobic overtones that appears throughout classical texts. These terms are problematic since, succinct as they are, they do not afford the flexibility and granularity necessary for describing a diverse and distinct set of independent city-states of the Levantine coast. They can be misleading as well, presenting the 'Phoenicians' as a monolithic ethnic group pursuing single political and economic goals in the ancient world. We need to keep in mind these factors as we discuss classical texts.

Some further issues affect our interpretation of Graeco-Roman writings and their usefulness for historical reconstruction. We have already mentioned the inherent bias engendered by the difference in cultures and economic and political competition. Additionally, we should point out that with rare exceptions (for example *The Phoenician Women* by Euripides), the Phoenicians rarely serve as a focal point of classical texts; they are invoked only when addressing other issues and topics of interest to the Greeks and Romans, such as regional and international warfare, trade or local events. Thus the coverage of the Phoenicians is patchy and incomplete. We should keep this in mind when considering classical texts.

Sources from Archaic and Classical Greece

To understand better the development of Greek attitudes towards the Phoenicians, we should start with the earliest texts.

Homer

Homer's *Iliad* is one of the first written descriptions of Greek encounters with the Phoenicians, masters of maritime exploration and crafts. Homer speaks of elaborate robes from Sidon and an exquisite silver mixing bowl, 'a work of art' brought over from Sidon by Phoenicians.[1] His descriptions are rather neutral and characterized by the distinction between the Sidonians and the Phoenicians, although the two words seem to be synonymous. However, in the *Odyssey*, another poem attributed to Homer, there already appears a shift in perspective. Though both the *Iliad* and the *Odyssey* are dated to the eighth century BCE, the latter work depicts a shift in attitude towards the Phoenicians, which may indicate changing sentiments as the economic and political situation in the Mediterranean became more volatile, marked by stiff competition in commerce between East and West. Some passages are unmistakably positive (*Odyssey* XIII:271–96 speaks of 'lordly Phoenician men'), but then we encounter passages where Phoenicians are characterized as 'well skilled in beguilements', 'gnawers at other men's goods' and not above using 'lying devices'.[2]

Some commentators do not regard the portrayal of the Phoenicians in the *Odyssey* as representative – rather, simply that some bad actors just happen to be Phoenicians.[3] However, just because a stereotypical character acts nobly at times, it does not negate the stereotype. In the passages above, the typical Phoenician is portrayed as cunning, always on the lookout for a profit, a deceiver crafty in commerce and a peddler of 'pretty things'. The passages are ruthless in their critique of famous mariners and merchants and betray 'partiality, preconceived mistrust and hostility'.[4] Such attitudes came to be fairly common in the representation of Phoenicians in Greek texts for centuries to come, as they served as succinct and relatable caricatures for the Greeks, with whom the Phoenicians competed in commercial and, later, political affairs.

Herodotus

The same elevated reputation of the Phoenicians as skilful mariners that we saw in the *Iliad* and the *Odyssey* can be traced throughout Herodotus' *Histories*. Herodotus of Halicarnassus (*c.* 484–*c.* 425 BCE) was a Greek historian who not only supplied a wealth of information on the history of Phoenicia in the Persian period during which he wrote, but filled in the gaps regarding much earlier times. The Phoenicians' mercantile and seafaring skills are the focus of Herodotus' accounts;[5] at one point he reports that the Phoenicians even circumnavigated Africa.[6] They were also the ones who supplied ships and personnel for the Persian fleet, which Herodotus calls simply 'Phoenician'.[7]

A few passages raise questions as to whether Herodotus was as tolerant and magnanimous towards non-Greeks, especially the Phoenicians, as he is often given credit for. Herodotus places the Phoenicians at the very beginning of his work. There, he recites an old myth of either Persian or Phoenician origin that lays the blame for the conflict between the Greeks and the Persians – the very centre of his historical inquiry – squarely on the Phoenicians. Either Herodotus appeased his readership by throwing in an easy-to-digest tale that would make sense of it all or, being the rational person he was, Herodotus was merely acknowledging what was known at the time, without taking sides.[8] However, we cannot discount the fact Herodotus was Greek, and he did take sides and frequently employed the term 'barbarians' to refer to non-Greek peoples (although he often chastised his own people, and their institutions, as 'barbarians'). In the grand conflict between the Greeks and the Persians, the latter were 'barbarians', and, by extension, so were those associated with them. The Phoenicians, of course, did just that, assisting the Persians during the Cypriot and Ionian revolts. As collaborators with the Persians, the Phoenicians were subject to all common denunciations. Herodotus' perspective is still the one of a Greek writer, and he is prone to reveal his bias towards the Phoenicians just as he did towards the Persians.

Nonetheless, Herodotus frequently portrays the Phoenicians in a positive light. In one instance, when Cambyses, king of Persia, commands the Phoenicians to set sail against Carthage, they refuse, citing the 'close bond' that united Phoenicia and Carthage and saying that it would be a 'wickedness' to wage war against one's 'children'.[9] Contrary to his lengthy ethnographical digressions about other peoples (the Egyptians, Persians and Scythians), Herodotus does not afford the same treatment to the Phoenicians. In *Histories*, they are very close to the Greeks and even serve as progenitors to some. The Phoenicians who came with Cadmus, the founder of Thebes, brought along the alphabet, too.[10] We can observe the same kinship in Euripides' *Phoenician Women*, where Tyre and Thebes are forever bound by the figure of Cadmus.[11] Given the closeness between the Greeks and Phoenicians, the Phoenicians for Herodotus often served as a trope to explore and articulate the Greek identity – both groups had similar interests in trade and seafaring, and the Greeks could enhance their own history by drawing upon the more splendid Phoenician heritage.[12]

Herodotus' use of the terms 'Phoenicia' and 'Phoenicians' deserves a short comment. For him, several city-states comprised the land of Phoenicia. One of them was Tyre and another Sidon; the latter receives considerably more coverage. Sidon is lauded for the quality of its ships and the skill of its naval officers in the service of Persian kings.[13] Its ships were the fastest, and the king of Sidon at one point receives the highest honours from Xerxes, king of Persia, for the military skill of his troops.[14] Despite these distinctions, the Phoenicians, as portrayed by Herodotus, comprised a single cultural entity on the Levantine coast; although they were administratively divided into several city-states, they remained united by their 'proclivity for trade'.[15]

Thucydides

Thucydides, another Greek historian from the fifth century BCE (*c.* 460–*c.* 400 BCE) and the author of the *History of the Peloponnesian War*, exemplifies the point that Greek authors covered the Phoenicians as long as they were active participants in the wars against the Greeks. At the time of the Peloponnesian wars, when conflict with Persia largely subsided and Phoenician participation in military actions was negligible, interest in the Phoenicians fell. Thucydides speaks of the Phoenicians in formulas, mentioning their piracy, the colonization of islands and their involvement in Darius's wars as experts in maritime affairs.[16]

Diodorus Siculus

Among other historians writing on the Phoenicians and the Carthaginians is Diodorus Siculus, a Sicilian who lived in the first

Naval manoeuvres during the Siege of Tyre. Illustration by André Castaigne, *c.* 1898.

century BCE. Although not technically representative of Classical Greece, in his *Library of History*, Diodorus looks back on the events of the fourth century BCE, supplying information unavailable elsewhere – some of his sources go back at least to that time. There are numerous doubts regarding the general reliability and historicity of his accounts. His vitriol against the Phoenicians is marked by his description of them as a 'rebellious and treacherous people, mindful of their own comfort'.[17] They are cruel barbarians par excellence and inventive in the ways of torture and extreme discomfort. According to Diodorus, when Alexander the Great besieged Tyre, the Tyrians dealt with the invaders by heating sand in bronze and iron shields and then catapulting them into the crowds of Macedonians. The sand got under their breastplates, scorching the skin and driving Alexander's fighters into excruciating pain.[18] At times, the Tyrians appear shockingly superstitious; during the same siege, afraid that the god Apollo would abandon them by withdrawing his much-needed protection, they chained his statue to its base.[19] The ruse did not work, of course, 'representing the victory of Greek rationality and might'.[20]

The Carthaginians are not spared by the Sicilian historian either. Historians have pointed out that for Diodorus there was little distinction between the Phoenicians and the Carthaginians since the Greeks had no special word for western Phoenicians.[21] For Diodorus, the Carthaginians are barbarians, prone to unusual and unnecessary cruelty. When relating an episode of the taking of Selinunte in Sicily in 409 BCE, he makes a point of them not being content in just looting the city but resorting to unimaginable brutality. The Carthaginians scattered throughout the city, burning homes with their inhabitants inside, putting women, children and old men to the sword and carrying their severed limbs in bunches, 'according to the practice of their people'.[22] To further malign the Carthaginians, Diodorus describes them even sacrificing children to Baal Hammon when they found themselves under siege by Agathocles in 310 BCE.[23]

The 'Periplus' of Pseudo-Scylax

Close to the classical histories are journey reports, exemplified in the case of Phoenicia by the *Periplus* of Pseudo-Scylax, a sixth- or fourth-century composition that probably took its final shape in the second half of the fourth century BCE. As a seafarer's manual, the *Periplus* (which literally means 'sailing around') describes, from west to east, the ancient cities starting from Iberia and West Africa. Pseudo-Scylax mentions the Phoenician city-states in his report, and he is one of the first to refer to the Phoenicians as an *ethnos*, a people, although divided between the individual city-states of Arwad, Sidon and Tyre.[24]

Other ancient Greek sources

Greek non-history writers used well-worn tropes as well, invoking the Phoenicians mostly because of their involvement in trade and the excellence of their craft (for example Euripides in *The Phoenician Women*, *c.* 408 BCE). The underlying sentiment, however, was still one of distrust, casting the Phoenicians in an unflattering light. In a quote attributed to Aristophanes, we read: 'I am becoming a true Phoenician: with one hand I give and with the other I take away.'[25] It is not entirely clear whether the character who makes this statement is a Greek or a Phoenician, but it really does not make much difference – the stereotype is still there. The *Republic* (*c.* 375 BCE) of Plato also carries a negative portrayal of the Phoenicians. When Socrates invokes the 'noble lie', he refers to it as '*Phoinikikon ti*', literally, 'the Phoenician thing' ('Phoenician tales' in the translation below):

> Now then, we spoke some time ago of useful lies. Could we contrive one now, a noble lie that might be believed by the rulers themselves, or at least by the rest of the city?
>
> What kind of lie do you have in mind?
>
> Nothing new. It is like one of those Phoenician tales telling of things that have happened before in many parts of the world – or so the poets assert and have induced men to believe. But it concerns something that is perhaps unlikely to happen in our own day, and it would certainly be difficult to persuade men to believe it.[26]

Some have tried to downplay the 'noble lie' concept,[27] but the gratuitous invocation of the Phoenicians in this context does not appear as anything but negative – they are portrayed as prone to engage nonchalantly in casual untruths.

A recent trend in the scholarship is to trace the rise of negative sentiment against the Phoenicians in Greek sources to the Battle of Himera, in which the Greek forces under the leadership of Gelon, king of Syracuse, and Theron, tyrant of Agrigentum, decisively defeated Carthaginian forces led by Hamilcar the Magonid. Greek sources date the battle to 480 BCE, the same day that the Athenians overpowered the Persians at the Battle of Salamis. Although untrue,[28] the date of the Battle of Himera coinciding with the great victory over another 'other' solidified a feeling of triumph, especially among the Syracusans, of the Greeks over a 'barbarian' people. The triumph was widely celebrated, especially in the poetry of the Greek poet Pindar.[29] Since there was no linguistic distinction between Phoenicians and Carthaginians, they came to be seen as one amorphous group, threatening and foreign, separate from the Greeks and their mores. Josephine Quinn points out that it was in this atmosphere of singling out the Phoenicians, whether from Carthage or from the Phoenician homeland, that the first identification of Phoenicians as 'barbarians' takes place in Thucydides' *History*, to be followed by Pseudo-Scylax and Diodorus Siculus.[30]

The Greeks did have other positive things to say about the Phoenicians and Carthaginians besides their maritime skills, and their contributions were sometimes lauded and celebrated. Strabo, a Greek geographer who lived in the first century BCE, had much to say about the Phoenicians' achievements in 'many beautiful arts', including astronomy, philosophy, arithmetic and geometry.[31]

Isocrates, writing in the fourth century BCE, praised the Carthaginians for having a very successful form of government which combined democracy, aristocracy and elements of monarchy.[32] Aristotle, in the fourth century BCE, also wrote positively of the Carthaginians, crediting them 'for the stability of their state, the loyalty of the populace to the system, and that neither civil strife nor tyranny has upset the governance of the realm'.[33] Polybius, a Greek historian of the second century BCE, mentioned in his *Histories* how Carthage compared favourably to the Roman Republic, combining monarchic, aristocratic and democratic elements.[34] Without doubt, Rome was the gold standard for Polybius, but that he chose Carthage against which to evaluate its political and administrative set-up confirms his admiration for the latter.

'The Capture of Carthage', engraving by Georg Pencz, *c.* 1539.

Punica fides

Things started to change with the advent of the Punic Wars between Rome and Carthage, and the notion of *Punica fides*, 'Punic faith', started to gain currency. As Rome began to engage with Carthage militarily, the Carthaginians quickly gained a reputation as breakers of oaths and treaties, although Rome was not above reproach in this sense either.[35] The sentiment was gathering steam by the early second century BCE, when we read in Diodorus how some Roman senators contemplated that it was 'not fitting for Romans to imitate Phoenicians, so as to overcome their enemies through deception and not through virtue'.[36] Erich Gruen locates the zenith of this notion at 146 BCE, when at the end of the Third Punic War, Rome crushed Carthage. The animosity at that time spilled over from simple political rhetoric to reach literary compositions as well. In a play by Plautus, *Poenulus* (known in English as *The Little Phoenician* or *The Little Carthaginian*), which was written a few years after the Second Punic War, the main character is fluent in many languages but 'knowingly pretends not to know', thereby being 'a true Carthaginian'.[37] Over time, the Carthaginian reputation for falsehood and treachery gets amplified, and we read in Cicero's speech to Scaurus at his trial in 54 BCE:

> All the monuments of the ancients and all histories have handed down to us the tradition that the nation of the Phoenicians is the most treacherous of all nations. The Poeni [Punics], who are descended from them, have proved by many rebellions of the Carthaginians, and very many broken and violated treaties, that they have in no respect degenerated from them.[38]

This passage is important for several reasons. First, 'the Phoenicians' in Cicero's speech are a distinct ethnicity, a people ('*genus . . . Phoenicum*' in the Latin). Second, this is the first instance in Latin in the first century BCE where 'Phoenicians' and 'Punes' are clearly distinguished, with 'Poeni' meaning 'western Phoenicians'. These points are important for our understanding of how Phoenicians and Punics were distinguished in antiquity.

There are less damning descriptions as well in imperial literature, such as a passage in chapter 79 of Sallust's *Jugurthine War* that tells the story of the Carthaginians giving their lives to protect their honour in the face of unreasonable Greeks.[39] Virgil's *Aeneid*, aimed at glorifying the Pax Romana (the 'Roman Peace' of Caesar Augustus), is generally positive towards the protagonist Dido, although from a literary point of view this could be a ploy to make the Roman victory appear more spectacular. Broadly speaking, though, irrespective whether the portrayal of Phoenicians and Carthaginians in Latin literature was negative or positive, the focus remained on their connection with the sea, as was the case with Greek literature.

THREE

AT THE SERVICE OF THE KINGS: PHOENICIANS IN THE BIBLE

Among the written sources from the ancient world, ancient Jewish writings, especially the Hebrew Bible, stand out. They portray the inhabitants of the Levantine city-states of Tyre, Sidon, Byblos and Arwad as advanced craftsmen, traders and, above all, masterful merchants traversing the seas. Many historians have used the Hebrew Bible to reconstruct the history of ancient Phoenicia or, at least, to supplement other historical sources. King Hiram of Tyre features prominently in many contemporary books on ancient Phoenicia, for example. However, reading the ancient Israelite literature as a historian is an entirely different enterprise from reading it theologically. Gleaning reliable historical information from the Bible requires a thorough understanding of its compositional process, its genres and its biases. In this chapter, we will assess the usability of ancient Jewish writings for historical information and summarize how they portray Phoenicia and the Phoenicians.

The Hebrew Bible as a historical source

The Hebrew Bible, the sacred texts of Judaism comprising the 24 canonical books, is also referred to as the Tanakh; the Protestant canon of the Old Testament consists of 39 books, and commentators traditionally use the Protestant canon to refer to specific books, as we will do here. The term 'Tanakh' is composed from the first Hebrew letters of its three main divisions, Torah (Teaching, or Law), Nevi'im (Prophets) and Ketuvim (Writings). These are thematic divisions, but these distinctions are also often used to draw conclusions regarding the provenance of the biblical books.

The Torah is a mostly self-contained document describing the primeval history, the patriarchs (Abraham, Isaac and Jacob), the Exodus from Egypt, the wandering in the desert, the core of the Jewish law and the preparations for the entry into the Promised Land. Because the Torah is such a seemingly coherent composition, its entire contents are often dated to the same period. The current consensus of critical scholarship is that the Torah, along with the entire Hebrew Bible, received its final form in the post-exilic period (sixth–fourth centuries BCE) or later.[1]

The Nevi'im and the Ketuvim do not appear so monolithic, as they reveal a variety of voices and corresponding biases. A rare exception is the books of the Former Prophets, consisting of the books of Joshua, Judges, Samuel and Kings, the first part of the Nevi'im. The Former Prophets narrative spans the taking of the land of Canaan by the Israelites to the destruction of the southern kingdom of Judah by the Neo-Babylonians in the sixth century BCE. The first two books, Joshua and Judges, tell the story of the settlement and the establishment of a loose confederacy led by tribal chieftains. The books of Samuel and Kings cover the emerging Israelite monarchy, with the first notable kings (Saul, David and Solomon), the division of the kingdom into the northern kingdom of Israel and the southern kingdom of Judah, the Assyrian devastation of the former and the subsequent Neo-Babylonian destruction of the latter.

What makes these books similar is their common theological point of view. These compositions are frequently called 'Deuteronomistic' – and the history told therein is almost universally referred to as the 'Deuteronomistic History (DtrH) – because they adhere to the formula first appearing in the Book of Deuteronomy, the fifth book of the Torah. There, one can observe a clear correlation between obedience to God's laws on the one hand, and well-being and retention of the land on the other. If the Israelites were obedient, they would keep the Promised Land and prosper. However, if they were disloyal and were to follow other gods, then various calamities would befall them, including being displaced from the land. The same framework underlies all the DtrH books, and the narrative appears to be driven more by theology than actual historical realities. The thinking goes that someone had to arrange the DtrH in such a manner, and we might therefore speak of the entire collection as having the same date, if not of writing then certainly for the final editorial process. The most likely time period for the books to have emerged as a coherent whole would of course be after the last events described therein; the Babylonian exile and the Persian periods seem to be the most likely candidates. We need to keep these points in mind when we discuss the coverage of Phoenicia in the DtrH.

There are several issues to be aware of when using the Bible for historical reconstruction. One of the most obvious is its theological nature. The overall focus of the Hebrew Bible is the divine history of God's dealings with the Jewish people. The biblical writers understood history differently from modern historians, and the historiographical conventions they employed differ from modern approaches. The events mattered and were reported only if they were connected with the overarching purpose of showing how God operated to carry out his will. Additionally, ancient history writing utilized orally transmitted stories that reveal a theocentric vision of the universe and humanity whereby natural phenomena are the direct acts of a powerful deity, where the supernatural is expected and frequent, and where humans are rewarded or punished by the deity depending on their compliance with his laws. The central people, of course, are the Jews, variably referred to in the Bible as Hebrews, Israelites and Judaeans. Other nations receive mention only as they interact with them, either in terms of opposition or cooperation. The Phoenicians are no exception, and the Hebrew Bible mentions them in terms of their usefulness to the kings of Israel and Judah in their projects and also as subjects of condemnation for their actions against God and his people.

One more issue has a bearing on any attempt to reconstruct history on the basis of the ancient Jewish writings: the question of the Septuagint, the Greek translation of the Hebrew Bible that also adds a few apocryphal books. The word means 'seventy' in Latin and refers to an ancient story about how the translation came into existence. According to a popular account from the historically unreliable Letter of Aristeas (*c.* second century BCE), Ptolemy II Philadelphus, king of Egypt from 285 to 246 BCE, commissioned Eleazar, the high priest in Jerusalem, to assemble a group of about seventy translators (six from each of the twelve tribes of Israel) to be sent to Egypt to translate the Hebrew Bible into Greek. He did this out of concern for the Jewish exiles living in his land, who no longer could read the text of their sacred scripture. The translators toiled for 72 days and produced 72 identical translations, which came to be known as the Septuagint (it is also frequently abbreviated in Roman numerals as LXX). Although the story seems too good to be true, in the absence of a more convincing explanation of the origin of the text, the LXX is usually dated to the middle of the third century BCE. What makes the translation particularly interesting is the fact that it is not entirely clear what sources lay behind it, since there are considerable discrepancies between the Hebrew and Greek versions. In the LXX, some books are shorter, others are longer, and there are notable differences in important passages, the spelling of names and so on.

Now we come to the important questions: in which books are the Phoenicians and Phoenicia mentioned, and what do those writings say about them? To answer these, we need to distinguish between the collective term 'Phoenicians' and 'Phoenicia' and more specific terms related to the Phoenician city-states – that is, 'Sidonians', 'Tyrians', 'Sidon', 'Tyre', 'Byblos' and 'Arwad'. The terms 'Phoenicians' and 'Phoenicia' rarely appear in the ancient Jewish writings. They can be found in the canonical Book of Obadiah (1:20) and in the non-canonical books of 2 Maccabees (3:5, 3:8, 4:4, 4:22, 8:8, 10:11), 1 Esdras (2:17, 2:24–7, 4:48, 6:3–7, 6:27–9, 7:1, 8:19, 8:23, 8:67), 3 Maccabees (3:150) and 4 Maccabees (4:2).[2] All these writings, except for Obadiah, are dated to the second century BCE or later, and by and large they do not tell us about Phoenicia. For example, the Books of the Maccabees tend to mention Phoenicia only as part of the set phrase 'Coelesyria and Phoenicia', an administrative unit in the Seleucid Empire. Apart from this identification, these books provide no additional information.

The situation is entirely different for the individual city names and the peoples associated with them. Phoenicia's two most important city-states, Tyre and Sidon, and their inhabitants are frequently mentioned. A simple search of the Hebrew Bible reveals a tendency of the writers to mention these city-states in three specific ways. First, some texts mention them independently of one another, with the city-state of Tyre being the politically stronger of the two. A telling example is the Book of Ezekiel, where the author dedicates three chapters (26–8) condemning Tyre and its royalty and only four verses to denounce Sidon and the Sidonians (28:20–23). The more extended denunciation conceivably reflects the elevated status of Tyre compared to that of Sidon. Second, in other books (1 and 2 Kings), the city-states are addressed separately as well, but in them it is the city-state of Sidon that appears to be stronger politically and economically. Third, in yet another set of writings (1 Chronicles and Ezra), the peoples of Tyre and Sidon are grouped together and used as a set phrase, 'Sidonians and Tyrians'. Notice how the writer of 1 Chronicles uses the phrase:

> David also provided great stores of iron for nails for the doors of the gates and for clamps, as well as bronze in quantities beyond weighing, and cedar logs without number – for the Sidonians and Tyrians brought great quantities of cedar to David. (22:3–4; NRSV)

The Chronicler does not make any distinction between the two peoples even if the writer of a somewhat similar story (with different details, however) in 1 Kings differentiates between them.

There are discrepancies among not only the individual books of the Bible, but the various versions of it. See, for example, how the same events are reported in the Masoretic Text (traditional Hebrew text of the Hebrew Bible) and the Septuagint:

The Masoretic Text (MT)	The Septuagint (LXX)
1 Kings 9:10–14, 26–8	
9:10 At the end of twenty years, in which Solomon had built the two houses, the house of the Lord and the king's house,	9:10 During twenty years in which Solomon was building the two houses, the house of the Lord, and the house of the king,
9:11 King Hiram of Tyre having supplied Solomon with cedar and cypress timber and gold, as much as he desired, King Solomon gave to Hiram twenty cities in the land of Galilee.	9:11 Chiram King of Tyre helped Solomon with cedar wood, and fir wood, and with gold, and all that he wished for: then the king gave Chiram twenty cities in the land of Galilee.
9:12 But when Hiram came from Tyre to see the cities that Solomon had given him, they did not please him.	9:12 So Chiram departed from Tyre, and went into Galilee to see the cities which Solomon gave to him; and they pleased him not. And he said,
9:13 Therefore he said, 'What kind of cities are these that you have given me, my brother?' So they are called the land of Cabul to this day.	9:13 What are these cities which thou hast given me, brother? And he called them Boundary until this day.
9:14 But Hiram had sent to the king *one hundred twenty talents* of gold.	9:14 And Chiram brought to Solomon *a hundred and twenty talents* of gold . . .
9:26 King Solomon built a fleet of ships at Ezion-geber, which is near Eloth on the shore of the Red Sea, in the land of Edom.	9:25–6 even that for which King Solomon built a ship in Gasion Gaber near Ælath on the shore of the extremity of the sea in the land of Edom.
9:27 Hiram sent his servants with the fleet, sailors who were familiar with the sea, together with the servants of Solomon.	9:27 And Chiram sent in the ship together with the servants of Solomon servants of his own, mariners to row, men acquainted with the sea.
9:28 They went to Ophir, and imported from there *four hundred twenty talents* of gold, which they delivered to King Solomon. (NRSV)	9:28 And they came to Sophira, and took thence *a hundred and twenty talents* of gold, and brought them to King Solomon.[3]

2 Chronicles 8:1–2, 17–18	
8:1 At the end of twenty years, during which Solomon had built the house of the Lord and his own house, 8:2 Solomon rebuilt the cities that Huram had given to him, and settled the people of Israel in them. 8:17 Then Solomon went to Ezion-geber and Eloth on the shore of the sea, in the land of Edom. 8:18 Huram sent him, in the care of his servants, ships and servants familiar with the sea. They went to Ophir, together with the servants of Solomon, and imported from there *four hundred fifty talents* of gold and brought it to King Solomon. (NRSV)	8:1 And it came to pass after twenty years, in which Solomon built the house of the Lord, and his own house, 8:2 that Solomon rebuilt the cities which Chiram had given to Solomon, and caused the children of Israel to dwell in them . . . 8:17 Then Solomon went to Gasion Gaber, and to Ælath near the sea in the land of Idumea. 8:18 And Chiram sent by the hand of his servants ships, and servants skilled in naval affairs; and they went with the servants of Solomon to Sophira, and brought thence *four hundred and fifty talents* of gold, and they came to King Solomon.[4]

A few things are worth noting here, and they demonstrate the tensions between the two different versions of the text on the one hand (the MT and the LXX) and the two books of the Bible that are conceivably talking about the same events (the Book of Chronicles is universally accepted as a late theological rethinking of the stories in the Books of Kings). The first is that the four versions cannot agree on the number of talents of gold brought to Solomon. Any discrepancy is meaningful if one considers that a talent equals about 60 kilograms. Also, the Chronicler in the MT version does not seem to know about Solomon's gift of twenty cities to King Hiram (he calls him 'Huram') and the dissatisfaction Hiram felt after inspecting them – the Chronicler only knows about the cities that Huram had given Solomon. The LXX version preserves an independent memory from the MT as it uses a unique spelling of the king's name ('Chiram') and does not maintain the same variants in spelling as can be found in the MT versions of 1 Kings 9 and 2 Chronicles 8. If we were to use these passages for any historical information about King Hiram of Tyre and his dealings with the Israelites, which versions would we use? Alternatively, if we can somehow explain these discrepancies and provide a plausible explanation, then we might develop an interpretative scheme for using these writings.

Phoenician city-states in the ancient Jewish texts

So, where do we start in talking about Phoenicia and the Phoenicians in the biblical materials? We have already noticed the changing voice that the ancient writers used in describing them. When analysing the texts that mention the Phoenician city-states individually, one should also distinguish between the two different genres: history and prophecy. The former, of course, aims to present a chronological sequence of historical events, even if the overarching aim is to demonstrate how God directed Israelite history and played an enormous part in it. Prophecy, on the other hand, seeks both to proclaim the mind of God to the people and to foretell the future. Although both are theological compositions, the two genres will have varying amounts of reliable historical information encoded in them.

'Historical' texts

Sidon gets the first mention, in the Table of Nations in Genesis 10, a fictitious and symbolic history of humanity as it originated from the descendants of Noah after the Flood. The writers mention Sidon as Canaan's first-born son; among Canaan's other descendants are the Jebusites, the Amorites, the Girgashites, the Hivites and other nations (10:15–20). The text clearly identifies the Sidonians as the Canaanites and further describes their territory:

> And the territory of the Canaanites extended from Sidon, in the direction of Gerar, as far as Gaza, and in the direction of Sodom, Gomorrah, Admah, and Zeboiim, as far as Lasha. (10:19; NRSV)

Stained glass window, depicting (from left to right) King Hiram, King Solomon and Hiram the 'Architect', Great Malvern Priory, Worcestershire, UK. Glass by Shrigley & Hunt, 1908.

For the writers of Genesis, then, the territory of Canaan extended from Sidon in the north to Lasha in the south. The location of Lasha is unknown, but it is likely that it was situated somewhere in the southern Levant, perhaps even by the Dead Sea.[5] If that was the case, then the land of Canaan would stretch from Sidon down to the Dead Sea, encompassing other sites such as Tyre, Dor and Sarepta. It is important to remember that the frequently voiced proposal that the Phoenicians self-identified as Canaanites is based solely on biblical tradition.

Following the Book of Genesis, the next set of historical materials, the DTRH, focuses primarily on the city-states of Tyre and

Sidon, presenting them as powerful and autonomous players in Iron Age Levant. The DtrH writers mention Tyre mostly in the context of two persons bearing the same name of Hiram: one was a king of Tyre, the other was a bronze-worker who contributed his skills to the construction of Solomon's Temple. King Hiram, the most interesting of the two for the history of Phoenicia, is said to have been a friend to both David and Solomon and a supplier of cedar wood (2 Sam. 5:11; 1 Kings 5:1–6). Solomon and Hiram reportedly drew up a treaty (1 Kings 5:12) according to which Hiram would provide the necessary timber to Solomon, and the latter would send food provisions to Hiram's household (1 Kings 5:9). It is curious that in the passage, the DtrH writers mention that no one was able 'to cut timber like the Sidonians' (1 Kings 5:6). Why would the Sidonians have anything to do with Tyre? If it is not a careless mistake that persisted for hundreds of years – and nothing seems to indicate this – it is an apparent confirmation of Tyrian superiority over the Sidonians in political and economic affairs in the Iron Age.

The DtrH authors continue to report on the Solomon/Hiram relations in 1 Kings 9:10–28. Ever grateful for receiving timber and an enormous amount of gold from Hiram, Solomon gifted Hiram twenty cities in the land of Galilee (9:11–13); the king of Tyre, however, was not happy with the 'Land of Cabul' for some unspecified reason. It was important for the DtrH authors to portray Solomon towering politically over Hiram, who appears subservient, weak and capricious. Later in the narrative, the DtrH also mentions Hiram sending his servants to staff the fleet that Solomon reportedly built on the shore of the Red Sea (9:26–7). The fleet was sent out to the mysterious land of Ophir (possibly somewhere on the eastern coast of Africa) and delivered from there 'four hundred twenty talents of gold' to Solomon (25,200 kilograms). From yet another passage, we learn of a joint expedition of Solomon's and Hiram's fleets to Tarshish (possibly Tartessos of southwestern Iberia[6]), whence they brought 'gold, silver, ivory, apes, and peacocks' (10:22).

Generally Tyre, through its royalty, receives very positive commentary in the DtrH. It is friendly with Israel, and it is a reliable and compliant partner in trade and travel. At times, Hiram attempts to counterbalance Solomon's superiority, as was the case with his displeasure at receiving the unwanted and questionable gift of twenty cities in Galilee from the overbearing Israelite monarch. Other than that unfortunate wrinkle, Tyre is generally presented as an enviable ally. For a theologically minded historian, ready to preach fire and brimstone against the gods and goddesses of other lands, the DtrH is curiously silent about the Tyrian deities. The answer to this puzzling omission lies in the goal of the Tyre narratives in the Books of Kings, which is to aggrandize Solomon's superiority by portraying a powerful and wealthy maritime city-state at the service of the great king.

Sidon is an entirely different matter as the DtrH speaks of it in a frequently menacing manner. Thus in the Book of Joshua, we find references to 'great' Sidon, an epithet never used for Tyre (11:8, 19:28). Also, Sidon and the Sidonians are frequently associated with foreign cults. Whereas the DtrH chose to ignore Tyre's deities, its wrathful rhetoric escalated when speaking of the Sidonian gods (Judges 10:6; 1 Kings 11:5). Interestingly, the passage from 1 Kings is in proximity to the Solomon/Hiram narratives we discussed earlier; it is as if the writers turned a blind eye to Tyre. At the same time, the DtrH writers seem to have an attitude of respect and even fear of the Sidonians. Consider the following passage from the Book of Judges:

> The five men went on, and when they came to Laish, they observed the people who were there living securely, after the manner of the Sidonians, quiet and unsuspecting, lacking nothing on earth, and possessing wealth. (18:7; NRSV)

The quiet, wealthy and sovereign Sidonians are clearly intimidating in some ways, and they are frequently spoken of as 'oppressors' (Judges 10:12), displeasing to Yahweh and, therefore, subject to expulsion by him (Joshua 13:4, 6). In general, they are a nuisance for the Israelites, intended as a test of their religious commitment (Judges 3:3). This is especially evident in the passage in 1 Kings 11:1, which lists many foreign women that 'Solomon loved'. The passage was intended to demonstrate both Solomon's diplomatic skills in securing favours from foreign rulers by entering into marriages with their daughters, and the debilitating effect such unions had on the king's devotion to Yahweh. By including the Sidonian women in the list, the DtrH sought to establish that the corrupting charms of the Sidonian women were nothing but a stumbling block for the Israelites whom they led astray. Even the eventual division of Israel into two kingdoms (the northern kingdom of Israel and the southern kingdom of Judah) after Solomon's death occurred to a large extent because of his worship of the Sidonian goddess Astarte (1 Kings 11:31–3).

Similarly, Jezebel, a daughter of King Ethbaal of Sidon and Ahab's wife, was the one who caused her Israelite royal husband to lust for other gods (1 Kings 16:31).[7] The DtrH explicitly reports that Yahweh's wrath against his people for their apostasy was directly

Frederic Leighton, *Jezebel and Ahab*, c. 1863, oil on canvas.

connected with foreign cults, first and foremost with the worship of Astarte. Even when the last 'good' king of Judah, Josiah, attempted to restore the worship of Yahweh, the first order of business was to eliminate any remaining trace of the worship of the Sidonian goddess (2 Kings 23:13).

How can these passages illuminate our understanding of Phoenicia and the Phoenicians? Once we situate the DtrH in the Persian period as a working assumption, then our task becomes a little easier. We have noticed already how the DtrH passages differentiate between Tyre and Sidon and speak of them as independent polities, with their distinct characteristic features and colourful personages. The term 'Phoenicia' and any derivatives, therefore, are not used, and whenever there is a need to identify the land occupied by Tyre and Sidon, the DtrH uses the indigenous term from the Ancient Near East, 'Canaan'.

It also appears that of the two, it was Sidon that appeared politically and economically stronger, with Tyre occupying the honorary second place. The picture corresponds well with the Persian period, the time of Sidonian pre-eminence in the southern and central Levant over numerous entities, including Judah/Yehud. Its coinage was widely spread and its trade interests involved the entire Levantine coast. Additionally, the cult of Astarte is well attested in Sidon in the first millennium BCE and, more specifically, in the Persian period. For example, the Tabnit inscription (KAI 13) identifies the central deity of Sidon as Astarte when it begins, 'I Tabnit, priest of Astarte, king of the Sidonians'.[8] The DtrH writers expressed their displeasure and concern regarding the encroaching cult of Astarte through theological condemnations.

The DtrH and archaeology

The discussion above presupposes a view that is squarely in conflict with some traditional interpretations of the DtrH. These postulate that the events concerning Tyre and Sidon described in the 'historical' texts corresponded mainly to the historical realities of the times of the Israelite kings. However, even the archaeological data casts doubt on the historicity of the biblical materials.

We can test the historical veracity of the DtrH using the passage in 1 Kings 9:11 that speaks of the gift of twenty cities in Galilee by Solomon to King Hiram of Tyre. 'The land of Cabul' mentioned in that text could possibly be identified with Khorvat Rosh Zayit (10 kilometres east of Akko). Such a handover, if it indeed happened, would not have occurred before about 900 BCE.[9] Traditional, conservative scholarship dates Solomon's accession to the throne to 970 or 960 BCE. Thus there appears to be a disconnection between the biblical materials and the archaeological evidence. More curiously, some may say that the handover never actually happened in the first place. Archaeologists have noticed that in terms of material remains, the city of Akko and its environs do not differ substantially from the other sites in Phoenicia for most of the first millennium BCE.[10] A change from one political and economic affiliation (from Israel to Tyre) would presumably lead to at least some changes in the material culture, but that cannot be established for Akko and other sites in its vicinity. How do we deal with the gift of lands, then? The most likely explanation is that the writers were keenly aware of the Tyrian dominance of the area and included the episode as yet another way to enhance Solomon's reputation as a benevolent and generous ruler. Additionally, Jerusalem and Tyre have been said to have close political and economic ties for many centuries.[11] Even in the Persian period, there was a Tyrian community living in Jerusalem that supplied fish and other products to the Jews (Nehemiah 13:16).

In short, the close ties of Jerusalem and Tyre throughout the first millennium BCE account well for the positive coverage of the latter in the DtrH writings. Sidon, on the other hand, a formidable force, especially under the Persians, evoked feelings of awe, fear and theological annoyance among the biblical writers.

Ezra, Nehemiah and Chronicles

The books of Ezra and Nehemiah cover the events in Judah in the Persian period. Ezra tells a story of the Judaeans returning from the Babylonian exile, rebuilding their temple and restoring the regular worship of Yahweh. Nehemiah is primarily interested in the building of the wall around Jerusalem to protect the community against outsiders.

The Phoenician city-states and their inhabitants are mentioned only once in Ezra (3:7). The Sidonians and Tyrians are mentioned together here, without a clear differentiation between the two. As we saw earlier, such a portrayal is characteristic of the late Persian or Hellenistic periods, when the polities were no longer seen as independent players in the Ancient Near East. Here, labourers from Tyre and Sidon are working on behest of the Judaeans to provide supplies for the rebuilding of the temple. Gone are the old grudges from both sides, and the Sidonians and Tyrians are happily assisting in building the temple of a religious tradition different from their own.

In the Book of Nehemiah, the Sidonians are absent altogether, but the Tyrians are said to have lived in Jerusalem at the time (the middle of the fifth century BCE) and routinely engaged in selling fish on the Sabbath to the people of Judah (Nehemiah 13:16). The passage is set in the context of Nehemiah renewing the keeping of the Sabbath by the Jews. Although the Tyrians were not obligated to keep the Sabbath and abstain from commerce on the holy day, in the text they are portrayed as setting a bad example to the Jews, who were tempted to do the same. For Nehemiah, obedience to God's law was of the utmost importance, something that should set the community apart and ensure its continued survival. The Tyrians selling fish on the Sabbath were deserving of reprimand and even condemnation.

The mention of the Tyrian enclave in Jerusalem deserves a mention. People from the Phoenician city-states establishing settlements in foreign lands is nothing new. Herodotus mentions the 'Camp of the Tyrians' at Memphis in Egypt, for example.[12] The description of the enclave in Nehemiah confirms the close cultural and economic ties between Tyre and Jerusalem that we first saw in the DtrH accounts. Evidently, such relations continued throughout the Persian period and beyond.

The Book of Chronicles is a Persian or a Hellenistic-era composition whose author(s) mostly reworked many of the biblical accounts (mostly the DtrH accounts) to serve their theological agenda. Because of the clear bias, the book is often seen as non-essential for historical reconstruction. However, if we attempt to remove the ideological layers, we can discern a distinct voice that can deliver some valuable historiographical information.

The Chronicler's tendentious writing can be traced through his portrayal of King Hiram, whom we first encountered in the DtrH. The Chronicler's use of the variant spelling 'Huram' is not an incidental idiosyncrasy as the writer uses a pun here, intentionally seeing the name as a form of the word *herem*, which means 'a devoted or set apart thing'. In this sense, King Huram is a 'righteous Gentile' wholly devoted to David and Solomon, the remarkable kings of ancient Israel (1 Chronicles 14:1, 2 Chronicles 2:3). The reason it is essential for the Chronicler to idealize David and Solomon, whom he depicts as pious and God-fearing, and to establish the idea of loyalty to them is to exemplify devotion to Yahweh and civil authority in his own time.

The Chronicler also corrects some information from the DtrH to emphasize the importance of Solomon in God's plan for Israel. Whereas in the DtrH King Hiram appears wilful to the point of dictating the terms of his agreement with Solomon, the Chronicler sets Solomon as the one who is in the position to impose demands on the treaty between the two royals (2 Chronicles 2:3–10). The Chronicler also changes at will DtrH's report of Solomon giving Hiram a gift of cities (2 Chronicles 8:1–2). Contrary to the Deuteronomistic account (1 Kings 9:11–14), it is Huram who gives the gift of twenty cities to Solomon. After all, the king favoured by God should be receiving gifts and being paid homage to rather than vice versa. The reversal of the gift-giving does not negate the fact that the cities were under the control of Tyre, even if such control manifested itself through cultural influence. If we treat the Chronicles as a composition dated to the late Persian or Hellenistic period, then we may assume that the author reflected both friendly relations with Tyre and the Tyrian influence in Judahite cities and villages of those eras.

In another departure from the DtrH, there is an almost complete and utter absence of the city of Sidon in the Chronicles. It is likely that by the end of the Persian period Sidon lost all relevance, following Artaxerxes III's raid against it in the middle of the fourth century BCE. The Chronicler dealt with the inconvenient historical information that he encountered in the DtrH regarding Sidon by entirely avoiding any mention of it. Sidon would also be a distraction from his general theological focus on the faithful and grateful Gentile – the city of Tyre.

Phoenicia in Jewish historical texts

In summary, the ancient Jewish historical texts show a movement away from distinguishing between the individual city-states of Sidon and Tyre, to their portrayal collectively – as in the phrase 'Sidonians and Tyrians – to referring to them together as 'Phoenicia'. Such progression reflects the historical events of the Babylonian, Persian and Hellenistic periods. The ancient Jewish texts inform us that for much of the Babylonian and Persian periods, the powerful city-states of Tyre and Sidon maintained their independence. Engaged in economic and political competition, the two city-states saw their fortunes change depending on the imperial powers that dominated the region. Tyre continued to have the political and economic advantage through the Babylonian period, only to see it fade in the subsequent Persian period when Sidon's fortunes vastly improved under the patronage of Persia. However, Sidon revolted against the Persians in the middle of the fourth century and was subsequently punished, and Tyre suffered destruction at the hands of Alexander the Great's army in 332 BCE. In the aftermath of those tragic events, Tyre and Sidon lost their economic and political independence and came to be referred to as 'Phoenicia', the name that the Greeks gave them when they referred to their arch-enemies in the political sphere and maritime trade.

We also have to conclude that much of the information in the 'historical' books of the Hebrew Bible is not reliable for the historical reconstruction of Iron Age Phoenicia since the texts were written long after the events they describe. This is especially relevant in regard to King Hiram of Tyre – although the biblical writers present some history, the details appear to have been added at a much later date, and the particulars of his reign are still elusive. The supposed historicity of King Hiram in the Bible is at times seen as confirmed by the writings of Flavius Josephus, a Jewish historian from the first century CE. Josephus cites two 'witnesses' to his stories, Dius and his *Histories of the Phoenicians* and 'Menander of Ephesus', both historians from the second century BCE.[13] Using them as his sources, Josephus mentions King Hiram of Tyre in his works *Against Apion* and the *Antiquities of the Jews*.[14] The stories there are largely reflective of the biblical accounts, although some additional details, including an exchange of riddles between Solomon and Hiram, are supplied. Yet historians are reluctant to accept the veracity of Josephus' accounts, questioning not necessarily him but the information from Dius and Menander, who were practically unknown among Josephus' Roman readers.[15] Dius' and Menander's information also appears too folkloristic to be taken seriously from a historical point of view. In the final analysis, Josephus possibly took Dius' and Menander's stories and infused them with the biblical themes and events to give the history of the Jewish people a weightier flare of antiquity – which was his purpose all along. It is hard therefore to accept the historicity of the information about Hiram, not only from the Hebrew Bible but from Josephus.

Tyre and Sidon in prophetic Jewish texts

The books belonging to the prophecy genre also frequently mention the Phoenician city-states, mainly Tyre and Sidon. However, prophetic books are notoriously difficult to interpret as the matters of authorship and the time of composition are exceedingly complex. Nevertheless, when we examine them through the historical prism of the late Iron Age and Persian periods, they can be useful for extracting some historical information.

For the most part, the prophetic books mention Tyre and Sidon in oracles condemning other nations for various transgressions against either Israel or Judah. Amos, the Judahite prophet of the eighth century BCE, pronounces judgment on Tyre for its many transgressions (Amos 1:9). In the passage, the phrase 'they delivered entire communities over to Edom' may refer to slave trade by the Tyrians.[16] Such trade is denounced in other biblical passages (for example Ezekiel 27:13 and Joel 4:6–7), and the sentiment sounds convincing since we have seen similar mention of a Phoenician slave trade in Homer and Herodotus. 'The covenant of kinship' may refer to the covenant made between Israelite and Tyrian kings, potentially confirming the DtrH's accounts regarding the ties between Solomon and Hiram – if, that is, the Book of Amos is dated to the eighth century BCE. However, the phrase can also refer to the ties between Judah and Tyre in the later Neo-Babylonian or Persian periods, and thus would not be supportive of the historicity of Hiram.

We find similar negative sentiments against Tyre expressed by Jeremiah (27:3; 47:4), Isaiah (23), Ezekiel (26:1–28:19) and Joel (4:4–8). Sometimes, the prophets mention the city-states of Tyre and Sidon together, as is the case with Zechariah 9:1–4, Jeremiah 47:4 and Joel 3:4. The last passage is of interest as it may have some historical value. The context of the passage is the prophecy of the future battle between Yahweh and Israel's enemies responsible for the destruction of Jerusalem. Because the fall of Judah is implied, Joel is frequently dated to the Persian period. What is interesting is that Tyre and Sidon are mentioned alongside Philistia ('What are you to me, O Tyre and Sidon, and all the regions of Philistia?'). It appears that the prophet was trying to mention all the entities on the West Asian coast of the Mediterranean, from north to south, but there is another intriguing possibility. Based on inscriptions and pottery, archaeologists have established that in the Persian period, the Phoenician city-states made significant inroads into the Philistine cities of Gaza, Ashdod, Ashkelon and Gath.[17] Classical authors (for example Pseudo-Scylax, who wrote the *Periplus* of the fourth century BCE) also note the control of Philistia by Tyre and Sidon, which undoubtedly led to some tensions between the indigenous peoples and the overlords to the north. Joel, however, mentions them together, in one context. From such a depiction we can propose that the prophecy reflects the time when the rivalry between Philistia and the Phoenician city-states dissipated because of the decline of the latter, late in the Persian or early in the Hellenistic period.

The Book of Ezekiel dedicates three long chapters (26–8) to Tyre, Sidon and, occasionally, Arwad, and it therefore deserves closer attention. There, Ezekiel prophesies the future siege and destruction of Tyre, the aftermath, the impact on Mediterranean trade and on the city-state itself, and the impending destruction of Sidon.

Ezekiel the prophet's active years fell in all likelihood in the first part of the sixth century BCE, and the date of the composition of his book was likely during the Babylonian exile or shortly after. The historical context of the book is unclear, though, since for historians the very fact of accurately 'prophesying' or predicting the actual historical event would be suspicious, whereas writing about it in its aftermath and giving it a prophetical flare would be more reasonable.

Ezekiel prophesies the forthcoming siege and destruction of Tyre by King Nebuchadnezzar of the Babylonians (26:7, 14). Historians suggest that the siege continued until 572 or 573 BCE; Ezekiel made a prophecy that at the end of it, the city would be destroyed by the mighty king. And yet, history does not confirm that the destruction indeed happened. The only event that literary and archaeological sources confirm is the deportation of the Tyrian elite to Babylon. Ezekiel's prophecy, it appears, is a case of wishful thinking. Having witnessed the siege of Jerusalem, the prophet imagines a time when the abominable Tyre would be besieged and destroyed.

Ezekiel's Chapter 27 (vv. 4–27) is particularly rich in describing Tyre's wealth, and we can deduce some historical clues regarding the city. It is an enviable maritime city-state with a strong presence in trade. Its neighbours, the coastal cities of Sidon, Arwad and Byblos, provide sailors for its ships (27:8–9). Others (Lebanon, Senir, Bashan, Cyprus and Egypt) supply various raw materials, especially timber (25:5–7). A third group (Put, Lud and Paras) provides troops for its defence (27:10). We have to take these lists with a pinch of salt, however, since it is highly unlikely that a prophetic passage written in poetry would aim to deliver accurate historical information. For example, the lands with which Tyre would have most likely traded – Tunisia, Malta, Sicily and Sardinia – are absent

Claude Lorrain, *Seascape with Ezekiel Crying on the Ruins of Tyre, c.* 1667, oil painting.

from the narrative.[18] It is entirely possible that the picture of Tyre contained in Ezekiel is that of a much weaker Tyre in the siege's aftermath of 573/572 BCE.

Ezekiel also mentions the city-state of Sidon in a series of oracles against other nations (Ammon, Moab, Edom, Philistia, Sidon, Tyre and Egypt) in 28:20–23. The passage is deeply ambiguous and short compared to that of the earlier oracle against Tyre, which goes on and on for almost three chapters. Sidon's inclusion in the list is seen either as a move to bring the number of the nations to the number of completion or fullness (seven) or to make sure that all coastal polities are sufficiently condemned.[19] Either way, Ezekiel's main umbrage against Sidon is its religious practices ('They shall know that I am the Lord when I . . . manifest my holiness in it'), and more specifically the cult of Astarte, for which we have ample evidence in the Persian period.

Ancient Jewish writings demonstrate the progression of the view of the Phoenician city-states. The biblical texts present the Phoenician city-states, primarily Tyre and Sidon, as individual economic and political city-states with their own distinct trajectories. The Jewish writers from the end of the Persian period and the following Hellenistic period, in the aftermath of the city-states suffering destruction and humiliation at the hands of the Persian kings, resort to a joint description of the two cities. No longer able to maintain their autonomy, Tyre and Sidon were considered a collective ethnogeographic unit, and the Jewish writings reflect that, resorting to the set-phrase 'Sidonians and Tyrians'.

For the most part, these writings are congruent with other literary sources from the ancient world. Though not devoid of ideological bias, they nevertheless point out the core qualities associated with the Phoenicians – their skill in maritime navigation, trade and their ability to manoeuvre the political landscape by making treaties with other royals. In treating Tyre and Sidon as independent city-states, the ancient Jewish writings also offer a unique Near Eastern, as opposed to Mediterranean or Homeric, view of Phoenicia and the Phoenicians.[20]

FOUR

RARE VOICES: PHOENICIAN WRITINGS

Few sources add more to our understanding of a people's identity than their own literary sources. Throughout time and place, humans have produced compositions that reveal themselves and their eras, complementing our understanding of their world view, aspirations, concerns and achievements. Among the memorable examples are the epic of Gilgamesh and the Enuma Elish from Mesopotamia; ancient Jewish writings; the *Iliad* and the *Odyssey* of Homer; and histories of Herodotus and Thucydides. Yet despite the abundance of writing in some cultures, several civilizations did not leave us much in terms of extended literary compositions. The Inca had neither writing nor literary heritage, and even the Persians, for all their might and well-developed ideology expressed through visual means, lack any notable lengthy literary heritage apart from occasional inscriptions, mostly from the royals, which are generally replete with pompous self-aggrandizing over military victories. In the past, historians defined a civilization by the presence of writing and thus excluded peoples and cultures without written records from the register of 'civilized' peoples. Consider for a moment the following quote from the renowned historian and author Barbara W. Tuchman, who wrote in the 1980s:

> Books are the carriers of civilization. Without books, history is silent, literature dumb, science crippled, thought and speculation at a standstill. Without books, the development of civilization would have been impossible. They are engines of change, windows on the world, and (as a poet has said)

'lighthouses erected in the sea of time.' They are companions, teachers, magicians, bankers of the treasures of the mind. Books are humanity in print.[1]

In more recent years, there has been a push to use the term 'symbolic communication' instead of 'writing' in defining a civilization, since ideas can be expressed through media other than letters and words. The aforementioned Inca are now believed to have used a system of knots of various colours to deliver important messages.[2] We also think of the Minoans as a great ancient civilization, although their Linear A script has not been deciphered yet; the very presence of symbolic communication, even if it is not understood, points to the sophistication of that culture.

The Phoenicians did not leave us much in terms of literary heritage. We assume that they were literate as they left a number of inscriptions on pottery and stone. However, longer works, which were in all likelihood written on easily degradable papyrus or parchment, succumbed to the destruction of time and fire. Those works were mentioned in antiquity, as Josephus tells of the archives of Tyre that were used by other historians (for example, Menander of Ephesus).[3] The Phoenicians also produced cosmogonies and theogonies, histories and mythologies, and itineraries and agricultural treatises – many are quoted or cited in Roman times and later, but none of them have survived in their original form.[4]

Whether literary works existed but were also lost to the passage of time is a moot point since we do not have anything to analyse, and probably never will have. What we have is a number of mostly short inscriptions that nevertheless illuminate our understanding of Phoenician identity, religion, politics and social history. We will try to sort them by the periods from which they emerged and identify the most important ones.

The alphabet and development of language

Before we get to explore the Phoenician inscriptions proper, the invention of the alphabet by the Phoenicians should be addressed.

The emergence of the alphabetical system, as opposed to a hieroglyphics or cuneiform type of writing, is significant, and the Phoenicians are frequently credited with it. Herodotus is the one who first voiced such a possibility when he wrote:

> So these Phoenicians, including the Gephyraians, came with Kadmos and settled this land, and they transmitted much lore to the Hellenes, and in particular, taught them the alphabet which, I believe, the Hellenes did not have previously, but which was originally used by all Phoenicians. With the passage of time, both the sound and the shape of the letters changed. Because at this time it was mostly Ionians who lived around the Phoenicians, they were the ones who were first instructed in the use of the alphabet by them, and after making a few changes to the form of the letters, they put them to good use; but when they spoke of them, they called them 'Phoenician' letters, which was only right since these letters had been introduced to Hellas by Phoenicians.[5]

According to Herodotus, the Greeks borrowed the writing system from the Phoenicians and, with time, adapted it to their own use by changing the shapes of the letters. The Greeks also willingly referred to the letters in their modified system as 'Phoenician',

(1) West Semitic Letter Names	(2) Egyptian Hieroglyphic Prototype	(3) Proto-Sinaitic (Sinai 375a) Catalog No. 89	(4) Izbet Sartah Ostracon	(5) el-Khadr Arrowhead #2 Catalog No. 91	(6) Mesha Stela	(7) Samaria Ostracon Catalog No. 90	(8) Greek Letters and Names
'aleph (ox)	(Gardiner F1)			—			A (alpha)
het (fence?)	(Gardiner O42)						H (eta)
kaph (palm)	(Gardiner D46)			—			K (kappa)
'ayin (eye)	(Gardiner D4)					—	O (omicron)

Script correspondence chart of several alphabetic signs.

overcoming hesitation about using anything originating from their long-standing competitors and antagonists.

Although such a tribute is both rare and welcome, coming as it does from Greek sources, the attribution of the invention of the alphabet to the Phoenicians is problematic as historians have determined the emergence of more stylized, as opposed to pictographic, shapes elsewhere in the Near East. The likely precursor to the Phoenician alphabet was the Proto-Canaanite script (appearing from the thirteenth century BCE on),[6] examples of which have been found on pottery and other objects in properly identifiable archaeological contexts. The script was a more stylized and simplified method of representing the basic sounds of a language compared to the pictographic symbols of Egypt.

Another development towards the emergence of a linear alphabet was a move away from the cuneiform shapes. By the first millennium BCE, the two processes converged and complemented each other, resulting in the emergence of a 22-letter Phoenician consonantal alphabet, 'corresponding to its phonological system',[7] read right to left (termed 'sinistrograde'). There were no vowels as the reader supplied them based on their familiarity with the vocabulary, grammar and context. Some linguists propose that, thanks in large part to trade and the colonizing activities of the Phoenician city-states, the simplified and user-friendly script was spread throughout the Mediterranean and was eventually adopted by the Greeks.[8]

Among the Phoenician city-states, Byblos became the first centre of alphabetic writing in the aftermath of the tumultuous

(1) Alphabetic Sign	(2) Ugaritic (Archaic Form)	(3) Ahiram Sarcophagus (Early Phoenician)
{g} gimel		
{š} samekh		

Comparison between Ugaritic signs and their alphabetic counterparts.

Phoenician
alphabet.

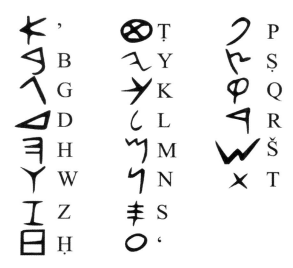

end of the Late Bronze Age and the beginning of the Iron Age.[9] Some scholars try to be even more precise, with one proposing that 'the pseudo-hieroglyphic script of Byblos was devised *c.* 900 BC, remained in use for the first two thirds of the ninth century, and was then replaced, *c.* 830, by the earliest monumental alphabetic inscriptions.'[10] Shortly thereafter, the dialect of Tyre and Sidon emerged as the standard 'Tyro-Sidonian' ('Phoenician') regional language that to some extent influenced the writings from Byblos. Then, about 900 BCE, the Phoenician alphabet was adopted in Cyprus by the settlers from the Phoenician homeland.[11] Eventually, a North African variant of the Phoenician language, known as Punic, came to be used in Carthage, a Phoenician (Tyrian) colony.

The Phoenician alphabetic script proved to be attractive, as both Hebrew and Aramaic speakers adopted the 22-letter writing system for their needs. Whether it was its simplicity, the prestige of the Phoenician script or something else is unknown. Confirming what Herodotus mentioned, the Greeks borrowed the Proto-Canaanite script sometime between the end of the second millennium BCE and the first quarter of the first millennium BCE.[12] Although Herodotus' account lacks sufficient information regarding the emergence of the alphabet (understandable on account of the evidence available to him at the time), for the most part he correctly identifies the chain of transmission of the writing system from the Phoenicians to the Greeks.[13]

The Phoenician system of writing was deciphered by the French writer and numismatist Jean-Jacques Barthélemy in 1758. Further work on the finalization of the decipherment was completed by the renowned German theologian and linguist Wilhelm Gesenius, who is credited with the creation of the field of Phoenician and Punic studies in the first half of the nineteenth century. Since that time, more than 10,000 inscriptions in Phoenician and Punic have been discovered and deciphered.[14]

Phoenician inscriptions

As carriers of indigenous voices, inscriptions from the Phoenician city-states can potentially reveal invaluable information regarding their societies, political climate and religious matters. In contrast to the available literary sources (mostly Greek) that reveal outsiders' points of view, the epigraphic evidence from the Phoenician home-land discloses how the writers saw their own identity and how they expressed it through the written word. The difficulty, however, is the dearth of written records from Phoenicia; for example, Tyre, the illustrious Phoenician city, yielded only a very small sample of inscriptions.[15] Mostly, historians have had to rely on the royal inscriptions of which we have a few samples. Household-level writing samples are very rare, and they are hardly revealing from the historical point of view. The damage to the existing archaeological layers, the impossibility of carrying out extensive excavations under-neath continuously occupied areas, and the absence of wide-ranging literacy are among the significant factors limiting the cache of existing Phoenician epigraphic evidence. Here we will provide a brief overview of the available evidence with the goal of extracting historical information and any data pointing to the identity of the writers.

Inscriptions from Byblos

Some of the oldest inscriptions emerge from the city-state of Byblos. During the French excavations of 1923, a limestone sarcophagus of

Sarcophagus of Ahiram, king of Byblos, *c.* 1000 BCE.

King Ahiram (also spelled as Ahirom[16]) was discovered (referred to as ANET 661). The sarcophagus was inscribed with an epitaph to Ahiram commissioned by his son, Ittobaal, usually dated to the early Iron Age (*c.* 1000 BCE).

The somewhat rough inscription (funerary inscriptions tend to be of lesser quality than those found on monuments) chiselled around the edge of the lid and the upper rim of the sarcophagus pronounces curses against anyone who disturbs the peace of the deceased. Historians have pointed out the iconographic connections of the imagery on the coffin (the lotus, for example) with Egyptian motifs, and some have even suggested that the sarcophagus was commissioned in Egypt and later imported to Byblos.[17] The Egyptian connection is not surprising as Byblos had maintained close political and economic ties with Egypt for the duration of its history. More revealing is the Byblian dynastic continuity confirmed through the words of the inscriptions, the son paying his dues to the departed father and pledging retribution on anyone who would venture to disrupt and violate Byblos along with his father's tomb. Thus the Ahiram inscription served both as a testimony to the viability of the dynastic succession and its eternal connection to Byblos as its homeland.

Traditional lotus imagery on the tomb of Hetpet at Giza, Egypt, from the Old Kingdom's Fifth Dynasty (2465–2323 BCE).

Notably, the curses contained on the sarcophagus were a characteristic feature of burials not only in Byblos but elsewhere in the Ancient Near East. There are several examples of curses on Egyptian tombs, most of which are of the following nature: 'Cursed be those that disturb the rest of Pharaoh. They that shall break the seal of this tomb shall meet death by a disease which no doctor can diagnose.'[18] Respect for the dead did not usually warrant spelling out the specific punishments, as it was considered unthinkable for them to be disturbed. The same sentiment can be observed in Herodotus' description of the inscription on the tomb of Nitocris, queen of Babylon: 'If one of the rulers of Babylon after me is in need of money, let him open my tomb and take however much he likes. But if he is not in need, may he under no circumstances open it; otherwise it will not be well for him.'[19] Although the context of the story in which the writing on Nitocris's tomb is mentioned is meant first and foremost as an illustration of Darius's greed, Herodotus is using here a well-known tradition of threatening curses against those who bother the dead. Byblos and its kings were deeply rooted in the culture of the Ancient Near East and they resorted to common conventions in burials and accompanying rituals.

Finally, the names Ahiram and Ittobaal echo the names Hiram and Ethbaal in the Hebrew Bible. Hiram was an illustrious king of Tyre who had extensive dealings with David, and Ethbaal was the father of Jezebel, wife of King Ahab of Israel. The question arises of whether the biblical writers were aware of the history of the Phoenician city-states and reflected that knowledge, however imperfectly, through the erroneous spelling of the names, or whether the names, with variant spellings, were common in the Phoenician city-states. The paucity of indigenous Phoenician inscriptions does not allow us to answer this question with any certainty.

In addition to the Ahiram inscription (and another minor royal dedicatory inscription, of Yehimilk of Byblos), we also have quite a few inscriptions from Byblos dated to the Persian period. The oldest of them are the two funerary inscriptions of Shiptibaal III (or his son) and another king. Both inscriptions contain curses against those who would potentially disturb the peace of the diseased. Of greater interest is the inscription of Yehawmilk (KAI 10), which is featured on a limestone stele discovered in the ruins of the ancient Temple of the Mistress of Byblos/Gubal in 1869. There, the goddess is depicted sitting on a throne, wearing an Egyptian-style garb with a winged disc on her head and holding a sceptre in one hand. With the other hand, she is blessing King Yehawmilk, who is extending a vessel, possibly a cup, in her direction. The bearded king appears to be wearing Persian-style clothing, which supports the fifth- or fourth-century date of the inscription.

The inscription describes the renovations to the Temple of the Mistress of Byblos in the Persian period. The Mistress of Byblos has been frequently associated with the city-state, and many have wondered about the origins of this female deity. She appears to have been equated with the Egyptian goddess Hathor since as early as the fifteenth century BCE.[20] Yet the most frequently voiced suggestion is that the Mistress is a syncretistic manifestation of aspects of the three female Canaanite deities Asherah, Astarte and Anath.[21] Such a view of the goddess casts the royalty of Byblos as being culturally connected to, and in some ways influenced by, the cultures of the wider Ancient Near East.

The inscription conveys a general sense of prosperity and stability. Undertaking a construction project of considerable scale amid ongoing disturbances or political turbulence would have been impractical. The Yehawmilk inscription therefore suggests instead the certainty on the part of the Byblian elite that the implemented renovations would endure despite any internal or external pressures on Byblos. The inscription also informs us of the irregular chain of ascension to the throne. Yehawmilk might have inherited the throne not from his father, Yeharbaal (who does not have a royal title), but from his grandfather King Urimilk ('I am Yehawmilk, king of Byblos, son of Yeharbaal, grandson of Urimilk, king of Byblos, whom the lady, Mistress of Byblos, made king over Byblos'[22]). The political life in Byblos appears quite bustling, and yet another Byblian inscription on a marble sarcophagus confirms just that. Usually referred to as the funerary inscription of Batnoam (KAI 11), the short epitaph also reflects minor shuffles in royal leadership – the inscription shows that Azbaal's father, Paltibaal, does not have the royal title but instead is said to have been a priest of the Mistress of Byblos ('In this coffin lie I, Batnoam, mother of King Azbaal, king of Byblos, son of Paltibaal, priest of the Mistress'[23]). Some have suggested that Azbaal founded a new dynasty as a challenge to the Persian imperial authorities; but the explanation may be simpler. It is evident that from time to time the royals in Byblos went through periods of inner political turmoil that may have been characterized by unexpected power grabs.

Inscriptions from Sidon

It is not surprising that most of the notable inscriptions from Sidon are dated to the Persian period. Sidon was the preeminent city-state on the Levantine coast, powerful both politically and economically, and its kings invested heavily in making the fact known far and wide. Especially resilient – surviving the passing of successive empires, natural destruction and the urbanization of ancient settlements – have been the inscriptions on Sidonian sarcophagi.

The most noteworthy inscriptions are those of kings Tabnit (KAI 13) and Eshmunazar II (KAI 14). They were discovered on two black basalt coffins that were imported from Egypt. Of interest

Sarcophagus of Eshmunazar II, king of Sidon (late 6th century BCE).

is the fact that Tabnit's sarcophagus had been used previously, whereas Eshmunazar's coffin was new. Tabnit's inscription, the main purpose of which is to deter potential looters, is usually dated to the second half of the sixth century BCE. The inscription clearly associates Sidonian royalty with the cult of Astarte; Tabnit here

Egyptian-style anthropoid sarcophagus of Tabnit, king of Sidon (early 5th century BCE).

appears to carry out both royal and sacerdotal (priestly) roles ('I, Tabnit, priest of Astarte, king of the Sidonians, son of Eshmunazar, priest of Astarte, king of the Sidonians, lie in this coffin'[24]). His son Eshmunazar II (grandson of Eshmunazar I), however, does not carry the same titles ('King Eshmunazar, king of the Sidonians, son of King Tabnit, king of the Sidonians, King Eshmunazar, king of the Sidonians'[25]).

The inscription of Eshmunazar II (the name means 'Eshmun has provided help') tells us that he ruled for a relatively short time – fourteen years – after the death of his father, Tabnit. When he ascended the throne, the king was too young, and his mother, Amotashtart, acted as regent while waiting for the boy to mature. Even when Eshmunazar II assumed royal responsibilities, Amotashtart was still very involved in the affairs of the city-state. The two of them oversaw the construction of the temples of Astarte, Eshmun and Baal. These three deities represent an expanded pantheon compared to the single Astarte mentioned in Tabnit's inscription, although both epigraphic compositions invoke dire warnings to those who would dare to disturb the tombs. Eshmunazar II's inscription also mentions the gift of lands given to the Sidonian kings by a Persian monarch, possibly Xerxes, for the Sidonian involvement in the campaigns against the Greeks ('the Lord of Kings gave us Dor and Joppa, the glorious lands of Dagon, which are in the plain of Sharon, for the great things which I have done'[26]).

Besides the extensive inscriptions of Tabnit and Eshmunazar II, there are a number of other, much shorter epigraphic materials from Sidon. Dozens of them are so-called Bodashtart inscriptions, discovered on building stones of the Temple of Eshmun, in the vicinity of modern Sidon. Most of them strengthen the thesis of the goddess Astarte and her cult being pre-eminent in Sidon, especially in the Persian period.

The last inscription from Sidon to mention here is the Baalshillem inscription. The inscription, a proclamation of praise to Eshmun, is located at the base of one of the statues of children near the Temple of Eshmun. The statues themselves were associated with well-being: the word 'Eshmun' is etymologically related to the roots meaning 'healing' or 'health'. That Eshmun appears quite frequently in the Sidonian inscriptions supports the notion that alongside Astarte, Eshmun was also the traditional deity of Sidon.

Inscriptions from outside the Phoenician homeland

A few inscriptions associated with the Phoenician city-states, usually by virtue of linguistic proximity, have been found outside Phoenicia proper. Two of them, the inscriptions of Kilamuwa, king of Ya'diya, and of Azatiwada, king of the Hittites, were discovered in what is now Turkey. They are both rather boastful proclamations of what Kilamuwa and Azatiwada accomplished. Although the inscriptions carry the familiar curses against those who would disturb them, they are not directly linked to the Phoenician homeland.

Several Phoenician inscriptions come from Cyprus, more specifically Kition and Idalion, traditional Phoenician colonies. Most of them are brief and fragmentary, however, and they do not provide much detail regarding the interactions between the inhabitants of the Cypriot sites and the Phoenician homeland. It is clear, though, that starting in the fifth century BCE Cyprus was drifting more and more into the Aegean cultural sphere, with Phoenician ties waning considerably. This process was not unexpected; the ongoing clashes between the Greeks and the Persians in the fifth century BCE affected the Phoenicians directly as they were known collaborators with the Achaemenid Empire by providing ships and soldiers.

Curious in the context of the relations between Greece and Phoenicia are two Phoenician inscriptions from the Greek mainland. Despite hailing from the formerly hostile land, the inscriptions show distinct connections with the Phoenician city-states, especially Sidon. Written in a style of a Greek resolution after a vote, the inscription from Piraeus (KAI 60) honours the crowning of one Shamabaʻal with a golden crown worth twenty darics for his services of rebuilding the temple court of the community of Sidonians. The major difficulty in using this inscription for historical reconstruction or socio-historical analysis is its unknown provenance. No Sidonian enclave was known to exist in Greece until at least 96 BCE, and there is therefore an understandable reluctance to date it to earlier. The mention of the darics, however, may place the date of the inscription either in the Persian period, when darics were used, or in Alexander the Great's time, since darics were known to be in currency even after the demise of the Persian Empire. Given this uncertainty, we can say only that there was once a community of Sidonians in Greece, and that those Sidonians showed a remarkable ability to assimilate to the prevailing culture by resorting to the same literary style of the resolution and the same procedure of voting on pressing issues that are known from existing Greek inscriptions. The unknown provenance of the Piraeus inscription prevents us from saying anything more about it and the community that generated it.

Another inscription that supports the notion that the Sidonians set up a settlement in Greece is a decree by Cephisodotus (Kephisodotus) to honour Straton (Abdashtart I in other sources), king of Sidon, dated to about 366–360 BCE. It was engraved on a marble stele that was discovered next to the Parthenon. It appears from the inscription that the Sidonians residing in Athens had a privileged status, as, for example, they were exempt from the Metic tax levied against foreign-born citizens of Athens. They were also acting as mediators between Athens and the Persians at the time when the latter's fortunes were dwindling under the weight of revolts and the structural weakness of the empire. It is quite possible that the Sidonians were eager to secure Athenian support for any future insurrection against the Persians, their former masters. Just a few years after the inscription was completed, Tennes, another king of Sidon, revolted against the Great King of Persia Artaxerxes III (c. 346/5 BCE).[27] Generally, the Cephisodotus decree provides a rare glimpse into the political and cultural developments in Persian-era Sidon, information not available from any other source. The Athenians showed great honours to the visiting king of Sidon – the same Sidon that over a hundred years earlier had heavily assisted the Persian kings in their campaigns against Greece.

Although we rarely hear indigenous voices from the inhabitants of the Phoenician city-states, the ones that are available to us shed some light on their self-identification and their place in broader Ancient Near Eastern history. The limitations of this information lie in the character of the inscriptions, which are mostly royal and funerary, and consequently tell us little about commoners, topics other than burials, or other aspects of the social life in the Phoenician city-states.

The major Phoenician inscriptions demonstrate that the loyalties of the inhabitants of the Phoenician city-states were first and foremost directed towards their cities of origin and almost never to coalitions, whether real or externally assigned. And although the writing system that they used was similar, they still maintained their distinct dialects.

Each individual city-state maintained its own religious pantheon. In Byblos, the Mistress of Byblos received constant veneration throughout the city's history, whereas the cohort of Astarte and Eshmun were the deities historically associated and prominently mentioned in the inscriptions from Sidon.

The individual city-states also successfully functioned in the cultural milieu of the Ancient Near East. Phoenician kings and queens resorted to the same cultural conventions as their neighbours, through the use of curses and blessings in funeral inscriptions and in showing preferences for the ruling tastes of the day, as was the case with the Egyptian sarcophagi of Tabnit and Eshmunazar II. The same social stratification between royalty and commoners as elsewhere in the ancient world was evident among the Phoenicians.

We should say a few words about literacy in Phoenicia. Starting in the eighth century BCE, writing and the ability to read spread beyond the royal elite in the Phoenician city-states.[28] Some have even proposed that, since the individual city-states placed inscriptions on seals and coins, it follows that literacy was widespread across large swathes of Phoenicia, at least during the time when coinage was introduced.[29] The factors that are cited in support of this are record-keeping, engagement in trade and the introduction of cursive writing.

However, the suggestion of widespread literacy in the city-states during the Persian period is not entirely convincing. The presence of letters on seals and coins does not necessarily mean that the user could understand what the writing said. The ability to recognize different signs and symbols is quite sufficient to determine the value of a coin or the identity of a seal-bearer. Similarly, merchants did not need to be literate to manage their record-keeping. Finally, cursive writing may have served as a means of maintaining the stratification between social classes, with cursive serving as a marker of a higher social status.

A more likely proposal regarding literacy in Phoenicia would be that it was comparable to the levels of literacy in the surrounding lands and cultures of the ancient world – that is, that it was the privilege of the elite and/or professional scribes who were entrusted with communicating messages from the royal authorities. Merchants and commoners might have 'technical literacy', the rudimentary skills needed to read and write the symbols meaningful to them for carrying out their activities. As a skill of the privileged, writing could possibly have served as a prestige marker, signalling the social status of the one who commissioned this or that piece of writing, whether on a stele or a sarcophagus.

Finally, the epigraphic evidence affirms the independent and autonomous character of the Phoenician city-states. It indicates that in Byblos, for example, the changes in royal leadership resulted from internal developments – or perhaps squabbles – with little outside influence. Similarly, the royals of Sidon appear to have plotted their own course in dealing with imperial authorities, mostly in the Persian period, by electing to lend their support to the Achaemenid campaigns, for which they were occasionally rewarded with gifts of lands.

FIVE

MONEY MATTERS:
PHOENICIAN COINAGE

Valuable insights regarding Phoenician identity, interactions with the power players in the Levant, and economic relations between both the Phoenician city-states themselves and the broader Mediterranean area can be gained through not only literary sources but numismatics. Phoenician coinage comes in different shapes, weights and materials, with the added differentiation of iconography, inscriptions and circulation. In a way, coinage is difficult for historians to interpret because its testimony is not as clear as the written word, and one has to resort to a fair amount of comparative analysis and employ a series of interpretative strategies to arrive at historical conclusions. In this chapter, we will briefly overview the history of coinage in general before describing coins from Phoenicia in all their variations. Of special interest to us are the changes that the coinage went through from one city to another, and also through time; those changes will be crucial to understanding the processes that were under way in the Phoenician city-states.

History of coinage

In the absence of royal decrees instituting the minting of coinage or diary entries of the people who actually produced it, we have to rely on the testimony of Herodotus in determining where and when the first coinage originated. Writing in the fifth century BCE, Herodotus reports that the Lydians in Asia Minor were the first to introduce coins as a monetary instrument: 'the Lydian way of life is not unlike the Greek. The Lydians were the first people we know of to use a gold and silver coinage and to introduce retail trade.'[1] Herodotus is describing how the Lydians were able to turn a natural alloy of gold and silver (commonly known as electrum) into currency. We have to keep in mind that Herodotus was not above fictionalizing events for the instruction of his readers. This passage concludes a lengthy narrative involving King Croesus of Lydia, a man known for his enormous wealth and his engagement with and eventual defeat by Cyrus the Great, king of Persia, in 546 BCE. Since coinage appears in Persia fairly shortly after the Persians defeated the Lydians, Herodotus' statement regarding the origin of coinage was meant to demonstrate the transfer of power and the irony of fate, where the greatest 'barbaric' empire of his day adopted the practices of the defeated, sophisticated Lydians.

Not entirely satisfied with Herodotus' account, numismatists have attempted to trace the earliest coinage production centres by carefully examining coinage hoards and collating them with literary sources. One proposal places the first attempt to mint silver coins in quantity on the Greek island of Aegina, located 40 kilometres southeast of Athens in the Saronic Gulf, in the first third of the sixth century BCE.[2] The Aeginates saw early on the value of currency for global trade, and soon their coins could be found across the ancient world. This wide circulation was aided in part by the uniform iconography, showing a sea turtle on the obverse. The minting practices of Aegina in time influenced those of other nation-states, which also strove for uniformity in iconography and weight.

Prior to the invention of coinage, precious metals (silver, gold and electrum) were in use for trade in the ancient world. In the Ancient Near East, for example, where archaeologists have discovered hoards of the precious metals in many locations, the weight of the primary monetary measure, the shekel, hovered around 8.26 grams.[3] Shekels in the form of stamped lumps of metal, silver ingots, were among the earliest examples of the pre-monetary instruments used in commercial and temple transactions. However, with time, coinage was recognized as a more convenient means of facilitating commerce, collecting taxes and making and receiving payments. Besides, coinage was minted by individual states that guaranteed its value. Although ancient coinage was typically made of precious metals, the value of a coin was higher than the value of the pure metal of the same weight, to compensate for the minting process.

In Greece, following the example of Aegina, Athens and Corinth began minting coinage soon thereafter, in the latter part of the sixth century BCE. By the end of that century, more than a hundred mints were producing coinage in the Greek world.[4] Coinage in Greece was primarily necessitated by the need to pay mercenary soldiers in an easily transportable monetary instrument, as well as to make legal payments of all kinds to the state.[5] The portability of coinage contributed in turn to the accumulation of wealth among the Greeks.[6] Some coinage – for example, of Athens – became popular not only among the states in formal alliance with Athens (such as the Delian League) but in other lands (Egypt, Palestine, Phoenicia, Bactria and Arabia).[7] In a way, the Athenian owl tetradrachm, the most commonly used, came to represent the city and its prestige.

Greek numismatics gave us a few important terms. First of all, the *obol* (literally, 'an iron spit') was a basic currency unit. Six obols equalled one *drachma* ('handful' in Greek). Four drachmas, or one tetradrachm, constituted one *stater* (literally, 'weight'), which could be minted in either gold or silver. All of these terms refer to the weight of the precious metals used, and the correspondence

Contemporary reconstruction of an Athenian coin.

between these currency units remained stable. However, the weight of the coins themselves fluctuated over time, not least because of the fluctuation of exchange rates between gold and silver.

Another boost to coin production in the ancient world took place in the Achaemenid period when the Persians commenced production of their own currency. Darius I, also known as Darius the Great, who ruled from 522 to 486 BCE, is generally credited with introducing a gold *daric*.[8] The daric equalled 20 silver *sigloi* (plural of *siglos*, which means 'to weigh'; the word is also etymologically related to 'shekel'). The daric weighed about 8.4 grams, had a high purity of gold (approximately 98 per cent) and corresponded with the Ancient Near Eastern shekel.[9] The siglos weighed 11.2 grams and was 94 to 97 per cent silver.[10] The characteristic feature of Achaemenid coinage was the depiction of the royal archer on the obverse as a personal statement of the power and prestige of the Persian kings. The vast Persian Empire embraced coinage as a convenient means of paying the mercenaries it employed during its numerous conflicts with the Greeks.

The Persians conducted a rather relaxed, laissez-faire style of governance and allowed their subjects a significant amount of economic and political autonomy. The lands under Persian dominion were able to retain their indigenous political set-ups and maintained their cultural trajectories under the formal leadership of Persia. In such a climate, many Persian subjects, including the Phoenicians, commenced to mint their own coinage to facilitate intra-state and international trade, to pay tribute to the Persians, and to compensate workforce and mercenaries. In doing so, they frequently used Greek and Persian coins as examples for their own, adopting both Greek and Persian weight standards.

Coinage in Phoenicia

Before we proceed to analysing coinage from the Phoenician city-states, we need to address a few important questions. The first of these are the dates of when the first coins were produced and the reasons why they needed to be introduced in the first place. Most researchers agree that the Phoenicians started producing coinage relatively late, sometime in the middle of the fifth century BCE, almost 150 years after the Lydians and the Greeks.[11] The four major mints were at Arwad, Byblos, Sidon and Tyre, and throughout the years there have been lively debates as to the order of their introduction. Coin hoards have been one of the primary ways to determine the date of coinage. Hoarding precious materials and coins was relatively widespread in the Ancient Near East, where the need to preserve wealth, considering the many conflicts, was high. By analysing the contents of a hoard and the presence or absence of coinage from a particular city, we can make reasonable conclusions regarding the timing of its introduction. For example, if there are several examples of hoards containing coinage of Tyre and Byblos but not Sidon, and then some later-dated hoards contain Sidonian coinage, we can conclude that Sidonian coinage appeared after minting had been introduced in Byblos and Tyre. The generally accepted sequence of introduction of coinage is as follows: Byblos, Tyre, Sidon, Arwad.

This brings us to the next issue: the need for coinage at all. Undoubtedly, coinage is a much more efficient means of economic exchange than barter or weighted precious materials. It is portable, it serves political purposes as it carries the insignia of the issuing authority, and it allows for more complicated and flexible commercial transactions compared to lumps of metal. These are definite advantages, but the timing of introduction of coinage is more significant. Why start minting coins at a particular time? We can answer this question if we look closer into the function of coinage.

Several possible reasons for the introduction of coinage exist. The first one is to facilitate local trade. In this line of thinking, the individual city-states would conduct mercantile exchanges by issuing their local currencies. The second reason concerns establishing local prestige and projecting power through the iconography on coinage. Whereas international trade in the Mediterranean was conducted mostly through the traditional use of precious metals in the form of ingots or other objects, the local economies were sustained by the use of locally minted currencies.[12] Disseminating image-bearing emblems of one's kingdom would make more sense in a more limited geographic area since distant lands would not immediately recognize the symbols and inscriptions.

The third suggested reason for introducing coinage is to have a precise monetary instrument to use in military campaigns and, more specifically, to pay mercenaries for their services.[13] According to this proposition, Sidon, for example, might have introduced their own coinage to pay for the rowers of the Sidonian boats during the Persian campaigns. The intensifying stand-off between the Greeks and Persians in the first half of the fifth century BCE led to the rise of a 'rower' economy, whereby a person, such as a farmer during the slow months of the agricultural year, could easily find decent employment rowing the triremes. That in turn led to a rising demand for a convenient form of payment.

The second and third suggestions are certainly plausible, but the first option is the most convincing. The Phoenicians, who were traders and mariners first and foremost, encountered coinage in Greece and emulated the Greeks by introducing their own. The limited distribution of Phoenician coinage suggests that they did not rely on it as the primary means of payment to mercenaries. Mercenaries

Model of the Athenian trireme.

would also be more likely to demand payment in a widely accepted currency than in coinage from the Phoenician city-states. Moreover, very little, if any, Phoenician coinage has been found in the interior of the Persian Empire, which casts doubt on the idea that the Phoenicians minted coinage to pay tribute to the Persians. If indeed they paid tribute using their coinage (as opposed to quantities of gold and silver) and the Persians then melted the coins for the precious metal, why would the Phoenicians go to the trouble of minting in the first place? The Phoenician city-states were autonomous in the Persian period, and they were given carte blanche by the Persian imperial authorities to maintain their economic activities as they saw fit. Coinage was convenient for the exchange of goods and services primarily between the various Phoenician city-states.

The chain of events leading to the inauguration of coinage among the Phoenician city-states would then look something like this. The Phoenicians actively supported the Persians in their wars with Greece. It was a natural alliance, fuelled by the animosity between the Greeks and Phoenicians throughout their histories and the cultural affinity of the Near Eastern peoples. The Phoenician city-states assisted the Achaemenid Empire by providing naval resources, such as ships and rowers. The Persian naval disasters such as the defeat in 480 BCE at the Battle of Salamis at the hands of the Greeks necessitated that Sidon, Tyre and other city-states replenish their fleets.[14] Most of the work was carried out in Phoenicia proper, using local materials and workforce. As the economic exchanges became more complex, the Phoenicians resorted to the Greek example and started minting their own coinage.

Several common features set Phoenician coinage apart. The Phoenician mints favoured maritime themes, reflecting both externally assigned and, undoubtedly, locally held traditions of seafaring. Additionally, all Phoenician coinage was struck on either silver or bronze (never gold, since it was the prerogative of Persian imperial authorities)[15] and adhered more or less, with some fluctuations, to a universal single weight standard, often referred to as 'Phoenician' (around 13–14 grams).[16] The standard fluctuated throughout the years, however, alongside the changing political and economic situation in the region.

The three major areas of interest, as far as Phoenician coinage is concerned, are iconography, metrology (study of weights and measures) and regional distribution. Iconography can potentially reveal information regarding political and religious affiliations, identity and relations to the Persian imperial powers. Both metrology and geographic distribution of Phoenician money can inform us about the economies of the various Phoenician city-states and their influence in the region. The more widely spread the coinage of a particular city-state, the more prominent its economic influence in the area and the more prestigious its position in the region.

Byblos

Although a relatively insignificant player economically and politically, judging by the number of numismatic finds there, Byblos is nevertheless credited with the honour of being the first to strike coinage in Phoenicia, around the middle of the fifth century BCE.[17] Byblos, which is not mentioned frequently as an active collaborator with the Persians, did not need to pay for mercenaries and yet it started minting coins. This fact strengthens the argument for the appearance of coinage based on the requirements of intraregional or local trade.

The first Byblian coins featured a crouched sphinx with a male head wearing the double crown of Egypt on the obverse and, variably, a lotus flower (sometimes interpreted as the lightning bolt of Baal Hadad, a Byblian version of the storm god), a helmeted head, an Egyptian sceptre or a lion on the reverse.[18] The use of Egyptian motifs is significant as the Byblian authorities reaffirmed their long-standing cultural ties with Egypt through the medium of coinage. However, they did so in the context of Persian imperial domination. Interpreted in such a manner, the first Byblian coinage serves as a means of affirming the city's autonomy in the empire. The chosen Attic weight standard of the first series was lighter than the standards that emerged later; with time, Byblos aligned the weight of their coinage with that of Tyre and Sidon.[19] It appears, though, that at first the main concern for the royalty of

Byblos was the correspondence of the Byblian coins with coinages of other lands (for example, Lycia), for ease of trade.

As time went by, the coins from Byblos changed both in their iconography and their weight. In the middle of the fifth century BCE, Byblian coinage began featuring a galley with three armed men on the obverse and a variety of animal imagery on the reverse.[20] The change of iconography in Byblos can be explained by its emergence as a maritime power. Historically, Byblos had been famous for exporting its cedar wood. With the rise of Persia, the authorities of Byblos decided that a more robust involvement in the military campaigns of the empire would be more lucrative. Following the examples of Sidon, Tyre and Arwad, Byblos established its fleet. The change from the Attic to the Phoenician weight standard also points to the rising prestige of Byblos as well as to more extensive trade within the region.

Throughout the Persian period, Byblian coinage production remained constant, without major interruptions. Such continuity suggests the stable economic and political atmosphere in the city-state as it successfully manoeuvred Persian politics and was able to gain financially from its cooperation with imperial authorities. The Byblian coinage, in tandem with inscriptions, also allowed historians to reconstruct the succession of the kings of Byblos in the Persian period: Shiptibaal III (525–501 BCE), Urimilk II (500–476 BCE), Yeharbaal (475–451 BCE), Yehawmilk (450–426 BCE), Elpaal (425–401 BCE), Azbaal (400–376 BCE), Urimilk III (375–351 BCE)

Coin of Azbaal, king of Byblos (r. 400–376 BCE).

Lion and bull scene on the Apadana at Persepolis, *c.* 5th century BCE.

and Aynel (350–326 BCE).[21] The long reigns of kings also supports the idea of stability in Byblos in the fifth century BCE.

In terms of iconography, Byblian coinage was syncretistic, as it frequently featured Egyptian, Greek, Sidonian and Persian images. Such variety suggests that Byblian authorities nimbly projected their alliances through iconography. Of particular interest is the changing lion. The lion appears in several series of Byblian coinage. Lions frequently represented the goddess Asherah; in Byblos, Asherah was better known as Baalat Gubal, or Mistress (Lady) of Byblos. It is unsurprising that the Byblians decided to show their veneration of the patroness of the city by featuring her likeness on their coinage. However, the goddess Asherah (Astarte in Greek) was also the traditional tutelary goddess of Sidon. In this way, the use of the lion motif could be interpreted as a way by which the

Byblian kings displayed deference to the then powerful city-state of Sidon and expressed respect for and acknowledgement of their mutually beneficial economic ties.

After a brief departure from the lion iconography in favour of a vulture standing over the body of a ram, the image returned in the second quarter of the fourth century BCE, this time in the form of the lion overpowering a bull.[22] The image may be interpreted as an attempt to covertly challenge Persian authority by emphasizing the prowess of the city-state, although imitation of traditional Persian iconography is more likely. The image of a lion attacking various animals (a bull, a goat, a deer, to name a few) was popular in ancient Iran, but in the Achaemenid period it came to symbolize the symbiotic relationship between power and abundance in the empire.[23] From such a viewpoint, the image would stand for the expression of compliance and humility in the face of the imperial authority on which Byblos relied for its protection and continued prosperity.

Overall, the iconography of Byblian coinage demonstrates the city-state's willingness to adjust to the changing power dynamics in the region. By projecting easily recognizable images on their coinage, the Byblian kings alternated between the show of strength, humility, deference and prowess.

Tyre

Tyre was second after Byblos to introduce coinage, around 450 BCE,[24] but the first to feature inscribed letters on it. As was the case with Byblian coinage, Tyrian money reveals multiculturalism and political and economic flexibility in dealing with other entities, both in the region and afar.

On the reverse, Tyrian coinage frequently features the image of an owl with an Egyptian crook and flail over its shoulder. Later, at the beginning of the fourth century BCE, coins from Tyre began featuring inscribed letters, possibly identifying the royal under whose tutelage the minting was carried out. The obverse of Tyrian coinage is more notable because of the variety of images used. Some of the earliest coins contain the images of a dolphin with three zigzagging waves underneath it, a murex shell, and, starting in the beginning of

Tyrian shekel featuring an owl on the reverse and a winged sea-horse with rider on the obverse, *c.* 425–394 BCE.

Tyrian ¼ shekel with a dolphin, *c.* 437–425 BCE.

the fourth century BCE, a human figure riding a winged sea-horse.[25] These images shed light on some of the markers of identity of the Tyrian kings. The owl is a multivalent image, occurring in indigenous Tyrian and foreign motifs. One of the obvious connections is with Athens, where the owl was popular from the mid- to late fifth century BCE as it was regarded as a symbolic representation of the goddess Athena. The inclusion of the owl may have been a move by the Tyrians to make their currency viable in Mediterranean trade by adopting the iconography of coinage that was already widely distributed in the region. The owl has cultural connections too with the iconography of Egypt, as it is supplemented by the depiction of the flail and the crook, common representations of kingship in Egypt. The dolphin, which reflects Tyrian maritime interests, is also featured on Greek coinage, especially on coins originating from Sicily. This signals Tyre's openness to using images popular in the eastern Mediterranean and a certain degree of cosmopolitanism and cultural astuteness. Finally, the murex shell is undoubtedly connected with the purple dye production for which Tyre was famous.

Tyre performed a switch in weight of its coinage by moving away from the previously used Phoenician standard and adopting the heavier Attic standard around 364–357 BCE. This change – which was carried out by all Phoenician city-states, in fact – was yet another example of how individual city-states adapted to changing political and economic conditions. The Athenian Empire in the fourth century BCE made a concerted effort to adopt a unified standard of coinage to facilitate collection of tribute from its subjects. Although Tyre and other Phoenician city-states were not accountable to Athens and not subject to its rule, they still adopted the Attic standard to facilitate commercial exchanges. Faced with the weakening Persian Empire, it was natural for the Phoenicians to seek potential allies elsewhere.

Another change that has been observed in Tyrian numismatics was the introduction of counterfeit coinage. Tyrian coins from the beginning of the fourth century BCE were not made entirely from silver but featured bronze cores plated with silver. One speculation as to why this was is that Tyre experienced fluctuations in its economy, and its authorities responded by passing counterfeit coinage for the real thing. Even in the climate of robust economic activity of which Tyre was part, economic downturns were possible. It is very likely that the economic success of Sidon, Tyre's neighbour to the north, necessitated Tyre to resort to counterfeiting its coinage. Tyre was simply unable to guarantee its currency with the silver on hand.

Sidon

Of all the finds from the Phoenician city-states, coinage from Sidon presents the most promising opportunity for historians to reconstruct the political and economic life of the city. As is the case with Byblos and Tyre, changes in weight and iconography supply valuable information about the role of Sidon in the Persian period and its interactions both with other Phoenician city-states and with the dominant powers in the larger Mediterranean region.

For such an economically significant player in the Persian period, Sidon resorted to minting coinage relatively late, in the third quarter of the fifth century BCE.[26] This is probably because Sidon was selling more goods than it was buying. Only when the economic exchanges became more complicated and required a more precise monetary standard did the authorities of Sidon introduce coinage.

Nonetheless, Sidonian coinage, once inaugurated, gained wide geographic distribution, both in the Levant and abroad, with samples having been found in Anatolia, Persia and Egypt.[27] Although it was regular, without major disruptions, the coinage weight did fluctuate throughout the Persian period, reflecting shifting allegiances and changing economic conditions in Sidon and Phoenicia at large. For example, towards the turn of the fourth century BCE, coinage from Sidon increased in weight from 12.83 grams to 14 grams, a similar weight to the Tyrian shekel. Whether a sign of solidarity with a neighbouring Phoenician city-state or an economic necessity, such a move was significant as the changed weight standard also corresponded to the Attic standard, thus indicating closer economic ties with Athens. A few decades later, the Sidonians switched the standard once again, resorting to the traditional Sidonian one, possibly because of yet another shift in economic circumstances.

It is iconography, however, that tells us the most about Sidon's involvement in imperial politics and the way the city authorities made a conscientious effort to navigate the changing political landscape in the region. Although Sidonian coinage features indigenous images reflecting maritime interests (for example, ships), of greater interest to us is a deliberate and broad adoption in Sidon of images associated with Persian imperial iconography. For a number of years now, historians have identified the existence of an artistic programme among the Achaemenid royals to project their authority. For example, Margaret Cool Root writes of their artistic programme as 'an integrated enterprise in which overarching principles of design, style, and iconography are devised, codified, and then applied in a way that yields a coordinated whole'.[28] Such a programme was conducted through a choice of meaningful images that signified Persian ideology and ultimately spread throughout the empire.

The royals of Sidon, eager to ingratiate themselves with the reigning imperial powers, resorted to appropriation of these images to make them appear loyal and malleable. The first noteworthy image is a chariot that was frequently featured on Sidonian coinage.

Sidonian coin of King Tennes (r. 351–347 BCE), with the chariot scene.

The chariot scene typically portrayed a chariot driver, a rider of great significance (usually indicated by his size) and a person following the chariot. While several interpretative possibilities exist, including the rider being identified with the king of Sidon or a local deity, the most viable reading of the scene is one of the king of Sidon humbly following the king of Persia on foot. Ernest Babelon, a French numismatist and classical archaeologist, describes

> The King of Persia standing in his chariot drawn by four horses galloping to the left; he is capped with the five-pointed kidaris and dressed in a candys; he raises and extends the right hand; the charioteer is in the chariot beside the king, holding the reins in both hands. Beneath the horses, the carcass of an ibex.[29]

The Persians used the chariot in their iconography widely, albeit without portraying the king riding in it.[30] Despite this, the actual chariot procession was quite possibly very meaningful for the royals and their subjects. As the Greek historian Xenophon thus describes in his *Cyropaedia* (c. 370 BCE), a biography of Cyrus the Great:

> Next after these Cyrus himself upon a chariot appeared in the gates wearing his tiara upright, a purple tunic shot with white (no one but the king may wear such a one), trousers of scarlet dye about his legs, and a mantle all of purple . . . And when they saw him, they all prostrated themselves before him, either because some had been instructed to begin this act

of homage, or because they were overcome by the splendour of his presence, or because Cyrus appeared so great and so goodly to look upon; at any rate, no one of the Persians had ever prostrated himself before Cyrus before.[31]

The king in a chariot was an affirmative image of power that instilled awe among friends and foes alike, and the Sidonian appropriation of the image in their iconographic repertoire is not accidental. By incorporating this image of power on their coinage, the Sidonian kings both reaffirmed the authority of the Persian royalty and expressed their respectful attitude towards the power under the aegis of which the city-state was able to rise to economic strength and prosperity.

Another image from the Persian imperial propaganda used on Sidonian coinage was that of a heroic encounter. The scene usually portrays a warrior defeating a mighty beast, most often a lion, and the image was widely used across the empire, including in Persepolis reliefs and the Persepolis fortification seals.[32] The combat motif was instrumental in cementing the idea of a victorious king overcoming seemingly insurmountable obstacles. Additionally, it was used to instil fear and awe in the subjects of such a potent monarch. King Darius of Persia speaks of himself in no uncertain terms:

This indeed is my activity: inasmuch as my body has the strength, as battle-fighter I am a good battle-fighter. Once let there be seen with understanding in the place [of battle], what I see [to be] rebellious, what I see [to be] not [rebellious]; both with understanding and with command then I am first to think with action, when I see a rebel as well as when I see a not- [rebel].[33]

The Sidonians almost certainly appropriated the image to strengthen their association with powerful Persian kings.

The last image on Sidonian coinage to consider is the archer. The archer was widely employed by the Achaemenid propaganda machine and featured on numerous seals and coins.[34] Historians have suggested that the ubiquity of the image – it was widely disseminated in subject lands – was tied to the Persian idea of the military power and prestige of the kings.[35] As was the case with the chariot and the combat scene, the archer is yet further confirmation of the Sidonian kings expressing their association with the powerful Persian Empire.

Arwad

We know very little about when coinage appeared in Arwad or the workshop that produced it. The start of production probably commenced around the end of the third quarter of the fifth century BCE.[36] Arwad produced coins in various denominations, from $\frac{1}{16}$ obols to staters, for the duration of the Persian period.

Some of the earliest examples of Arwadian coinage bear the image of a marine deity (a manifestation of the ubiquitous Baal) on the obverse and a warship on the reverse. These are familiar maritime themes that are found on coins from other Phoenician city-states. Later, around 400–380 BCE, the image of the marine deity is accompanied by a sea-horse, possibly an attendant to the deity, and they become more detailed, as does the warship, which is enhanced by the depiction of waves, letters and numbers.[37] The head of the deity undergoes some stylistic changes in this period too, as it becomes more 'Hellenized'.

The fourth century BCE also saw the introduction of bronze Arwadian coinage, as opposed to the silver that was in use previously. Bronze coins were intended to provide smaller change for larger denominations in a climate of bustling economic activity. Moreover, the weight changed as well, shifting from the previously used Persic standard to the Attic standard.[38]

Against a background of scant information about Arwad in the Persian period, coinage provides some clues as to the character of the city-state. Its orientation to the West rather than the East towards the end of the Persian period is notable, in line with other Phoenician city-states. The development is not surprising as the Persians found their power challenged throughout many of their controlled regions at the time. Another possibility is that

Stater from Arwad, *c.* 348/7–339/8 BCE.

Arwad was unsuccessful in subcontracting their services to the empire and looked towards Athens as a more lucrative trading partner. This conclusion is supported by a considerably wide but numerically limited distribution of Arwadian coins; Arwadian trade simply could not compete with Sidonian trade, as it was largely confined to Arwad itself.

The coinage surveyed in this chapter helps historians make several conclusions regarding the Phoenician city-states. The iconography suggests that they drew upon their individual repertoires of meaningful and symbolic images, mostly involving maritime exploits and the representation of gods, and used them to accentuate separate identities. The royals also used coinage to project images of power, compliance and reverence, while at the same time negotiating relationships with the Persian Empire, to which the Phoenician city-states were subject, and with the larger Mediterranean world. To the Persians, the Phoenician city-states pledged allegiance and compliance; their coinage signalled to the world at large that they served the Persian kings and therefore shared their imperial strength and protection. Imagery changed in the fourth century BCE, with traditional Greek iconography appearing with increased frequency, suggesting a shifting orientation to the west as Persian power was continuously challenged and the Phoenicians shrewdly replotted their course of trade towards Greece. Metrology of Phoenician coinage, with the change from the Persic to the Attic weight standard, supports this conclusion.

six
CITIES OF GODS:
PHOENICIAN RELIGIONS

As seen in Phoenician inscriptions, the Phoenician city-states throughout their histories exhibited a strong preference towards specific deities. Each city-state, for a variety of historical and cultural reasons, preferred unique deities and divine cohorts that were considered benevolent patrons and were invoked in times of both prosperity and distress. Religious loyalties in the Phoenician city-states were characterized by continuity, and nowhere is this so clearly seen than in the duality of the divine cohorts, male and female. In Tyre, that duality was exemplified by Melqart and Astarte. The population of Byblos worshiped Baal Shamem and Baalat Gubal (Mistress of Byblos), and the divine pair of Eshmun and Astarte found veneration in Sidon. On the other hand, we know little of the Phoenician religions. The existing epigraphic evidence does not supply us with crucial information, such as written prayers or extensive god lists. Other sources of information, such as archaeological finds, are lacking in this regard as well.

In this chapter, we will examine what we do know of the major gods of the Phoenician city-states and religious material artefacts, and we will place the religions of Phoenicia in the larger context of the Ancient Near East. If possible, we will also try to reconstruct and sketch the religious understanding of life and afterlife in the Phoenician city-states.

Astarte

Astarte, whose name we have seen mentioned in the Phoenician inscriptions, most notably those from Sidon, was revered widely throughout the Ancient Near East. Astarte's cult has been observed in such places as Ugarit, Egypt, Mesopotamia, ancient Israel and Phoenician colonies, where she was worshipped under a number of different names, including Inanna and Ishtar.[1] The etymology of the name Astarte is not definitively agreed on, but the consensus is that the name alludes to Venus, the planet associated with femininity. Indeed, Astarte's domains generally are procreation and sexuality, in addition to royal patronage, warfare and seafaring. The goddess most certainly represented the feminine aspect of the divine and that could explain the popularity of Astarte in the ancient world.

Much information about Astarte in Phoenicia comes from Philo of Byblos' 'Phoenician History'. These writings, from about 100 CE, were chiefly preserved in Greek in Eusebius' *Praeparatio Evangelica* (Preparation for the Gospel, fourth century CE). Philo, in his turn, said that he prepared his 'Phoenician History' based on the writings of another Phoenician writer by the name of Sanchuniathon, who is said to pre-date the Trojan War (thirteenth century BCE). Such a convoluted chain of transmission would normally give significant pause to historians, but the intriguing part is that much of Philo's (or Sanchuniathon's) information has been confirmed by fourteenth-century BCE documents recovered from Ugarit (Ras Shamra, in modern-day Syria).[2] In Eusebius' work we read that Uranus, the god of the sky, sends Astarte, his daughter, along with her two sisters Rhea and Dione, to kill the god of time (and his own son), Kronos. Kronos, however, caught them, and although they were his sisters, he married them. Astarte and Kronos had seven daughters, referred to collectively as the Titanides or Artemides, and two sons, Pothos (Desire) and Eros (Love). Later in the story we read that

> Astarte, the greatest goddess, and Zeus Demarus, and Adodus king of gods, reigned over the country with the consent of

Kronos. And Astarte set the head of a bull upon her own head as a mark of royalty; and in traveling round the world she found a star that had fallen from the sky, which she took up and consecrated in the holy island Tyre. And the Phoenicians say that Astarte is Aphrodite.[3]

Although there is a connection of Astarte with Tyre, it is Sidon that is most often associated with Astarte. Judging from Tabnit's and Eshmunazar's sarcophagi, the goddess was a divine patron of the city, ensuring its continued strength and status in the region. That King Tabnit was a priest of Astarte is telling since we can surmise that the royal and priestly roles were combined in Sidon. Whether it was a regular arrangement or not is unclear, but it appears that Tabnit's wife Amotashtart served as Astarte's priestess as well, according to the inscription on the sarcophagus of Tabnit's son Eshmunazar. With the rise of Sidon's economic and political prominence in the Persian period, the cult of the city's chief deities, Astarte and Eshmun, gained more prominence in the neighbouring city-states. We can observe such development in the religious life in Byblos, where the traditional deity Mistress of Byblos (Baalat Gubal) syncretically adopted several features of Sidonian Astarte. Astarte was also worshipped in Tyre, although her consort deity was Melqart, the local manifestation of the ubiquitous Near Eastern Baal.

Baal

Whereas Astarte and other goddesses are quite often interpreted as manifestations of the female in the Near Eastern pantheon, Baal usually represents the male divine aspect. The name means 'lord', 'master' or 'owner'. There are debates over whether Baal was a unique divinity or an epithet of the deity Baal Hadad, the weather god of Mesopotamia. It appears, though, that Baal was worshipped as a distinct deity among the Canaanites and, later, Phoenicians, before spreading around the Mediterranean region as a result of the colonizing efforts undertaken by the individual Phoenician city-states.

Stele with storm god Baal Hadad (Arslan Tash, reign of Tiglath-Pileser III, 745–727 BCE).

The wide presence of the 'Baal' element in the many theophoric names in Phoenicia and elsewhere in the Ancient Near East can be attributed to a number of domains for which he was considered responsible. The cache of ritual texts from Ugarit previously mentioned reveals some of his more prominent attributes.[4] Baal is a king and a judge. His might manifests in his lordship over the weather and clouds, storms and lightning. He is in charge of supplying rain, and therefore he is responsible for harvests and sustenance in general. Still subject to the annual cycle of rebirth and decline, Baal's disappearance into the shadowy underworld and reappearance reflect the yearly crop cycle. He is also a protector from enemies, both on land and at sea, in this life and beyond. It is the status of Baal as a protector of those who are deceased that has given rise to the notion that Baal is a chthonic deity, presiding over the realm of the dead. We do not have exhaustive confirmation that Baal's theogony from the Ugaritic texts was shared by all the peoples who included Baal in their pantheon. It is reasonable, however, to assume that some, if not all, the mythology of Baal contributed to his cult in the Phoenician city-states and elsewhere in the Ancient Near East.

One of the names containing 'Baal' is Baal Zaphon (sometimes spelled as Saphon). The name means Lord or Master of Mount Zaphon and refers to the enigmatic but very real sacred mountain of Jebel al-Aqra (Mount Kasios/Casius), near the mouth of the Orontes river in modern Syria. The texts from Ugarit identify the mountain as the abode of Baal; the form 'Baal Zaphon' may have been a more descriptive name for Baal, but there is evidence that Baal Zaphon was worshipped separately from other Baals.[5] Judging by the stone anchors found near the Temple of Baal in Ugarit, the god's major domains were the weather and sea storms. In this light, seafarers would appeal to Baal Zaphon for protection from storms and bad weather in general. It is of interest that the etymology of the word 'typhoon' can possibly be traced to 'Zaphon', but it is far from certain, since 'typhoon' could also have been derived from the Cantonese term *taifeng*, meaning a big wind. In any case, the maritime connection is telling, as the veneration of Baal Zaphon is attested as far from Ugarit as Tyre and even Carthage, both renowned for their seafaring efforts.

Finally, another deity mentioned in relation to Phoenicia is Baal Shamem (Lord of Heaven). The god was a popular northwest Semitic deity, most notable for his temple in Palmyra dated to the second century CE, which was destroyed in 2015 by the Islamic State of Iraq and the Levant. In Phoenicia, the earliest mention of Baal Shamem is from a minor inscription of Yehimilk, king of Byblos, dated to the mid-tenth century BCE. There, the king asks Baal Shamem to protect his reign in exchange for having rebuilt several temples to the god. The deity is also mentioned in the Esarhaddon Treaty of the seventh century BCE, in which King Esarhaddon of Assyria made a pact with Baal, king of Tyre. In enumerating various possible curses on any party that would break the treaty, Esarhaddon writes:

> May Baal Shamem, Baal-Malage, and Baal Zaphon raise an evil wind against your ships, to undo their moorings, tear out their mooring pole, may a strong wave sink them in the sea, a violent tide . . . against you.[6]

Example of cultic stone anchors found near the Sea of Galilee.

Storm god brandishing lightning (Homs area, Late Bronze Age).

In this context, Baal Shamem, along with the other two Baals, is most certainly responsible for activities related to seafaring, such as storms and winds, a connection expected in Tyre and Byblos, where he was the subject of veneration.

Baalat Gubal/Mistress of Byblos

As the feminine form of 'Baal', 'Baalat' is frequently rendered as 'lady' or 'mistress'. She is most often associated with the city of Byblos as a consort to Baal Shamem. Gubal (or Gebal) was the name that the inhabitants of the city called it, whereas 'Byblos' is a designation given by the Greeks. We have seen her name mentioned in the inscription of Yehawmilk, and we also have a visual representation of the goddess. As many have pointed out, the image of Baalat Gubal on the Yehawmilk Stele is strikingly similar to the Egyptian goddess Hathor, and, given the long history between Byblos and Egypt, this is not surprising.[7] However, in the context of pantheons from the Phoenician city-states, it is reasonable to interpret the Mistress of Byblos as a local manifestation of the goddesses Astarte, Asherah and Anath, and, in general, as a personification of the female divine.

Eshmun

Eshmun is regarded as a god of healing and well-being and was popular in the Eastern Mediterranean from the early first millennium BCE.[8] Artefacts connected to Eshmun dating from as early as the eighth century BCE have been found in several places, including Syria, Palestine, Egypt and those connected with Phoenicia, namely Cyprus, Carthage and Punic sites. In Phoenicia, Eshmun was the chief deity of Sidon starting in the sixth to fifth centuries BCE. Etymologically, the name Eshmun is reminiscent of the Semitic word for oil, which was said to possess healing qualities.[9] His cult in Sidon, and the timing of his emerging cult there, can be connected with the rising popularity of a similar deity, Asklepios, in Greece by the sixth century BCE.[10] Whether it was a cultural borrowing is not clear, but the syncretic amalgamation and adoption of various deities was at play in Sidon at the time. After all, Eshmun was revered not only as a healer god but as a 'dying and rising' or resurrecting god,[11] similar to Baal. Several sites near Sidon, including Eshmun's temple at Bostan esh-Sheikh, feature inscriptions connecting Eshmun with Astarte as a divine couple.[12] The kings of Sidon eagerly incorporated the worship of Eshmun by frequently including his name in their own theophoric names (for example Eshmunazar).

Melqart

The dying and resurrecting god, a reflection of the cyclical quality of nature, found its place in the pantheon of not only Sidon but Tyre as well. There, the patron god Melqart, along with his consort Astarte, gained prominence, and they were elevated to the status of the protectors of the city during the Iron Age. Even Melqart's name (meaning 'king of the city') bound the god and the city-state. Herodotus, who supposedly travelled to Tyre himself, mentions Melqart and the importance of the deity to the city of Tyre.[13] Herodotus, however, calls Melqart by the Hellenized name Heracles, a practice that became widespread in the Persian period when cultural interactions between the East and the West grew exponentially, even if brought about by conflicts, primarily between the Greeks and the Persians. It is curious, though, why the priests themselves would call their patron god of the city by the Greek name. One possibility is that they tried to provide a corresponding name that would be comprehensible for the Greek traveller who wasn't fluent in their language. It is also possible that Herodotus simply equated the two gods and proffered the Greek name to his readers (whom he scolds in the passage for their gullibility and, in other passages from *Histories*, for their ignorance in many historical and cultural matters). Regardless, the story does reflect the long-standing worship of Melqart in Tyre and a common equation, at least in the Greek world, of Melqart and Heracles.[14]

Melqart, just like Eshmun, was worshipped as a god of dying and eventual rejuvenation, as several sources indicate.[15] For example, Josephus mentions how King Hiram of Tyre, after building the temples of Melqart and Astarte, set up a celebration of Melqart's 'awakening' (*egersis*).[16] It is conceivable that Astarte played a role in Melqart's resurrection, but the details elude us.

The death and resurrection aspects of Melqart (and Eshmun) are also echoed in yet another deity, Adonis, worshipped at Byblos.[17] Although an important figure in Greek mythology, etymologically 'Adonis' is derived from a Semitic word, *adon* (lord). The basis of the Adonis cult is the myth of an exquisitely handsome youth who was the beloved of Aphrodite, goddess of love. After he had been killed by a wild boar, Aphrodite pleaded with Zeus to allow Adonis to spend half the year with her and half the year in the underworld. It is apparent that the duality of Adonis' existence, caught in the cycle of dying and rising, reflects the agricultural context in which his worship originated. The cult of Adonis was particularly popular among women, who celebrated the god during an annual Adonia festival in Athens. In Byblos, there was also an annual celebration of Adonis' death (accompanied by mourning). Most of this information comes from Lucian, a Greek writer from the second century CE, who also described in his *On the Syrian Goddess* how the participants in the rituals dedicated to Adonis were required to shave their heads, and those women who refused were penalized by having to prostitute themselves in front of the temple.[18] We should note, however, that this is a rather late text from a visiting Greek author interpreting a foreign ritual, and whose account could have been coloured by the already existing Christian framework of the dying and rising god. Even in Lucian's work there is little evidence that Adonis was expected to rise again. After all, the women participating in the rituals are required to shave their heads as a symbolic act of mourning – the corresponding act to greet the risen god is absent. Many historians are reluctant to treat Adonis of Byblos as a typical dying and rising deity.

As a local manifestation of Baal, Melqart embodied several characteristics, including the dynastic protector, agricultural and maritime helper, and a chthonic deity in charge of the netherworld. However, his status as the protector of Tyre was his most important role. For the Tyrians, it was a way of differentiating themselves culturally from the Sidonians, who worshipped Eshmun as their chief deity. As the commercial and colonizing activity of Tyre intensified, the cult of Melqart spread to Cyprus, Malta, Italy, Spain and other locations in the Mediterranean, as suggested by iconographic and epigraphic evidence.[19]

Tanit

The goddess Tanit (the name most probably means 'face of Baal') is most frequently attested in Carthage and at other Punic sites, where she was regarded as a consort of Baal Hammon.[20] She was quite often represented by an isosceles triangle (the body) with a horizontal bar on top of it (portraying the outstretched arms) and a disc above (the head). Tanit was regarded as the protector of Carthage and a guide to sailors. Curiously, since the image of Tanit was most often installed over the remains of animals and, quite often, children, placed in tophets (burial urns),[21] this has led many to speculate that the Carthaginians were involved in child sacrifice.[22] The written evidence describing child sacrifice comes primarily from Roman sources, and this is often debated. Engaged in prolonged competition and frequent campaigns against Carthage, the Romans often represented their enemies in a very unflattering light. It is possible they 'othered' the Carthaginians by portraying them as cruel to the point of sacrificing children. However, recent discoveries suggest that this may not have been the case, and that even though the Carthaginians may have practiced human sacrifice from time to time, tophets were also used for other purposes.[23] What the researchers discovered, based on the analysis of more than three hundred burial urns and the remains of more than five hundred individuals, is that the tophets were used to a large extent for burials of children who died shortly before or after birth, which is consistent with available data on perinatal mortality. Carthage was not immune to numerous diseases that plagued many cities of the ancient world, and when children died, they were buried in tophets.[24]

In Phoenicia proper, Tanit was worshipped for the most part in Sarepta, where the temple of Tanit-Astarte was located. The nature of the association of Tanit and Astarte is not entirely clear, but, just like Astarte, Tanit had a complex personality and was responsible for a number of domains. From Carthage, the base from which we derive most of our knowledge about Tanit, her cult spread to the Mediterranean, Sardinia in particular.

Tophet from Carthage dedicated to Baal Hammon with the Tanit symbol, 300–200 BCE.

Maritime deities

Most of our information regarding Phoenician maritime deities comes from archaeology. We have evidence of the specialized religion of mariners through excavations of harbour shrines, ship-wrecks, tombs and burial sites. The testimony of written sources also confirms the reliance of sailors on the benevolence of gods. For example, in the treaty of Esarhaddon, where the curses for breaking the treaty (or destroying the stele upon which it was written) are listed, we read about the invocation of Baal Shamem, Baal Malage and Baal Zaphon upon those who would dare to do so. The three gods seem to be regarded as responsible for both positive and negative aspects of seafaring; just as they could assist in delivering sustaining winds, so could they bring destructive storms. The weather and maritime aspect of the three gods is unmistakable.

Among the gods who were worshipped at sea by Phoenician mariners are various manifestations of Baal, Reshef-Melqart and the goddesses Asherah and Tanit. Although popular as land-based deities, placed in the maritime context they acquire a range of attributes, from assisting in navigation to protection from the weather. Their images were often placed in shrines erected near important promontories – the shrines possibly served as landmarks for navigation and as marks of freshwater sources.[25] Figurines and images of ships and their parts, especially prows, anchors and rudders, were used as celebratory amulets, tributes to the protective powers of the gods, and archaeologists have discovered incense burners in shipwrecks off the coasts of Ashkelon, Gadir, Nora and Pisa.[26] It has been suggested that even the ships' masts, which were constructed solely of cedar wood, were fashioned to resemble 'Asherah poles', sacred poles or trees accompanying Canaanite religious sites that we know of from the Hebrew Bible. In a way, the masts shared both 'a common physical form and metaphysical function',[27] serving as physical substitutes for the goddess, who may have functioned as yet another assisting deity, providing protection and navigational guidance. Phoenician priesthood resided primarily on land, and it is unlikely that the great variety of Phoenician ships would have had a religious officiant on board. It

Statuette of a
storm god from
the Syrian coast,
1500–1200 BCE.

is quite possible that there was an arrangement whereby religious functions, including the pronouncement of prayers and incantations, would be carried out by someone already on board who was skilled in matters of spirituality.[28]

Given the importance of seafaring to the Phoenicians, it is not surprising that the favour of the gods was petitioned through the cult of particular deities. It is worth stating that a separate pantheon for maritime activities was something that seafarers have possessed throughout history. One example is the veneration of Mary among Christian sailors, who assigned to her, along with traditional attributes of comfort, mercy and compassion, the qualities of aid and protection for those at sea. At times, Mary was metaphorically thought of as a 'ship for those who wish to be saved'.[29]

Ritual life and worship

When discussing temples in the Ancient Near East, it is customary to use the term very widely, to include not only the shrine but the entire architectural complex, including any sacred statuary. The temple in general is considered an abode of the gods, a place of worship and sacrifice, tended to by priests. Shapes, sizes and forms of temples vary widely throughout the world, and even in the Ancient Near East there are differences. In Phoenicia, accurate reconstructions of temples are hampered by the destruction of the layers belonging to the Late Bronze and Iron Age periods, with the structures undergoing considerable reconstruction in the subsequent Hellenistic and Roman eras. The major surviving Phoenician temples, with varying degrees of degradation, are the Temple of Eshmun in Amrit (also referred to as the Maabed complex), the Temple of Eshmun at Bostan esh-Sheikh, near Sidon, and the two-temple complex at Umm el-Amed, south of Tyre. This is by no means an extensive list, and one has to resort to comparative typology from other sites associated with the Phoenicians in the eastern Mediterranean to draw conclusions regarding the plans and usage of temples in the Phoenician homeland.

Phoenician temples are usually sacral complexes consisting of one or more structures: an open area or courtyard, which archaeologists working in the Levant identify as a *bamah*, and an enclosed sanctuary. Our main source of information for the bamah is the Hebrew Bible, but its testimony is too general to speak confidently about what a bamah actually was. The Mesha Stele, dated to the ninth century BCE and from the ancient kingdom of Moab (located in what is now Jordan) mentions a bamah in the context of worship of the Moabite deity Chemosh: 'And I made *this high place* for Chemosh'. Bamah is usually translated as a 'high place'; as the term implies, the bamah was usually set on a high ground and was shaped as an open courtyard, in the middle of which was a cultic installation of some kind. It was also customary to have a sacred well in the courtyard, the tradition taken with the Phoenicians as they set up their colonies in the Mediterranean.[30] Phoenician temples also frequently featured ablution basins.

Mesha stele, 9th century BCE.

The enclosed temple would frequently feature pillars, covered porticos and rear chambers (as in the 'holy of holies' of which we read in the Hebrew Bible).[31] The temples were modest in size, and if any renovations were undertaken, as we read in Josephus concerning the building activities of King Hiram of Tyre, they were most likely constructed vertically rather than horizontally due to the land constraints in busy cities.[32] Because of the biblical allusions to King Solomon being assisted in the building of the temple by King Hiram of Tyre,[33] a frequently advanced suggestion is that the first Israelite temple at Jerusalem was inspired by the temples that existed in Tyre (and, possibly, other Phoenician city-states), although the questionable historicity of the Bible and the lack of viable remains of temples both in Jerusalem and Phoenicia mean it is hard to make such a point with confidence.[34] Additionally, the Bible mentions the Tyrians primarily in the context of bronze-working rather than providing any kind of programmatic architectural assistance to the construction of the temple itself. Undoubtedly, there were processes of cultural exchange that could have made it possible for the builders of Solomon's Temple to be acquainted with the architectural and religious heritage in Tyre, Sidon and other Phoenician city-states. However, to state definitively that the Jewish temple is an example of Phoenician architecture is unwarranted.

Courtyard of the Amrit temple, late 4th century BCE.

The Baalat Gubal temple in Byblos, *c.* 2800 BCE.

The choice of the temple location was an important factor in striking the right balance between a place pleasing to gods and one that would also deliver a meaningful connection between the landscape and the sacred space to worshippers. The association of Phoenician deities with the celestial bodies, where Baal would be identified with the Sun and Astarte with Venus, is well known.[35] The two bodies were seen by the Phoenicians as closely connected, thus representing the assumed marriage between Baal and Astarte.[36] For this reason, historians have suggested, on the basis of comparative typology of temples found in Phoenician (Tyrian) colonies, that the temples were constructed in such a manner so that some elements (altars) would align with the summer solstice sunrise and the winter solstice sunset.[37] Unfortunately, the paucity of archaeological data prior to Roman times prevents us from knowing whether such alignment was followed throughout the Phoenician city-states, but the suggestion is nevertheless intriguing.

Temples in Phoenicia, just as throughout the ancient world, were serviced by priests. As indicated in inscriptions, at times Phoenician royalty served in this role. Overall, though, the priesthood was hereditary, and priests came from aristocratic families residing in the city. Again, in the absence of detailed pre-Roman information from the Phoenician homeland, we need to resort to comparative typology from later time periods and from Phoenician colonies. A limestone stele from Umm el-Amed dated to Hellenistic times (fourth to second centuries BCE) depicts a male priest, who is 'clean-shaven, dressed in a turban-like bonnet and a long, pleated linen tunic with wide sleeves; a folded stole of thin cloth, a priestly attribute, is suspended from the left shoulder'.[38] Presumably, the same garb would be an accurate reflection of the traditional priestly attire that was in use in centuries prior. Some indication of what the priests looked like and what their vocation involved can be gleaned from the work of the first-century Latin writer Silius Italicus, who described the Temple of Melqart at Gadir in his *Punica* (Book III):

> Further, those who are permitted and privileged to have access to the inner shrine forbid the approach of women, and are careful to keep bristly swine away from the threshold. The dress worn before the altars is the same for all: linen covers their limbs, and their foreheads are adorned with a head-band of Pelusian flax. It is their custom to offer incense with robes ungirt; and, following their fathers' rule, they adorn the garment of sacrifice with a broad stripe. Their feet are bare and their heads shaven, and their bed admits no partner; the fires on the hearth-stones keep the altars alight perpetually.[39]

If we assume that homeland traditions were exported to the colonies, we can deduce that the priests in the Phoenician city-states customarily shaved their heads, walked barefoot and practised celibacy.

Other information about temple activities can be gleaned from comparative sources. For example, Herodotus mentions the practice of sacred prostitution in Babylon, noting that similar customs

A Phoenician priest on the stele of Baalyaton, 4th–3rd century BCE.

existed in Cyprus.[40] Such a practice would appropriately correspond to the cult of Astarte – the goddess of love – at the Cypriot Phoenician sites of Kition, Amathus and Paphos.[41] Archaeological information gleaned from Kition suggests that Phoenician temples there employed a good deal of personnel, including scribes, butchers, bakers and sacrificers. The last were undoubtedly involved in slaughtering and burning sacrificial animals, primarily sheep and lambs.

One of the most ancient and widely spread institutions in the Ancient Near East, which, judging from the evidence from Cyprus, was also popular in Phoenicia, was *marzeaḥ*.[42] The word usually denotes a feast in honour of a deity or a temple, but it can also refer to the group of people taking part in the celebration. The feast would involve chanting, playing of music, praying and singing, with, additionally, an element of heavy drinking.[43] It can be thought of as a sacred banquet attended by higher-class functionaries. Interestingly, the inscription from Piraeus in Greece mentions *marzeaḥ* ('On the fourth day of the feast [*marzeaḥ*], in the fourteenth year of the people of Sidon, it was resolved by the Sidonians in assembly'[44]); there, the term was used as an important date marker, thus pointing to the weight and importance the feast had in the community.

The absence of textual sources forces us to sketch the religious practices of commoners by resorting to the iconography from material remains. Glenn Markoe, an expert in classical and Near Eastern art, was successful in reconstructing such practices from the decorations on Phoenician metal bowls.[45] They frequently feature dancers and musicians, at times masked, in a procession before a deity or a priestess. Among the instruments used in such worship were double-pipes, tambourines and lyres.[46]

Offerings and incense burning were important pious acts in Phoenicia, and these activities are frequently featured on pictorial relics and on seals. They were done primarily inside the temples in front of *asherahs*, columns representing sacred woods, or *betyls* (pillars; literally a 'dressed stone') that were meant to represent the deity. Betyls could stand as high as 1.5 metres tall, as finds at traditional Phoenician sites in Motya (Sicily) and Mogador (Morocco) demonstrate, and they were enduring elements in the Phoenician temples, surviving well into Roman times.[47]

Childbearing, well-being and divine protection were most likely the primary concerns of domestic worship, as they were in many ancient societies. The iconography of artefacts associated with domestic worship suggests the veneration of Astarte and deities who were Egyptian in origin (Amun, Bes, Osiris, Isis and Horus). However, since many religious artefacts (figurines,

Egyptian god Bes, Saqqara, Egypt, 30th dynasty (380–343 BCE).

statuettes and so on) are not inscribed, it is difficult to make any conclusive judgements based on iconography alone. One exception is the Egyptian god Bes, whose prominent ears, sizeable belly and pronounced eyes are hard to mistake for anything else. The ambiguity of depiction and identification of Phoenician deities has led many to advance the idea of aniconism ('no image') in Phoenician religion.[48] Among the cited evidence, the Temple of Eshmun at Sidon is remarkable in this sense since no representation of either Eshmun or Astarte have been found in the area. For the most part, the religious artefacts there include thrones, stone urns and stone markers. The Phoenician avoidance of the depiction of the deities, both in the homeland and among the Punic colonies, would fit in well in the Near Eastern tradition of aniconism, which manifests, for example, in the prohibition of using the images of Yahweh in ancient Israel. Markoe noted that the use of betyls may have been incorporated as a symbolic substitution for images of the deities.[49]

Funerary artefacts, practices and beliefs

Phoenician funerary artefacts are numerous, and they allow us to say a few words about the practices accompanying burials of the dead. Burial practices have also revealed a distinct social and economic stratification existing in Phoenicia.

Sarcophagus and tomb of Abi-Shemu of Byblos, 19th–18th century BCE.

Anthropoid sarcophagus from Ain el-Helwe, 5th century BCE.

The Phoenicians practised two major burial methods, inhumation and cremation, although the former became the primary burial approach in the Persian period.⁵⁰ Cremation is thought to have been practised in the areas closest to Israel, and it may have served as an identity marker to distinguish the Phoenicians from their neighbours to the south.⁵¹ There is a pronounced difference in the burials of commoners and wealthier persons. Whereas the average Phoenician would be buried in either a shallow oblong pit or a vertical grave, a person of means or authority would be buried in a decorated sarcophagus that would be placed in a rock-cut tomb. Commonly, the Phoenicians used anthropoid sarcophagi, which were either imported from Egypt or produced locally but with strong Egyptian characteristics, especially in the finishing of the headgear. Also significant is the use of funeral masks, sometimes made of gold, by the wealthier strata of society.

A variety of implements found in and around burials (food utensils, fragrance containers, clothing, figurines and so on) and the iconography on the sarcophagi strongly suggest the expectation of an afterlife. The Phoenicians believed that the dead would continue their existence in some capacity after death, and the living had a responsibility to care for the spirit of the dead by offering 'food, libations of water, and the celebration of commemorative rituals to evoke the name of the dead person, whose spirit continues to exist in the form of an ancestor'.[52] One suggestion is that the dead would assume the role of 'chthonic healers' who could be invoked by the living in times of distress.[53] The lotus is an important icon in determining Phoenician views on death and the afterlife. A traditional Egyptian symbol in tomb depictions, the lotus was 'sniffed by the deceased and his family members in a gesture aimed at ensuring the symbolic rebirth of his soul in the afterlife'.[54] The same lotus flower is depicted on the sarcophagus of Ahiram; his son Ittobaal lifts the flower to his face as if to smell it. Interpreted in such a way, the lotus flower featured on the Ahiram sarcophagus would encapsulate forever the belief that Ahiram transitioned safely to the afterlife.

Phoenician religion, when reconstructed using the scarce archaeological finds in the Phoenician homeland and more ample finds throughout Phoenician colonies, appears to combine two distinct elements: beliefs and practices similar to those of other Near Eastern religions, and distinctive elements that contributed to the individual identities of the Phoenician city-states. As was the case in many other ancient societies, Phoenician religious beliefs and practices served to express their dependence on gods' favours in both everyday tasks and maritime endeavours. Gods were supplicated, nurtured and appeased through rituals and temples, through prayers and religious objects. Afterlife was a perennial concern as well, hoped for and insured through burials. At the same time, each Phoenician city-state maintained and nurtured its own cultural identity through the devotion to a divine couple, unique to each city, their cohort possessing a remarkable symbiosis of their combined supernatural powers.

The Phoenicians also demonstrated a notable flexibility in their openness to borrowing elements of religious beliefs and iconography from other nations, as the appropriation of the worship and image of the Egyptian deity Bes suggests. The royalty, both kings and queens, played a significant role in religious affairs in Phoenicia. They supported the development of temple infrastructure and assumed priestly responsibilities as well.

SEVEN

MASTERS OF CRAFTMANSHIP: PHOENICIAN ART AND TRADE

Having established Phoenicia as comprising a conglomerate of individual and independent city-states, the question arises as to whether we can speak of 'Phoenician art' as possessing a distinct set of features that would distinguish it from other Near Eastern styles.[1] Museums are full of artefacts that are identified as 'Phoenician', yet their provenance is frequently missing. The paucity of excavated pre-Roman archaeological layers is a significant factor that complicates matters, while the dominant, but changing, notion that the Phoenicians comprised a cohesive ethnic and cultural entity is evident, in part driven by the assumptions of classical authors. Some known examples of the misattribution of artefacts are Cypriot bowls assigned to the Sidonians by Homer in the *Iliad*, and the bronze-wheeled stands in Solomon's Temple which the Hebrew Bible claimed to have been supplied by Hiram of Tyre. Historians have identified the 'Orientalizing' process through which the Greeks and others, unaware of the true origins of art objects, imparted a special, mythical status to those considered Phoenician.[2] The same process is still at work today and can be observed in the way many artefacts are labelled.

Another complicating factor is that many of the objects identified as Phoenician were produced primarily for export, and, when found in contexts outside of the Phoenician homeland, it is difficult to definitively identify them as Phoenician by their styles and typological qualities. Historians tend to focus on the dominant stylistic features of 'Phoenician' artefacts, referring to them as: A) 'Egyptianizing' (using common elements of Egyptian art, such as 'the regular spacing of figures; figures that are depicted in profile; large expanses of undecorated flesh or clothing; symmetry in regard to motifs, symbols and patterns; decoration with colours that were common to the Egyptian palette; or incorporation of specific motifs that were common to Egypt'); B) 'Assyrianizing' (using 'Assyrian-style lions, clothing, hairstyles, deities, demons, emblems of royal office, or winged sphinxes; giving predominance to animals and nature scenes; or depicting human figures as relatively rigid and static'); C) 'Syrianizing' ('utilising symbols and motifs that were common to Anatolia; presenting figures from a frontal perspective; and depicting distinctive facial features such as large eyes and noses, receding chins and pinched lips') or D) 'Cypro-Phoenician' ('having characteristics that are common to both Phoenician and Cypriot artistic traditions; displaying a largely Phoenician sense of organisation and layout; utilising certain common decorative motifs; drawing heavily upon Assyrian traditions').[3]

Given such abundance, Phoenician style is characterized by, on the one hand, eclecticism and openness to foreign styles, and, on the other, the continuity of artistic traditions in Phoenicia with the styles preferred in the Levant from the Late Bronze Age to the Iron Age. Phoenician artisans drew upon the existing repertoire of styles and artistic elements, creating a unique blend of features that came to be identified as 'Phoenician'. Glenn Markoe defined Phoenician art as 'an amalgam of many different cultural elements – Aegean, north Syrian, Cypriot, Assyrian, and Egyptian – and it is this strongly eclectic quality that complicates any attempt to categorize strictly on the basis of style'.[4] Artisans in Phoenicia also masterfully navigated their consumers' changing preferences and tastes to supply products that would do well not only in the internal market, but in the international market, thus cementing the unique and nimble style we refer to as 'Phoenician'.

Pottery and ceramics

Pottery in Phoenicia, and the ancient world in general, is indispensable for reconstructing time periods and the processes of cultural exchange. The ebb and flow of style and colour preferences and distribution of particular samples throughout geographic regions can be of substantial assistance in reconstructing history. However, the pottery associated with Phoenicia is frequently considered unremarkable and mediocre, even conservative, both in the colour palette used, their morphological and decorative styles and the quality of production.[5] We should keep in mind, however, that not all pottery samples are equal, and that a distinction should be made between pottery types used for consumption (products meant for everyday use) and for industrial purposes (products used in activities such as agriculture, fishing, raising livestock and so forth).[6] Consumption pottery was used in a number of situations (domestic, ritual and funerary) and settings (private and public, urban and rural), depending upon specific socio-economic needs.[7] There are several characteristics that define this kind of pottery:[8]

1. They exhibit the continuity of shapes dictated by the intended use of the vessels.
2. They are morphologically similar to metallic vessels of similar shape; consumption pottery represents social stratification, with lower classes using more affordable clay vessels but in the shape of more expensive, metallic wares.
3. The repertoire of shapes is limited, and it becomes more so in the Iron Age.
4. The function of the vessels is difficult to determine as similar vessels were used in both domestic and ritual contexts.
5. Both single-purpose and multipurpose vessels could be used in the same context.
6. The quality of vessels depended greatly on the context in which they were used, and the shape often correlated with the production quality. Those types of ceramics used in a banquet setting (decanters, for example) would often, but not always, be of higher production value than those used every day (such as bowls).
7. Consumption pottery appears to be socially less prestigious than metallic vessels imported from the Aegean or Cyprus.

Overall, domestic consumption wares were regarded in Phoenicia first and foremost for their functionality, and this may underlie their unremarkable nature in decoration and form. They were poor imitations of much more prestigious metallic vessels, and they would only be appreciated more highly if they were imported.

The varieties of pottery types used in industrial, as opposed to domestic, contexts are dependent on their usage. Francisco Núñez, a prominent historian and archaeologist of Phoenicia, identifies two major types of containers: those used in the production and transformation of products (such as the fermentation of grains and grapes) and those intended for storing, transporting and selling various raw materials.[9] Whereas the first type would not require much uniformity in shape or design, the second would, in order to facilitate an orderly flow of trade and commerce. The two different pottery contexts affect not only the quality and shapes of vessels but their production, depending on their demand and distribution.

Archaeologists have identified pottery workshops in Tell Rachidiyé and Tyre, but the most important find is the industrial quarter in Sarepta, which contained several pottery workshops continuously running from the Late Bronze Age II (1400–1200 BCE) to the Persian period.[10] The workshops were well organized, with a number of kilns and special drying rooms, suggesting that pottery production was done there on an industrial scale. If we transpose the Sarepta model to other Phoenician city-states on the basis of the continuity of archaeological remains and their geographic proximity, we can conclude that pottery production was a viable and bustling industrial activity in the Phoenician homeland.

Several specific types of pottery are associated with the Phoenician homeland. They are usually classified either by their colour and style (bichrome, black-on-red and red slip) or shape (bowls, flasks, jugs (notably mushroom-lipped ones) and various kinds of pitchers).[11] These classifications are not exclusive as there is some overlap between styles and shapes. The oldest type of Phoenician pottery is bichrome (two-colour) ware that first appeared in the middle of the eleventh century BCE and disappeared roughly two centuries later.[12] Some believe that the emergence of this type of pottery marks the beginning of the

Phoenician civilization, and that the early Phoenicians began creating dual-colour wares to deliberately diversify and beautify their items – in contrast to the monochrome pottery styles of the previous eras. Bichrome vessels, mostly globular jugs, feature alternating broad dark-red and narrower grey bands, arranged horizontally. The horizontal arrangement of bands is mostly because of the use of the potter's wheel.

The second style, referred to as either black-on-red or Cypro-Phoenician, replaced bichrome wares in the middle of the ninth century BCE. Vessels of this type are usually of finer quality than bichrome pottery and are characterized by 'a reddish slip and

Example of a bichrome terracotta amphora from Tell Rachidiyé (Iron Age II).

black horizontal or concentric lines'.[13] The style gradually fell out of favour, losing its exquisite features in the process, before disappearing by the seventh century BCE. It was succeeded by red slip pottery, one of the most common types of Phoenician pottery, found in Cyprus, North Africa and the Mediterranean.[14] Its inauguration in the ninth century BCE coincided with the beginning of the westward Phoenician expansion. Mushroom-lip jugs are most widely attested examples of this style.

The three types of pottery are used to determine both the chronology and the 'Phoenicianness' of archaeological sites. Since these are products that literally stand the test of time because of their durability, samples can help reveal their age. They are also used to determine the ethnicity of the people inhabiting the sites. If a particular type of pottery is considered 'Phoenician', then the people who used it could potentially be identified as Phoenician as well. There are numerous problems in using pots as identity markers, however, since pottery could have been imported, and serious questions regarding the practice, especially as applied to the studies of Phoenicia, have recently been raised.[15] Clearly, there is need for a more considered approach when tracing connections between archaeological remains and the ethnicities of those who used them.

Generally, the Phoenician potter excelled in two distinct kinds of objects, closed and open. Closed vessels have their body wider in diameter than their rim. Among the types associated with Phoenicia are 'amphorae, kraters (vessels used to mix wine and water), cooking pots, strainer-spouted jugs, trefoil pitchers and neck-ridged jugs'.[16] Strainer-spouted jugs are notable as the spout, protruding at a 90-degree angle from the main body, allowed for the pouring and straining of heavier liquids such as wine. The trefoil pitcher echoes more refined metallic vessels and was possibly intended as a cheaper alternative meant for everyday use by commoners. Amphorae made storing and shipping products much more efficient. With time, Phoenician amphorae gained uniform shape and standardized capacity, which substantially facilitated Phoenician trade. Among open-form vessels are cups, plates and goblets.[17] Often, pottery vessels had their jar handles decorated

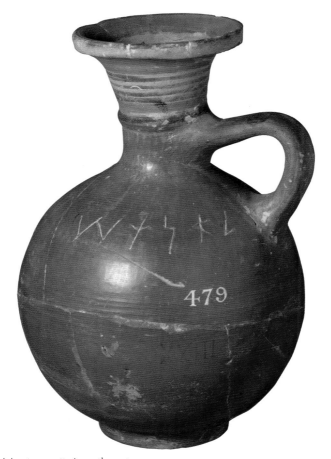

Phoenician terracotta jug, 7th century BCE.

with stamped images of quadrupeds, scorpions and rosettes, among other images.[18] In the Persian period, stamped amphorae handles from Sidon feature the image of a ship, undoubtedly inspired by the might of the Sidonian fleet.

Finally, a few words about the way pottery was produced. Using contemporary observations at the Lebanese village of Beit Shehab (also spelled Beit Chabab), historians have suggested that the process is similar to the one used by ancient Phoenician potters.[19] First, the clay is sourced from nearby terraces, and then it is kept for four to five months in settling basins before being placed

---

in a cellar. The finished vessels are allowed to dry for a few weeks. During the firing process, the kiln is kept at 800 degrees Celsius for eight days before its contents are removed.

Glass

Phoenician glass was known throughout the ancient world, and Sidon particularly was associated with its production. Pliny the Elder, writing in the first century CE, even credited the Phoenicians with the invention of glass.[20] Although the discovery by archaeologists that the Mitanni had produced glass in the sixteenth century BCE overturned the claims by Pliny, the association of Phoenicians with glass production provides a strong indication that the Phoenician contribution to the popularization of glass was significant.[21]

At first, glass products were produced for the domestic market, but with time, as the quality increased, exports to the western Mediterranean became more widespread. Earlier glass samples from Phoenicia are relatively crude as the vitreous paste would be stretched around the core and then moulded according to the desired design.[22] Decoration could be added later using different coloured pastes. With the invention of glass blowing, more refined glass pieces, both in colour and quality, appeared. The most common types associated with the Phoenicians are alabastra (plural of 'alabastron', a small pottery type used for storing oil and perfume) and hemispherical vessels.[23] Most of the examples of these pottery types come from the remains of temples, palaces, tombs and residences of the elite, which suggests that they were prestige, luxury items. The Phoenician glass repertoire was broad, though, and included amulets, lucky charms and glass inlays in wood and ivory items, 'apotropaic pendants in the shape of demon masks, animals and anthropoid heads',[24] and faience (glazed pottery). Faience objects could be moulded into a wide range of charms, which included scarabs (*Scarabaeus sacer*) and amulets echoing Egyptian symbols and deities.[25] These ubiquitous products were mass produced in local workshops in the Phoenician homeland, on Cyprus and on Rhodes. Homer even referred to such products

Phoenician glass alabastron, 625–600 BCE.

as *athyrmata* ('baubles' or 'trinkets') in the *Odyssey*, indicating that they were in wide use throughout the ancient Mediterranean world. We need to keep in mind that, as with most Phoenician products, faience items produced in bulk for the popular market were of much lesser quality than those aimed at the luxury market.

Ivories

The Phoenicians were not the first to use ivory for crafting works of art, but when they did start, around the ninth century BCE, they quickly gained renown for their skill.[26] There is overwhelming evidence of Egyptian motifs in Phoenician art in general and in ivories in particular, owing to the significant Egyptian influence in the broader Levant during the latter years of Egypt's Twenty-second Dynasty.[27]

Most Phoenician ivories come from outside Phoenicia proper, although some have been discovered in Byblos and Sarepta. Among the locations yielding the greatest number of examples are Assyria (at Khorsabad), northern Syria (Arslan Tash and Zinçirli Höyük), northern Palestine (Samaria), Punic sites (Carthage, Palestrina, Carmona, Gadir) and northern Iraq (Nimrud, ancient Kalhu).[28] We can distinguish between two stylistic groups of ivories, Phoenician and northern Syrian. The Phoenician group, generously represented by the findings at the palace of King Ashurnasirpal II in Nimrud, stands out for its portrayal of traditional Egyptian motifs, such as 'the birth of Horus, a cow suckling a calf, youths binding a papyrus, a lioness on a papyrus thicket, a griffin trampling a fallen Asiatic'.[29] The winged disc on the panel is also an Egyptianizing element. Among the Phoenician-style techniques are ajouré (perforated openwork panels) and, much more numerous, champlevé (raised reliefs with a removed background). Ivories could also be supplemented with cloisonné work, comprising inset colour glass paste and semi-precious stones. Ivories were often used as furniture inlays for beds, chests and tables, among other items, and individual pieces of larger compositions frequently featured Phoenician lettering serving as assembly and arrangement instructions.[30]

Ivory furniture plaque with Egyptianizing figures from Assyria, 9th–8th century BCE.

Northern Syrian ivories, characterized primarily by greater detail and a lack of Egyptian features, are represented primarily by the corpus from the same palace of King Ashurnasirpal II.[31] In all likelihood these were spoils captured by the Assyrians, conceivably from Phoenicia itself, but from a workshop different from the one producing Phoenician-style ivories. Another suggestion is that relocated Phoenician artisans produced them *in situ*, in Nimrud. To support this idea, Markoe cites a case of the discovery in Nimrud of unworked Egyptian faience paste that was used as an ivory inlay.[32]

Phoenician ivories have most often been found in the context of palaces, which underscores the prestige associated with the material, especially when it was carved by skilled artisans. Although we will never know for certain, the existing examples of ivories suggest how Phoenician palaces and temples might have looked by indicating the spaces where they would be placed. Although many iconographic motifs feature elements echoing the Egyptian visual language, Phoenicians used Egyptian motifs to express their own traditions and beliefs, as Eric Gubel has pointed out.[33]

Phoenician ivory production petered out around the early seventh century BCE because of the diminution of elephant herds in Syria. This was not the only factor, however, since the Phoenicians still maintained a close relationship with Egypt and the newly founded colony at Carthage, both able to supply the tusks necessary for producing ivory products. Another reason for the decline in ivory work might be the sack of Sidon and Tyre's diminishing economic activity in the early seventh century BCE, accompanied by the steep reduction of the circulation of Phoenician luxury goods in the west.[34]

Metalwork

Metal bowls were and still are considered the pinnacle of 'Phoenician' craftsmanship. Homer mentions a 'mixing bowl of silver, a work of art' made in Sidon, to be given as the highest prize to the winner of a foot race held in honour of Patroclus.[35] For years, many of the exquisite bowls hailing from the ancient world were considered 'Phoenician'. Whether they were found in Cyprus, Italy, Iran, Syria, Spain or other places, they were determined to be 'Phoenician' based on the uniformity of the iconographic language used: a central medallion, either a rosette or a hunting or other scene, and one or more concentric circles.[36] The process of so-called 'Phoenicinizing' of bowl attribution culminated in 1988 during the exhibition *The Phoenicians* at the Palazzo Grassi in Venice, when all

Phoenician bowl with a hunting scene, 8th century BCE.

metal bowls were displayed under the title 'Phoenician', regardless of any accompanying finds or archaeological context, or whether they were parts of burials or larger collections.[37]

Despite the 'Phoenician' attribution, ancient bowls vary in style and themes. The earliest bowls, mostly of bronze, appear about 700 BCE, followed by silver ones, which were often gilt. The form followed the function of the vessel. Shallower bowls were used either in religious contexts for libation or as decorative objects, with many, usually from private settings, featuring a puncture hole that suggests that they were suspended for display.[38] Heroic combat, floral motifs and various animals were common themes. Frequently they featured 'Egyptianizing' elements. These include depictions of groups of women in Egyptian garb, Egyptian deities, papyrus boats and scenes involving reeds. It is likely that artisans selected themes with Egyptian elements deliberately, with an eye to the export market. Egyptianizing elements, including nonsensical hieroglyphics, could have been a way to attach cultural prestige and aesthetic appeal to the bowls intended for export.[39] Comparable examples of prestige iconography include 'Assyrianizing' elements, meaningful at the time of the Assyrian domination of the Near East in the first half of the Iron Age, which include winged sphinxes and hunting scenes.

Given the wide distribution of Phoenician bowls throughout the ancient world, and the absence of finds in the Phoenician homeland, the following four hypotheses have been proposed:[40]

1. The bowls were produced in the Levant and from there were disseminated throughout the Mediterranean. One justification for such a proposal is that both the iconography and the shape of the existing bowls are decidedly Near Eastern.[41] Such a hypothesis does not at all explain the complete absence of specimens originating unmistakably from the Levant.

2. The second proposal, currently enjoying the widest support, postulates that the bowls were produced by travelling artisans. As Phoenicians were exploring the Mediterranean to find sources of metal to pay tribute to the Assyrian kings, some craftspeople set up shop away from their homeland. Although this would explain the absence of bowls in Phoenicia, some are not convinced. The historian James Muhly wrote, 'I very strongly believe that the whole idea of immigrant craftsmen is something of a British fantasy and I like to see scholarship moving in another direction.'[42]

3. Some, including Muhly, have suggested that the vessels were produced where they were found.

4. The final suggestion explains the geographic spread of the bowls in the Mediterranean by the processes of commercial trade and exchange alongside those of tribute and the spoils of war. In this line of thinking, an object would be produced in one location but would then travel far and wide, changing hands, its movement most probably propelled by its intrinsic value and status as a prestige item.

Baal figurine from
Ugarit, *c.* 1350 BCE.

The last hypothesis is very attractive as it takes into account the exchange of ideas and knowledge in the ancient world, where themes depicted on the bowls (for example, the heroic encounter motif) would either appeal to sensibilities regarding kingship and the status of a hero or instruct about them. Additionally, a synthesis of various styles (Aegean, Assyrian, Egyptian) would make an object, no matter where it was produced, widely desirable. As Nicholas Vella states, 'Calling the metal bowls "Phoenician" should only serve as shorthand to understand the mobile and mutable world that was the Mediterranean in the Archaic period.'[43]

Besides bowls, other metal objects associated with Phoenicia include bronze figurines and votive razors, although the latter appear only in Mediterranean, rather than formally Phoenician, contexts. The figurines were intended to be offered in temples and domestic shrines. Most of the time, they portray either standing or sitting male and female worshippers or gods dressed in Egyptian-style garb, sometimes wearing enigmatic, omega-type (O-shaped) necklaces and often posed with their palm extended in a gesture of blessing. Some were overlaid with gold, as can be seen in the example from Ugarit. Most of the figurines were discovered outside Phoenicia, although Markoe has proposed that they were exported from the Phoenician homeland.[44]

Seals

Two kinds of instruments were frequently discovered in Phoenician tombs: cylinder seals and stamp seals. Cylinder seals, popular in the Ancient Near East since the Middle Bronze Age, were small stone cylinders engraved with hunting or royal scenes that featured a drilled hole through their length for wearing on a string or a pin.[45] Their primary purpose was to represent a signature – the bearer of the cylinder seal would roll it over wet clay to leave an impression of its image. By the turn of the first millennium BCE, the invention of the Phoenician script led to a shift from traditional Near Eastern clay tablets (which were perfect for cuneiform) to papyrus scrolls.[46] Light and easy to transport, papyrus proved to be an excellent material for all kinds of private and official correspondence. The change in materials necessitated a change in the sealing instrument, and thus smaller stamp seals were introduced. To safeguard its contents, the scroll could be rolled and tied with a string, which could then be sealed by placing a piece of clay over it and impressing the stamp seal. The great majority of stamp seals were carved from steatite, a soft stone, although jasper, carnelian, agate and other materials were used as well.

Almost from the time of their introduction, Phoenician stamp seals featured the scarab, an impression in the image of the beetle, which in ancient Egypt could be used to symbolize regeneration; in later renditions the anatomy of the beetle became simplified to the point of becoming a simple oval (referred to as a scaraboid).[47] Other Egyptian images too were featured on stamp seals: the ankh (a cross-like symbol but with a loop instead of the top bar), the falcon, the sacred serpent and the Eye of Horus. Egyptian religion often informed the Phoenician seal engraver, especially the theme of rebirth. However, the seals of the eighth to seventh centuries BCE frequently echo the iconography found on bowls and ivories.

The apex of seal production fell in the fifth to fourth centuries BCE, when seal engraving expanded into the western Mediterranean. There, locally sourced materials were used for the production of seals. The city of Tharros on Sardinia became a major source of production and distribution; seals from Tharros are sometimes made of green jasper. With the shift of production westward, the iconographic repertoire changed, absorbing Cypriot, Euboean, Persian, Greek and Etruscan imagery,[48] and the featured gods expanded to include Heracles and a bull-headed Baal. Animal combat scenes became popular as well, most certainly due to the cultural influence of Persia, where such scenes were connected with the notion of kingship.

Terracotta

Unlike most of the objects we have considered, terracottas are products primarily emanating from the Phoenician homeland, bearing unmistakable connections with Phoenicia and the Levant. Terracottas – usually crude representations of human figures and floral motifs – are not known to have been exported; they were intended for religious and domestic use and meant for local markets. The major centres of terracotta production were Sidon, Achziv, Sarepta and Beirut.

The production processes of terracotta items (mostly figurines, protomes and masks) reveal not only the economic stratification of the societies in which they were produced, but the social contexts in which they were used. Phoenician coroplasts (modellers of terracotta figurines) produced their works using the three major techniques: by hand, on a potter's wheel and with various moulds. Naturally, handmade products were relatively crude, and they did not require much skill to make. They were in all likelihood produced by amateur artisans for use in domestic settings

Phoenician
terracotta shrine
with nude Astarte,
7th–6th century BCE.

as amulets or other apotropaic items. Wheel-produced terracottas appear more standardized in shape and style, with their 'tapering conical torsos, moulded heads, and handmade arms of rolled clay'.[49] However, the artisans who produced them, as was the case with handmade products, do not appear to be emulating or incorporating styles from elsewhere in the ancient world. Moulded terracottas, on the other hand, evince outside artistic traditions, owing to their use in temple and funeral settings. Most moulded figurines are represented by ex-votos (votive offerings to a god or a goddess) and funerary accoutrements found among ruins of sanctuaries and cemeteries, although some came from the antiquities market.

Two frequent motifs on moulded terracottas are 'Breast Astarte', a naked woman cupping her breasts with her hands, and the veiled pregnant goddess, both nods to the importance of fertility in ancient Phoenician iconography at least until the sixth century BCE.[50] Other popular representations are clothed versions of Astarte (of Syrian style, from the Persian period), enthroned or seated deities (Melqart, Eshmun, Baal), Bes figurines, 'hollow trumpet-shaped' male and female figurines of worshippers holding either animals or children or playing musical instruments, 'divine horsemen', charioteers in chariots pulled by horses, busts and life-size statues.[51] As becomes clear from this list, most of the terracotta objects belonged to the religious sphere, assisting in rituals or paying homage to the deities of the Phoenician pantheon.

Most of the clay masks from Iron Age Levant come from Phoenicia.[52] Terracotta masks enjoyed uninterrupted use in the Levant from the end of the Middle Bronze Age to the Persian period, and because most of them were found in funerary settings

Clay funerary mask from Tyre, 7th century BCE.

Carthaginian clay mask from Tunisia, 5th–4th century BCE.

or temples (although some were discovered in industrial or secular settings), they are most likely to have been used in religious settings. Phoenician masks represent female and male humans (variously beardless, short- or long-bearded and wrinkled), but never other animals. The age progression observed in male masks may well allude to some rite of passage, and cut-out mouths, frequent features of these masks, suggest that the worshippers who wore them were probably chanting or praying, although posthumous use cannot be discounted either.[53] As Phoenicians expanded into the western Mediterranean, they took their mask-making skills with them. However, western mask samples from such places as Motya, Ibiza and Carthage show that new iconographic motifs were introduced there with time, with the grinning face gaining much popularity.

Stonework

Stone artefacts are much more prevalent in the Phoenician home-land for the simple reason that they do not travel easily. Several distinct categories of stonework are attested in Phoenicia: statuary in the round (where sculptures are presented in a three-dimensional form without accompanying background), stelae and sarcophagi. Phoenicia lacked the more durable kinds of stone necessary for high-quality sculpture production, and artisans made use of materi-als found in abundance locally: limestone and sandstone. Although these kinds of stone were easy to work with owing to their plasticity and softness, the resulting products were often more fragile and of lower artistic quality compared to those found in Egypt and Assyria, for example. The Phoenicians did start to import Greek marble, however, in the sixth century BCE, which allowed them to produce exquisite pieces aimed primarily at more affluent patrons.

Statuary in the round appeared in Phoenicia around the Persian period, and, as usual, Egyptian styles heavily informed the masons' work. However, the Phoenicians did not follow stylistic conventions of contemporaneous Egyptian sculpture but rather those of the earlier Twenty-second Dynasty from the ninth cen-tury BCE. The surviving examples of statuary in the round are mostly religious in nature. The most famous examples of votive statues are 'Temple Boys' (and girls) found in the ruins of the Sidonian Bostan esh-Sheikh sanctuary (dated *c.* 430–380 BCE). The figures there bear an unmistakable Greek resemblance.

Statues from the Eshmun temple near Sidon, 6th–5th century BCE.

Colossus from Byblos, *c.* 300–200 BCE.

The unfinished limestone colossus from Byblos may serve as a rare example of the monumental sculpture portraying divine subjects. The statue evinces strong Egyptian motifs in the figure's stance (one leg in front of the other, as can be seen in numerous Egyptian sculptures), the Egyptian wig and the supporting black pillar.[54]

Stelae in Phoenicia are represented primarily by funerary monuments, both inscribed and blank, which have been discovered in Khalde (near present-day Beirut International Airport), near Sidon; the site of Tell el-Burak south of Sidon; and the Al-Bass cemetery in Tyre.[55] The last yielded the largest number of stelae and *cippi* (a cippus is a small round or rectangular pedestal or pillar). Some cemeteries did not feature any stelae at all, as with Tell Rachidiyé, while others, such as Achziv, had many. It is possible that the stelae were reused in later construction projects or were overlooked during excavations since many were roughly hewn and blank and could be mistaken for building stones.[56] Compared to Phoenicia, stelae are much more numerous in the Punic world, where the tradition of using votive and funerary tombstones was more systematic.[57] Finally, many more stelae were discovered in southern Phoenicia and northern Palestine than in the areas in or north of Beirut. The explanation for this may lie either in the quality of excavations (where stelae were overlooked) or in the differences in funeral customs between various Phoenician sites.

Since the stelae and cippi were hewn of limestone or other soft materials, the quality of iconography and inscriptions from Phoenicia is lacking. Some images, such as the ankh, are easier to discern than others, and generally the iconography is of the following types: anthropomorphic (featuring faces and busts), Egyptian hieroglyphs, the sign of Tanit (a stylized figure of the goddess with raised hands), betyls, free-standing letters, astronomical symbols (the winged disc proving a popular choice), geometric figures, shrines and floral motifs.[58] Such a cornucopia of iconography suggests the great importance religion played in the everyday life of the Phoenicians. As products meant for the average citizen, low-quality stelae and cippi are in contrast to objects associated with the royals and those meant for export.

Although common citizens might have been satisfied with a modest stela or cippus over their grave, more affluent Phoenicians preferred the sarcophagus. Scores of sarcophagi have been discovered in Phoenicia, mostly in Arwad and Sidon. One of the earliest examples of Phoenician sarcophagi is the Ahiram sarcophagus, dated to the early first millennium BCE and viewed by many as one of the major examples of early Phoenician art. One reason for this status is the prevalence of Levantine features (the garments, beards and hairstyles, for example, of the engraved characters) and relative absence of Egyptian influence, such as the lotus-and-bud decorations or offerings on the ritual table that one would normally expect to encounter. What we find in the Ahiram sarcophagus is a reduction of Egyptian elements in favour of indigenous iconography and style. Such a departure might have been a wilful move by the Byblian royalty because of some unknown political development. The Egyptian iconography returns in force in the ensuing periods, coinciding with Egypt's Twenty-second Dynasty. Most of the sarcophagi discovered in Phoenicia date to the fifth to fourth centuries BCE, and their styles still show a strong Egyptian influence.

Sarcophagi in Phoenicia were made of basalt and marble, and they were not only locally produced, but imported from Egypt, and, in turn, were sometimes reused. Such 'recycling' of burial instruments showed the high prestige associated with imported goods from Egypt among the elite. One of the most popular and fascinating types of coffin is the anthropoid sarcophagus. These were composed of two parts, the box and the lid, and the latter has been most useful in tracing changing tastes. Egyptian types dominated Phoenician sarcophagi prior to the fifth century BCE and would feature a crudely fashioned body and a carefully rendered head with a hairstyle corresponding to the gender of the deceased. However, the sarcophagi produced in Sidon and Arwad in the following period abandon their body-shaped forms, instead being replaced by a clean slab of material; the male heads on the sarcophagi also adopt Greek elements such as thick hair and curly beards. It is likely that the iconography of the face was generic, without reference to the actual likeness of the deceased individual.

Jewellery

A number of exquisitely rendered jewellery items in gold, silver and bronze have been associated with Phoenicia and the Phoenicians, although very few items can be traced to Phoenicia proper. Such limiting factors as the lack of undisturbed burials and the impossibility of carrying out controlled archaeological excavations in the Phoenician homeland hamper any attempts to tie specific finds squarely to Phoenicia.[59]

The overwhelming number of jewellery finds come from the Punic west, especially Carthage and Tharros, which were major production centres beginning around the seventh and sixth centuries BCE.[60] It has been suggested, however, that many Mediterranean products were fashioned after the models from the Phoenician homeland, on the basis of their similarity with the few samples there, especially from the burials around Sidon dated to the Persian period. Based on this, we can draw a few conclusions about Phoenician jewellery production and the evolution of tastes in the homeland region.

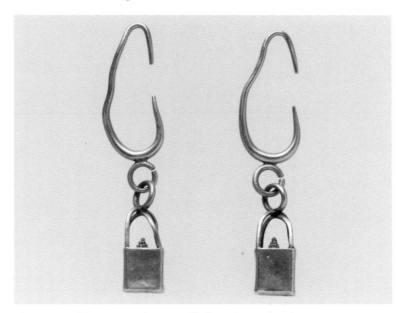

Phoenician gold earrings with cage and ball pendants, 7th–6th century BCE.

Phoenician jewellery dates to at least the Bronze Age, and with time the Phoenicians were able to achieve great skill in working with metals, creating objects of unprecedented quality and attention to detail. Granulation (using small granules of metals for decorative purposes), filigreeing (using gold or silver wire to produce intricate patterns) and embossing were techniques in widespread use by the Phoenician jeweller. Coloured glass, lapis lazuli, carnelian, amethyst and hematite were often inserted to create a finished piece. Affluent buyers sought gold and plated silver objects, whereas the demand of the broader market was satisfied with bronze jewellery with gold and silver foil overlays.[61]

Popular items such as amulets, necklaces, earrings, pendants and finger rings were either fashioned into or were decorated with several images that served magical, apotropaic functions. Often, the jewellery makers turned to the available Egyptian repertoire of symbols, some of which we have already encountered: the ankh, the Eye of Horus, the scarab beetle and a winged disc. The Phoenicians were fond of adding pendants to necklaces and earrings in various shapes, including pomegranates, female figures, lotus flowers and shrine-shaped discs with embossed or granulated embellishments.[62] Finger rings served the double function of housing the bearer's stamp seal. In the western Mediterranean, earrings were leech- or boat-shaped with added granulation.

Phoenician glass head pendant, 650–550 BCE.

Textiles and dyeing

Phoenician textile production and trade were famous throughout the ancient world. Homer mentions the 'elaborately wrought robes' produced by Sidonian women.[63] The Assyrians highly valued Phoenician textiles, which they collected as tribute.[64] The prophet Ezekiel in the Hebrew Bible mentions that Tyre both imported and exported textiles (Ezekiel 27:7, 16, 18). Archaeologists have also determined that Phoenician ships carried wool in the Persian period.[65] Sadly, almost no textile artefacts exist that would inform us about what those garments looked like or how they were constructed. Based on the surviving artworks (such as reliefs) that portray Phoenicians, we can surmise that they preferred to wear ankle-length, loose-fitting robes decorated with embroidered designs and fringed hems.[66] However, we have ample evidence regarding the dyeing industry that flourished in Phoenicia.

In antiquity, purple was considered the colour of royalty and power and the unmistakable sign of wealth and status. For example, throughout his epics, Homer frequently mentions heroes wearing garments of purple. Phoenicia was the pre-eminent centre of purple dye production, and mythical accounts even situate Tyre as the place where the purple dye industry originated. Julius Pollux, a Greek scholar and rhetorician from the second century CE, retold a tale of how Heracles was walking on the shore of Tyre with his dog, and the dog bit into a sea snail, thus dyeing its mouth Tyrian purple.[67] According to Pollux, this incident happened a few hundred years before the Trojan War, during the reign of the legendary King Phoenix, who was the first to wear garments dyed with Tyrian purple. Contemporary consensus, however, places the invention of the dye much earlier, during the Middle Minoan I–II (2160–1700 BCE).[68] Pliny the Elder attributed to Tyre the best-quality purple dye and emphasized how the dye propped up Tyre's fame and fortune.[69] Finally, Strabo mentioned how Tyre excelled economically because of its dye industry (and how unpleasant the city was to live in because of the smell associated with its production).[70] Even the Greek word *phoinix*, from which Phoenicia

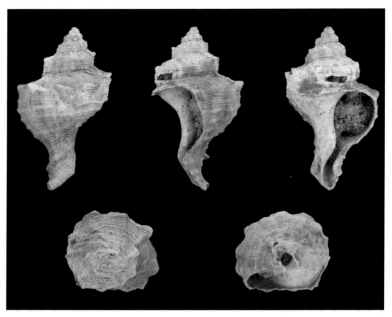

Shells of the medium-sized sea snails *Hexaplex trunculus*, known for producing royal blue dye.

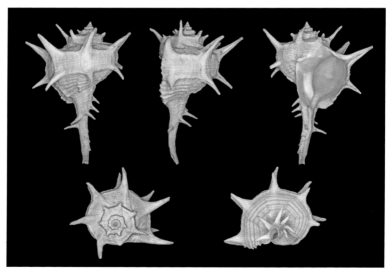

Shells of the medium-sized sea snails *Bolinus brandaris*, known for producing 'Tyrian' or 'imperial' purple dye.

gets its name, is derived from *phoinós* for 'red', an allusion to purple dye production, as well as a reflector of ethnic stereotypes.

Phoenicians used two types of Mediterranean mollusc, *Hexaplex trunculus* (also referred to as *Murex trunculus*) and *Bolinus brandaris* (also known as *Murex brandaris*), for dye production. *Hexaplex trunculus* produced a royal blue dye, whereas *Bolinus brandaris* was reserved for 'Tyrian' or 'imperial' purple.[71]

Pliny describes how the purple dye was made.[72] It was produced by collecting murex snails, breaking them open, extracting the glands and heating them for ten days in large vats filled with saltwater. When the dye was eventually released, it was colourless but turned purple when exposed to air again.

Archaeology has substantiated the connection between purple dye and Phoenicia. Beirut, Sidon, Tyre, Sarepta, Shiqmona (also spelled Shikmona), Apollonia, Dor, Akko, Tell Keisan and Arwad all yielded evidence of murex harvesting, processing and dyeing.[73] Both Tyre and Sidon were conveniently located for the collection of murex shells in large quantities. However, in times of great demand when larger-than-usual quantities of shells were needed, Phoenicians resorted to importing them from faraway places such as Mogador in Morocco.

The prestige of purple dye was in part due to the enormous quantities of shells required for its manufacture. In order to produce just 1.4 grams of dye, sufficient only to dye the trim of a single garment, 12,000 *Bolinus brandaris* shells were needed.[74] Accordingly, the dye was worth more than its weight in gold.

Minor arts and crafts

Several arts and crafts defy easy categorization, but because of their esoteric, novelty qualities it is worth mentioning them here. Ostrich eggs with either engraved or painted designs are found mostly in the Punic world, where they gained popularity around the seventh century BCE.[75] It has been suggested, though, that the western examples echo older models that appeared in the Phoenician homeland around the eighth century BCE.[76] As the practice of decorating ostrich eggs spread around the ancient

Mediterranean, artisans used local designs. Again, the Phoenician connection here is tenuous since no samples from the Phoenician homeland have been mentioned in the existing literature.

We can observe the same with Indo-Pacific *Tridacna squamosa* (fluted giant clam) shells adorned with images of plants, animals and humans, the focal point of the piece being the female or bird's head carved in the umbo, the highest part of the shell. They have been discovered in both the east and west but not Phoenicia proper.[77] Their decoration echoes bowls and ivories and for the most part is indicative of the fact that they were produced by a single workshop or a close association of workshops at an unknown location. Although we have no solid evidence, a site along the southern Phoenician coast is a strong possibility.

Phoenician arts and crafts were characterized first and foremost by an openness to a wide range of styles and motifs and an ability to combine them eclectically into what came to be identified as 'Phoenician art'. This is not to say that the Phoenicians themselves did not develop their own artistic language and skills in crafts – they did so by masterfully marketing their products far and wide, with an eye to differentiating between less demanding consumers and those with more discerning tastes (and deep pockets).

Another notable element of the Phoenician artistic heritage is that lines are very much blurred between products emanating from the Phoenician homeland and those from the wider Punic world. Because of the lack of material remains from Phoenicia proper, any product exhibiting eclecticism of styles or being in one way or another connected with who the Phoenicians were believed to be was automatically considered 'Phoenician'. This process of 'Orientalizing' affects both ancient and modern commentators; whenever art objects defy expectations and accepted stylistic norms, they are considered 'Phoenician'. It is understandable that it is much easier to classify as 'Phoenician' any objects produced by Phoenicians colonizers, but at what point do the colonizers sufficiently depart from their eastern roots and develop their own artistic language?

EIGHT

Travels and Trade: Phoenician Westward Expansion

The Phoenicians were considered masterful navigators of the seas among allies and enemies alike. Their maritime achievements were unprecedented in the ancient world. By the tenth and ninth centuries BCE, they engaged in establishing colonial outposts across the Mediterranean, venturing even into the Atlantic coast of the Iberian Peninsula. We have those colonies to thank for much of what we know about the Phoenicians. As our overview of material remains has shown, western Phoenician colonies supply much of our knowledge about Phoenician arts, for example. In this chapter, we will survey the major Phoenician colonies in Cyprus, the Aegean, the Italian Peninsula, Sardinia, Sicily, Malta, Ibiza, the Iberian Peninsula, Portugal and northern Africa. We will start, however, with some general observations about Phoenician maritime abilities and achievements and examine why the Phoenicians, more than any other entity of the ancient world, ventured into overseas expansion.

Phoenician shipbuilding and navigation

For the peculiarities of Phoenician shipbuilding, we have to rely on non-Phoenician accounts (Egyptian, Greek and others) and iconographic sources such as Assyrian reliefs and Phoenician coins and seals that portray Phoenician ships. Also useful are several shipwrecks that preserved not only some technology used in shipbuilding but the ships' contents. Many maritime technological innovations came from outside Phoenicia, but the ingenuity of the

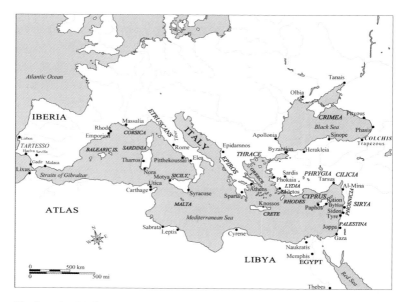

The Iron Age Mediterranean.

Phoenicians allowed them to bring these inventions to market, thus revealing a considerable knack for adopting useful innovations and trends (as was the case with arts). Mortise-and-tenon joinery, the earliest example of which is dated to the fourteenth century BCE, gained popularity in the first millennium BCE. It was considered a Phoenician invention (the Romans called it *coagmenta punicana*, 'Phoenician joints'). Here is how Jeffrey Emanuel describes it: 'This technique, which replaced sewn-plank joinery, consisted of linking planks (mortises) by their edges via a tenon, which was inserted into the two connecting planks and secured with a wooden peg or nail – an edge-to-edge fastening method commonly used in the ancient Mediterranean.'[1]

Another 'borrowed' invention was the brailed rig and loose-footed sail, which appeared at the end of the Late Bronze Age; the first visual representation of the rig and sail appears on the walls of the mortuary temple of Ramesses III (r. 1184–1153 BCE) at Medinet Habu in Egypt.[2] The technique allowed for an efficient lowering and raising of sails like a Venetian blind, enhancing the manoeuvrability of the ship. Finally, by the end of the eighth century BCE, the Phoenicians made their own contribution to the art of shipbuilding as they invented a bireme, a two-banked galley that allowed for greater maritime speeds without extending the length of the ship.[3]

The Phoenicians were masters of navigation. Homer spoke of them as 'famous seafarers',[4] and Herodotus gleefully related an account of how the Egyptians hired a Phoenician fleet to circumnavigate Africa.[5] One of several reasons for venturing outside the Phoenician homeland was the lack of resources and any discernible hinterland – the Lebanon Mountains effectively left just the coastal area for any productive economic activity. Some have argued that the Phoenicians, ever pragmatic, did not start an overseas expansion to broaden their geographic horizons and knowledge but to seek better markets for what they produced, while at the same time scouting for raw materials.[6]

We have already seen in our discussion of Phoenician religious practices how much attention was paid to astral bodies. That attention undoubtedly stemmed from the experience of navigating the uncharted waters of the Mediterranean, and because of that, every effort was made to appease celestial bodies and secure their direction, both metaphorically and figuratively. Strabo mentioned how the Phoenicians used various constellations for navigation.[7] Diodorus Siculus described how the Phoenicians were the first to sail beyond the Pillars of Heracles (the Strait of Gibraltar) into the Atlantic and to discover the Madeiras or the Canaries.[8]

The Phoenician expansion into the western Mediterranean was gradual, with the lands closest to established Phoenician outposts the first to be explored and settled, and from where the process would be started all over again. After Cyprus, the island of Crete was possibly the first Phoenician outpost. On the way to Crete, Phoenicians might have stopped on the island of Rhodes. Moving further west, we notice that the Phoenicians were not interested in the Adriatic region at all, possibly because of an existing Etruscan population.[9] They did, however, resume a sizeable settlement activity starting from Sicily and beyond.

The pinnacle of Phoenician maritime prowess is their legendary circumnavigation of Africa. Herodotus tells the story in his

Histories, noting how the Phoenicians would make occasional stops to sow seeds and wait for the harvest before resuming their voyage around Africa.[10] According to Herodotus, the endeavour took place during the reign of Necho II of Egypt, which lasted from 610 to 595 BCE. Undoubtedly, Herodotus' account seemed believable to ancient readers – Africa was considered a small continent in antiquity. It seems plausible to contemporary commentators as well, but for different reasons. As reported, the journey would have taken place when the Phoenician city-states still enjoyed economic prosperity. Also, the voyage of over two years, covering an estimated distance of 20,000 kilometres, is credible.[11] Even if the Phoenicians did not complete the journey, they still went much further south than many of their contemporaries.

One unintended consequence of the journey was the projection of the Phoenician navigational prowess onto other discoveries of distant lands. Studies appearing as far back as 1535 suggested that either the Carthaginians or the Phoenicians landed in the Americas before anyone else.[12] These claims seem to have been founded on the simple notion that both the Phoenicians and the Carthaginians (as 'relatives' of the Tyrians, who founded Carthage) were the pre-eminent maritime entities of their time. That little was known about either of the peoples before the nineteenth century did not hurt either. Arguments vacillated between the Phoenicians and the Carthaginians, assigning voyages to the Americas before 600 BCE to the former, and those after 500 BCE to the latter based on the fact that the Carthaginians barred any ship, including those from the Phoenician mother country, to sail through the Strait of Gibraltar from about 509 BCE.[13]

It appears that regarding the question of whether the Phoenicians discovered the Americas, all one had to do was believe. In 1872, the apparent evidence for such beliefs came to light – the Paraíba Stone. It was discovered near the Paraíba river in Brazil, and it had an enigmatic inscription in an unknown language carved upon it. The man who found the stone, Joaquim da Costa, transcribed the inscription and sent a copy to Rio de Janeiro to be deciphered. It turned out that it seemed to be written in a Semitic language. Since no specialists in ancient languages were to be found in Brazil, a naturalist by the name of Ladislau Netto took up the task of deciphering the stone. He determined that the writing appeared to be in Hebrew, which he learned for this very task. Finally, the inscription could be read:

> We are sons of Canaan from Sidon from the city of the king. A storm cast us on this distant shore, a land of mountains, and we gave a young man to the gods and goddesses, in the nineteenth year of Hirom, our great king.
>
> We went from Ezion-geber on the Red Sea and departed with ten ships.
>
> We were at sea together two years circling the land belonging to Ham but were separated from the (protecting) power of Baal and were no longer with our company. We arrived here twelve men and three women in the new shore of which I Mat'aštart, the captain, have taken possession. May the gods and goddesses grant us grace.[14]

Had the inscription been genuine, it would have opened a new chapter in our knowledge about the Phoenicians. However, it is widely regarded as counterfeit. We have absolutely no surviving documents in which the Phoenicians identified themselves or used terms that referred to the Phoenician peoples collectively as 'sons of Canaan'. Eventually, Netto had to publish a retraction of his conclusions in which he attempted to lay the blame on five possible forgers. Other circumstances give historians serious pause as well. For one, Costa vanished along with the stone, and no credible scholar has ever seen it. Even the location of the find is ambiguous since there are two distinct Paraíba regions in Brazil.[15]

One would think this would have dissuaded the believers. Not so. Theories persisted: the Phoenicians landed in the Americas by sailing down the Red Sea, then crossing the Indian and Pacific oceans.[16] Sometimes the Phoenicians are thought to be the Hebrews, a belief infused with ideas from the Book of Mormon, which talks about the ancient Hebrews fleeing the destruction of Jerusalem by the Babylonians by getting into ships, crossing the Atlantic Ocean and forming the peoples that later came to be known as Native

Americans. A great deal of theorizing regarding the Phoenician discovery of the Americas, without any concrete archaeological evidence (but many fake coins[17]), is fuelled by the simple fact that the Phoenicians were great seafarers who were capable of long-distance travel. Of note is a recent report from Puerto Rico, where a set of enigmatic inscribed stones known as las piedras del padre Nazario (The Stones of Father Nazario) came to be associated with the Phoenicians, although, as usual, the evidence is slim.[18]

Being associated with or believed to be a descendant of a noble, capable people is seen as an honour, and this desire drives those who propose that the Phoenicians discovered and inhabited other lands. Josephine Quinn speaks of 'Phoenicianism' as a tendency in North Atlantic islands from the sixteenth to nineteenth centuries to turn to the Phoenician heritage in search of one's national identity and consciousness.[19]

As with the discovery of the Americas, the evidence is scant, and there exists only one artefact that contentiously connects the North Atlantic islands with Phoenicia – a graffito on a tile from Holt in Wales mentioning the name 'Macrinus', a first- or second-century CE Roman soldier of African descent who served in Imperial Rome's Twentieth Legion, stationed at Chester. The inscription is in Neo-Punic, fitting the North African birthplace of the soldier; Macrinus would have been able to write his name (if nothing else) in his native tongue, 'perhaps as a kind of joke to mystify his fellows'.[20] Despite this weak evidence, theories connecting Britain and other lands with Phoenicia still flourished well into the nineteenth, and even the twentieth, century. Quinn provides many fascinating examples of how the Phoenicians were associated with such places as Stonehenge and Cornwall, the British tradition of painting one's body with woad, and 'Punic dress' and 'Punic huts' in Wales; how the Phoenician language was considered the mother tongue of the Celtic languages of northwest Europe; and how Ireland was supposedly the colony of the Phoenicians. In a way, Phoenicia and the Phoenicians advanced British and Irish concepts of identity by appealing to the heritage of the renowned Levantines.[21]

As fascinating as discussions of possible or fictional voyages and colonizing efforts by the Phoenicians can be, we need to look closely at the more reliable data emerging from the Mediterranean and the Atlantic coast of Iberia and northern Africa. The evidence of Phoenician expansion there can greatly assist us in understanding how Phoenician colonization took place and what data helps in identifying this or that place as 'Phoenician'.

Cyprus

Situated about 240 kilometres from the coast of modern Lebanon, the island of Cyprus served as a launch pad for Phoenician expansion westward; additionally, its copper resources were of much interest to the Phoenicians, who were in dire need of raw materials. The relationships between the Phoenician city-states and Cypriot kingdoms were sporadic, experiencing rises and falls due to cultural, economic and political developments in the ancient world. Cyprus (or Alashiya, its Late Bronze Age name) established solid and wide relations with the Levant, Egypt and the kingdom of Ugarit long before we can speak of Phoenician expansion into the island. Known for its copper ('Cyprus' is derived from the Greek word *kúpros*, for copper) and bronze, kingdoms in Cyprus were successful on the international scene, trading in metals and pottery.[22]

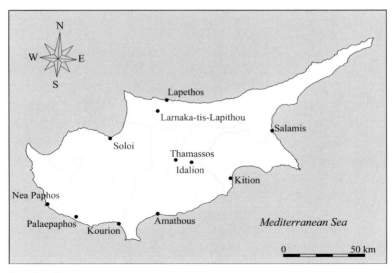

Iron Age Cyprus.

Starting in the eleventh century BCE, Phoenician exports to Cyprus grew steadily. Two hundred years later, the Phoenician presence on the island became much more pronounced, with the rise of the city-state of Kition (also referred to as Qart-hadasht, Punic/Phoenician for 'New City'),[23] near Larnaca in modern Cyprus. Epigraphic evidence dated to the eighth and seventh centuries BCE discovered both in Cyprus and in Assyria places a governor vassal of the king of Tyre at the helm of Qart-hadasht between about 730 and 670 BCE. Inscriptions refer to the city as the capital of a Cypriot kingdom accountable only to the Great King of Assyria. Although the evidence is not overwhelming, it suggests that Qart-hadasht was the name of Kition with the Phoenicians at the helm until it fell under Greek influence (the last time the name Qart-hadasht appears on the Rassam cylinder of the Assyrian king Ashurbanipal, dated to 664 BCE, which contains records of his conquests); from the fifth century on, Kition becomes the only geographical name for the city. It is more appropriate to speak of the Cypro-Phoenician kingdom of Kition rather than calling it a Phoenician colony because of the unique mixture of local and Phoenician traits there.

The settlement at Kition had existed since the thirteenth century BCE. The city found renown in the ancient world; even the Hebrew Bible (Numbers 24:24) mentions it under the name 'Kittim'. Curiously, the Bible uses another name for Cyprus as well, Elishah, derived from Alashiya, Cyprus's ancient name, which may indicate a different independent tradition or commercial networks. Conveniently located in a harbour, Kition was the point of contact between the entire island and the Levant. The major artefacts that connect Kition with Phoenicia are pottery and terracottas appearing in the eighth century BCE. They were either imported from Phoenicia or were produced on site by the potters who relocated from Phoenicia to Kition, in all likelihood training apprentices to satisfy demand.[24] Local potters also started imitating Phoenician types and shapes, making it difficult to distinguish between local products and imports from the Phoenician homeland. In Kition, even Phoenician cultural conventions were borrowed. Sabine Fourrier mentions the process of 'Phoenicinizing' traditional

Cypriot drinking bowls with handles. Phoenician-period vessels from Cyprus have handles that are barely usable, suggesting that even the mainland style of drinking – by placing a vessel in the open palm – was imitated in Kition.[25]

Another form of evidence of Phoenician influence or presence is epigraphic. Inscriptions found in Cyprus suggest that the Phoenician alphabet appeared on the island around the ninth century BCE.[26] Most of the epigraphic evidence since that time appears in the Phoenician alphabet, rather than the Cypro-syllabic script. Many inscriptions mention the Phoenician deities Astarte, Melqart, Eshmun, Anath, Reshef and the Cypro-Phoenician god Mikal. Overall, though, the epigraphic evidence does not allow us to speak with any degree of certainty about the nature of contacts between Cyprus and the Phoenician homeland.[27]

The Persian period, especially the fifth century BCE, marks the rise of Greek influence on the island. Cyprus was caught in the middle of the animosities between the Greeks and Persians, and there was a concerted effort on the part of Greek writers to incorporate Cyprus into the Greek cultural milieu.[28] The tension between and the pull of two different cultural traditions, Greek and Phoenician, are also apparent in the mixture of styles of funerary stelae, coffins and sarcophagi – both Ionian and Phoenician types are observed in Kition. The orientation of Kition towards Greece was accompanied by political and economic developments in the fifth century BCE as well. First, the king of Kition absorbed another Cypriot city, Idalion, possibly through military conquest in the middle of the century. A hundred years later, Kition expanded again, this time by acquiring Thamassos. Such expansionism positively affected the economic prosperity of Kition. Archaeological evidence from Kition revealed three main building phases, suggesting a bustling economy in the city in the fifth and fourth centuries BCE.[29]

Besides Kition, Idalion and Thamassos, other sites in Cyprus evince Phoenician connections. Among them are Kourion, Lapethos, Salamis and Amathus. Of note is the preference among the Cypriot elite for products produced in Phoenicia prior to the fifth century BCE, as many of them were placed in Cypriot tombs.[30]

Outside Kition, new settlers from Phoenicia did not integrate into local societies completely but kept their customs, including maintaining their own funerary grounds.

With the rise of Alexander the Great and Cypriot kingdoms falling under Ptolemaic rule, all traces of the Phoenician language, one of the more reliable markers of the Phoenician presence on the island, disappear. The island, and especially Kition, continued to be engaged in lively commerce with the outside world, actively trading with Phoenicia, among many other territories.

The Aegean

Both literary sources and archaeological finds show that the Aegean, with its multitude of islands and coastal settlements, interested the Phoenicians mainly because of the area's natural resources, mostly metals. Classical authors make numerous mentions of the Phoenicians as traders, sometimes bandits, slave traders, as well as unsurpassed mariners. Earlier literary sources, especially the Homeric poems, extol Phoenician achievements in crafts and seafaring, but they do not mention specifically the Phoenicians settling in the Aegean. Later authors, however, do mention the Phoenicians making more permanent settlements. For example, Herodotus relates how the Phoenicians came to Thasos to colonize the island and to mine for gold, and in the process turned the entire mountain upside down.[31] Herodotus

The Iron Age Aegean.

also mentions the temple to Astarte built by the Phoenicians on the island of Cythera, lying to the southeast of the Peloponnese peninsula; with time, the temple evolved into a classical temple to Aphrodite. Ergias of Rhodes, a historian from the fourth century BCE whose works are cited by the second-century CE rhetorician Athenaeus, mentions the Phoenicians settling in Ialysos, on the island of Rhodes.[32] Diodorus Siculus relates an episode of Phoenicians stopping on the island of Rhodes on their way to Crete.[33] Ancient sources also mention the Phoenicians arriving in Argos and the North Aegean.[34] Finally, Thucydides, Josephus and others suggest that the Phoenicians, especially the Sidonians, settled in northern harbours of the Ancient Near East and south and southwest Anatolia, especially Cilicia.[35] Overall, ancient literary sources suggest that the Phoenicians mostly traded in the Aegean and settled in locations that were undoubtedly advantageous to their commercial interests. It is conceivable that the currents and winds contributed to their choice of settlements, too.

Archaeological evidence, on the other hand, is not very clear about the Phoenician presence and trading activities in the Aegean because claims regarding Phoenician involvement in the area are frequently based on artworks that are considered 'Orientalizing' and 'exotic' and, therefore, foreign and most likely originating in Phoenicia.[36] Determining the processes by which such artefacts ended up in the Aegean is often impossible since they could be either produced on site or imported from elsewhere, including the Phoenician homeland. The very notion of Orientalizing art is vague since the implied Phoenician attribution of an object can be misleading and erroneous. Also, the physical presence itself can be of several kinds, including sporadic commercial contacts, sustained continuous presence in ports, a settlement for reasons besides commercial interests, and, finally, an extended cohabitation side-by-side with indigenous communities, resulting in amalgamation, assimilation and exchange of ideas.[37]

Rhodes is a natural stop on the voyage into the western Mediterranean, and it is not surprising that its archaeological record includes many Phoenician artefacts, although it is unclear whether the Phoenicians settled there. Among the objects classified as Phoenician and upon which we can assess Phoenician trade are luxury items dated to the late eighth and seventh centuries (ivories, tridacna shells and gold and silver jewellery).[38] Some have suggested that a workshop on Rhodes produced luxury items and small perfume bottles imitating Phoenician and Cypriot prototypes. Most of the items seem to originate from Ialysos, suggesting that the workshop was located there; the testimony of classical authors supports such a notion as well. On the nearby island of Cos, the discovery of black-on-red unguent flasks attests to Cypriot-Phoenician trade of such items with the island in the ninth century BCE.[39] Similarly, the island of Samos yielded exotic artefacts (figurines, toys, amulets and bronze and glazed vessels) with origins in the Near East and the Levant near the temple of Hera.[40] Whether there was a production centre on Samos is unclear, but trade in these items with the Levant and Phoenicia is possible.

The islands of Rhodes and Cos were on the Phoenician route through the central Aegean, of which the Cyclades were part.[41] The numerous islands (about 220 in total) did not yield much in the way of Phoenician artefacts, but connections with Phoenicia are still present. The island of Paros was famous for exporting its marble to Sidon in the Persian and Hellenistic periods.[42] Also, an influential Phoenician community of merchants found their home on the island of Delos. The island was an influential trading and banking centre where the Delian League kept its treasury. Delos was also a sacred centre and a major pilgrimage site as it was considered the birthplace of Apollo. So sacred was Delos, in fact, that all burials and births were forbidden there. The Phoenicians appear in the epigraphic record of the island in the fourth century BCE, when they dedicated images of Tyre and Sidon on the island, and Philokles (also spelled Philocles), 'King of the Sidonians', 'dedicated golden crowns at Delian sanctuaries and sponsored a Soteria festival in his honour about 280 BCE'.[43] The presence of shrines dedicated to various Levantine gods and endogamy (intermarriage) between the Phoenicians all point in favour of Phoenician settlements at Delos in the third and second centuries BCE.

In our discussion of epigraphy, we have already mentioned the Phoenician inscriptions from Greece which state that the Sidonians set up camp in Athens in the fourth century BCE, and how they had special rights and privileges. Phoenician and Greek inscriptions from the Piraeus area (about 12 kilometres southwest of the city-centre of Athens) also imply the presence of Tyrian and Kitian settlements.[44]

The Phoenicians chose where to settle based primarily on their trade routes. The island of Crete was conveniently located on the southern Aegean Phoenician commercial route, which allowed them to bypass the Greek mainland,[45] and several classes of objects found on the island support the notion that the Phoenicians visited and settled on it. First, there was the arrival of some unknown metalworkers to Knossos, the centre of the Minoan civilization and the most significant city in Crete, around the ninth century BCE; the metalwork found there bears a strong resemblance to the Phoenician repertoire.[46] Also, abundant samples of exotica (ivory, toys, amulets, faience objects, scarabs and other easily transportable artefacts), classified as both Phoenician and Cypro-Phoenician, increased on Crete in the span of the ninth and eighth centuries.[47] Even if we consider these objects Phoenician, it is impossible to say for sure that they were indeed brought by the Phoenicians themselves. Cemeteries on Crete, on the other hand, provide more substantive data concerning the Phoenician presence. In addition to Phoenician-style pottery from the cemeteries of Knossos, Kommos and Eleutherna and metal vessels and jewellery, the discovery of cippi (three at Eleutherna and two at Knossos) proved valuable. The cippi were not used by the local population but have parallels at the Al-Bass cemetery in Tyre and other Phoenician sites,[48] which suggests a stronger case for a more extended presence of the Phoenicians who lived and died on Crete. They might have chosen Crete for the same reasons they selected Kition, where Phoenician artisans set up their workshops to satisfy market demands with their goods and to teach apprentices.

Sicily

Moving further west, Sicily was the next logical stop into the Mediterranean (and beyond) for the Phoenicians. That Phoenicians lived all over Sicily was well known to ancient writers, including Thucydides.[49] His account suggests that because of the pressure from the Greeks, who had their own expansionist designs, the Phoenicians relocated to the northwest of the island and settled in the towns of Motya (modern Marsala), Soluntum (modern Solunto) and Panormus (modern Palermo), maintaining close and cooperative relations with the native Elymians. Markoe suggests that the Phoenicians, unlike the Greeks, nurtured their relationships with the indigenous populations to maintain the flow of commerce rather than to claim territories.[50] Archaeology supports the dating of Thucydides' narrative, locating the early stages of the settlement of Motya in around 720 BCE, shortly after the earliest Greek colonies were established in Naxos (734 BCE) and Syracuse (733 BCE).[51] Thucydides also mentions that the Phoenicians abandoned their earlier eastern settlements in favour of the more northwesterly locations; a plausible idea since Naxos could have been a convenient port location for ships navigating the toe of Italy from the north.

The town of Soluntum, yet to be thoroughly excavated (an ancient necropolis discovered there is dated to no earlier than the sixth century BCE),[52] was destroyed in the fourth century BCE by the Greek tyrant Dionysius I, only to be rebuilt on Monte Catalfano a few years later.[53] Panormus (literally meaning 'all port' in Greek) revealed the ancient necropolis, but no settlement. Although the foundation of the city is dated to the eighth century BCE, the oldest artefacts come from layers that date to a century later. The continuous occupation of the city for thousands of years precludes large-scale excavations, and archaeology has not provided definitive answers regarding the Phoenician settlement there.

Motya, however, is another matter. The site is located on the island of San Pantaleo, about 160 kilometres from Carthage, and it was one of the closest departure points in the direction of mineral-rich Sardinia.[54] Archaeology has provided much information regarding the nature, development, organization and identity of this Phoenician city on Sicily, although we should note that only a few parts of the town have been excavated: the necropolis, the tophet, the Cappidazzu sanctuary, the North Gate, the southern fortification, the Kothon and the temple at the South Gate.[55] The earliest inhabited sites date to the eighth century BCE, and the tophet is dated to the eighth or seventh century BCE. Although tophets are largely associated with Punic traditions, its date places the artefact in the Phoenician cultural sphere. Overall, Phoenician artefacts in Motya are scarce, which suggests that there was a process of 'continuous infiltration of Phoenicians in already existing local society instead of a new foundation by Phoenicians'.[56]

There are numerous signs that Motya significantly expanded in the middle of the sixth century BCE, a process connected with the encroachment of Carthage in the western Mediterranean.[57] In its quest for territorial expansion, Carthage engaged in hostilities not only with Greeks and Etruscans but with older Phoenician settlers as well. Inscriptions from Motya and other sites in western Sicily dated to the sixth and fifth centuries BCE often mention the cults of Baal Hammon, Astarte, Tanit and Shadrapha – all deities frequently encountered in the Punic pantheon. However, Melqart, a major Phoenician deity, makes little appearance in the epigraphic evidence, showing up only on isolated coins. Burial customs in Motya are dissimilar to those in the Phoenician homeland as well. They are marked by the transition from inhumation to cremation, starting at the end of the fourth century BCE, and echoing the same transition as in Carthage. Even in the layout of the house, Mediterranean traditions are more pronounced, showing little connection with the Levantine east. All these factors point to the 'Punification' of Sicily. Phoenicians may have stopped for a time in Sicily, and some stayed, but their final destination was further west.

The Italian Peninsula

The Phoenician presence in Italy and Sardinia has been taken for granted for some time, but it can be premature to speak of permanent Phoenician settlements there, owing to several factors. First, the discovery of what was considered 'Orientalizing' artefacts in Italy and Sardinia sheds little light on who actually created them and how they ended up there, as we discussed earlier. Another factor is a strong emphasis on the Greek world in the twentieth century, which overshadowed any genuine inquiry into the Levantine presence in Italy.[58] As a result, while there is nuance in identifying Greek pottery (Euboean, Corinthian and so on), the term 'Phoenician' is applied with little differentiation between cities and regions. In recent years, there has been a move away from Hellenizing towards examining a more local and more complex web of interactions, where fluidity and connectedness is emphasized over rigidity and stasis.[59] The implications of such a move for the study of Phoenicians in Italy are twofold: a reassessment of the role Phoenicians played in central Italy, and of the importance of the Tyrrhenian Basin over the island of Sardinia 'in developing Phoenician contact in the early and mid-first millennium BCE'.[60] This change in approach is still very new, so its assessment is yet to bear fruit, but time will tell.

Phoenicians first landed on the Italian Peninsula (primarily Campania and Etruria) in the early to mid-eighth century BCE,[61] following the Mycenaean trading routes that had been sustained by their close collaborators the Cypriots.[62] From Campania and Etruria, Levantine artefacts spread all over the Tyrrhenian seaboard, only to subside after the middle of the seventh century BCE. Considerable evidence exists of Levantine–Euboean collaboration in the exploration of the Tyrrhenian Sea; the two groups used the same trading techniques, which often were based on the concept of gift-giving.[63] This assumption is made based on luxury goods such as ivory, silver or bronze bowls, and large vessels that were given to local elites to ensure their assistance in acquiring commodities they required. After securing the patronage of local elites, the large-scale trade in *athyrmata* (trinkets) commenced.[64]

Consensus holds that the Phoenician interest in the Tyrrhenian Basin was mostly propelled by their interest in the plentiful deposits of copper, lead, iron and silver there. However, some areas where traces of the Phoenicians were discovered had none (for example, Campania). This factor has led some to reassess Levantine trade and the forms it took, emphasizing that the Phoenicians sought contacts primarily with socially complex societies rather than being interested in 'cultural exchange' with just about anybody.[65] Others explain the draw of the metal-deficient locations by proposing that the Phoenicians were attracted, at least in the initial phases of contact, by agricultural products and human resources.[66]

Some of the areas exhibiting Levantine contacts are Torre Galli and Francavilla Marittima in Calabria in the south, Pontecagnano, Montevetrano and Pithekoussai in Campania in the southwest, Castel di Decima, Palestrina, Laurentina, Veio, Cerveteri and Tarquinia in Lazio near Rome, Vulci in Latium in central-western Italy and Chiusi, Marsiliana, Vetulonia and Populonia in Tuscany in central Italy.[67] Among them, the ancient settlement of Pithekoussai on the island of Ischia (a short boat ride from Naples) serves as an example of the interconnectedness of different Mediterranean communities; the Phoenicians at Pithekoussai appear to have existed alongside and within the existing indigenous and Greek populations. Burials at the site feature a rich mixture of pottery types, both Phoenician red slipware and 'Rhodian transport amphora with Aramaic graffiti', and there is evidence of a mixture of rituals performed in the same burial sites.[68]

Sardinia

As we have seen, Phoenician efforts overseas were not solely based on the search for ore-rich regions, but we cannot underestimate their interest in securing metals; Sardinia serves as a good example. The island is rich in copper, iron and silver-bearing lead, and as such it attracted traders from the fourteenth and thirteenth centuries BCE, when Mycenaeans first arrived there.[69] The Mycenaeans were followed by Cypriot traders, who made their mark on Sardinia in the late twelfth or eleventh centuries by producing bronze there. The Levantine arrival, in turn, followed the refinement of iron technology in the eleventh and tenth centuries.[70] The island was important for the Levantine exploration of Sicily and North Africa, and Sardinia also played an important role as a springboard for venturing into the Italian Peninsula.

When Levantine traders first arrived on Sardinian shores, they encountered the indigenous Nuragic population, and contemporary studies focus on the interaction between the two peoples.

A well-developed bronze industry of the Nuragic civilization along with the emergence of native urban settlements resulted from the Phoenician presence on the island. The Nuragic culture gradually declined, beginning in the seventh century BCE. They were either incorporated into the Phoenician population or, having missed out on the new economic opportunities provided by the Phoenician Mediterranean trade, withdrew to focus on traditional agriculture.[71]

The earliest evidence for the Phoenician presence on the island is a monumental inscribed stele found at Nora, a southern coastal site. Epigraphists date it to the end of the ninth or early eighth century BCE and interpret the inscription, though not without detractors, as a commemoration of the erection of a sanctuary to the Phoenician deity 'Pumay'.[72] If the dating and the interpretation are correct, the stele bears the earliest mention of the island's modern name and the erection of the stele falls squarely within the period when both Carthage and the site of Kition were founded; connections of the archaeological finds at Nora with Cyprus suggest that it was the Phoenicians from Kition who settled there. Of interest is the fact that the deity Pumay is associated with Cyprus as well.[73]

The island of Sant'Antioco in the south of Sardinia is yet another site that bears evidence of Phoenician settlement, dated to the second quarter of the eighth century BCE.[74] Among the finds on the island are a necropolis and pottery samples that comprise a mix of Nuragic, Phoenician and imported Greek, suggesting a mixed population.

The last two major Sardinian sites associated with the Levantine settlement are Tharros and Othoca. Based on pottery samples, archaeologists have established that Phoenician settlements were established atop pre-existing Nuragic sites. Of the two sites, Tharros stands out, since by the sixth century BCE it transformed into a burgeoning urban centre, an international port, and a major production and distribution centre for funerary sculpture, terracottas and jewellery.[75]

Historians have identified the emergence of a distinct 'Mediterraneo-Phoenician' culture in Sardinia, which produced pottery and other objects with styles that significantly departed from Levantine prototypes. Whereas earlier, pre-seventh-century pottery samples tended to be identified as 'Tyrian', the same cannot be said of the products emerging in the seventh century. Not only did Levantine colonizers influence indigenous populations of Sardinia (and other places), but the reverse process was under way as well.

Malta and Gozo

The Maltese archipelago's location was beneficial for the Phoenicians as it lies halfway between two major commercial routes in the Mediterranean, one to the north towards the southern coast of Sicily and one to the south, along the North African littoral.[76] Diodorus Siculus mentions that the islands provided a refuelling and servicing station for Phoenician ships.[77]

The two major islands of the archipelago are Malta itself and Gozo, and both provide archaeological evidence not only of Phoenician visits but Phoenician settlement. Archaeology places the earliest Phoenician settlement in Malta in the early ninth century BCE, and by the eighth century the Phoenician presence on the archipelago was widespread. In Gozo, the Phoenicians settled primarily in the interior highland and the southern coastal port, and on the main island of Malta, on a central highland plateau and around the large bay of Marsaxlokk.[78] The sites of Rabat and Mdina formed the nucleus of the community, and Marsaxlokk served as a natural centre of commercial trade, as two Phoenician temples to Melqart (at Ras ir-Raħeb) and Astarte (at Tas-Silġ) suggest.[79]

Phoenician sites on Malta.

Just as with Sardinia, the mixture of wares in the archaeo-logical record, especially at the inland sites of Mdina and Rabat, suggests that the Phoenicians seem to have forged close ties with the indigenous populations of the Maltese archipelago. Lacking in metal-bearing ores and developed agriculture, the area stood apart as a Phoenician settlement, with little lasting cultural input from the Levant, Carthage or the Phoenician western Mediterranean, as novel pottery types, including 'handmade pots and thistle-headed beakers', attest.[80] Such finds suggest a process of acculturation into the local landscape, such as through embracing new diets and 'commensality', thus creating a new, regional collective identity that departs from the Levantine and other roots.[81]

The Phoenician presence in Malta is broad and well attested, as well as frequently celebrated. Ever since the seventeenth cen-tury, a steady flow of finds has emerged from Malta. Among the earliest discoveries are a sarcophagus (discovered at Rabat) and two bilingual inscriptions on cippi; the latter were instrumental in Jean-Jacques Barthélemy's deciphering of the Phoenician script.[82] In spite of this, Malta has yet to yield many of its treasures con-nected with Phoenicia and the Phoenicians, as many of the finds remain to be published and numerous sites are still to be excavated properly. Among the most promising are the sanctuary site of Tas-Silġ, Punic farmsteads at San Pawl Milqi, a Punic shrine at Għar ix-Xiħ and an early seventh-century BCE shipwreck with a cargo of amphorae and mill stones.[83]

Ibiza

Ibiza, as well as the Balearic archipelago of which it is a part, came to be an important location for colonists from the Atlantic straits and, later, for settlers from the Punic lands. The island is located some 90 kilometres off the eastern coast of the Iberian Peninsula, and it played an important role for the Phoenicians traversing the Mediterranean and for the colonists who settled in what is now Spain. The name 'Ibiza' is derived from Punic 'YBŠM (possibly vocalized as 'Yboshim), which means an 'isle of the Balsam-tree'.[84] The Catalan name, Eivissa, most certainly comes from Ebusus, the

Phoenician sites
on Ibiza.

name given to the islands by the Romans, who transliterated and adapted the ancient Punic name.

Although agriculture is very limited on Ibiza because of the low fertility of the soil, the island's main natural resources are lead and silver ores at s'Argentera mines in the east.[85] There, remains of a blast furnace used in the production of iron have been found, and Phoenicians were known for processing iron ore. The earliest evidence indicating that the western Phoenicians visited and settled on the island is dated to the eighth century BCE, with the sites of Sa Caleta and Puig des Molins in the southwest dominating the archaeological landscape. Whereas it is unclear whether the earliest visits were temporary, the more permanent settlements are dated to the mid-seventh century BCE, the date first mentioned in Diodorus' writings.[86] The processes we observed in Sardinia and Malta, whereby newcomers merged with indigenous populations, are not observed in Ibiza, since no traces of significant indigenous communities have been located on the island.

The Sa Caleta settlement was probably founded by the Phoenicians who had settled in Alicante, on the 'Levante' (eastern Iberian coast).[87] Some regard Sa Caleta as a settlement functioning akin to a factory, aimed at collecting and processing local and foreign raw materials. Among the finds associated with Phoenicians are domestic products and objects related to metalworking. The site of Puig de Vila, although roughly contemporaneous with Sa Caleta, appears to fit a more urban, rather than industrial, layout. A necropolis at the nearby site of Puig des Molins yielded many burial goods and several dozen cremation urns deposited into cavities hewn in rock or buried in pit graves. An interesting inscription from the site mentions a person by the name Eshmunab(i) making a votive offering to the deity Eshmun-Melqart.[88] The inscription may signal the existence of an Ibiza temple dedicated to the syncretistic veneration of the principal gods of Sidon (Eshmun) and Tyre (Melqart).

In the sixth century BCE the involvement of the western Phoenicians on the island waned, most likely due to the rise of Greek trade. Sa Caleta was abandoned about 600–575 BCE, the population relocating to the Ibiza Bay enclave, which became a centre of Phoenician-Ibizan ceramics production.[89] However, the styles of pottery produced there were more akin to examples from Sicily, Sardinia and Carthage, which may be an indication of the island turning towards Carthage in its orientation. From the last quarter of the sixth century BCE, we no longer speak of the western Phoenicians operating on the island but of the Punic presence that dominated it until the Roman times.

The Iberian Peninsula

The entire southern Iberian coast was known in antiquity as Tartessos, a semi-mythical city rich in natural resources, especially tin (some identify the 'Tarshish' of the Hebrew Bible with Tartessos). Judging by the Phoenician sea-routes and the amount of archaeological evidence coming from the southwest of the

Iberian Peninsula, Gadir was the ultimate destination for the sea-faring people. Unlike other Mediterranean sites, the area allows us to speak of not just an amorphous and unspecific 'Phoenician' presence but, more specifically, a Tyrian one.[90] Such a precise designation is significant as it paints a more detailed picture of the Phoenician exploration and colonization of the Mediterranean and the Atlantic coast of Iberia. Owing to this, we can speak more confidently of the Tyrian quest for metal-rich ores – gold, copper, iron, tin and silver – not only in the Iberian Peninsula but in the entire western Mediterranean.

In the last few decades, intensified excavations have revealed Phoenician settlements and necropolises along much of the Iberian coast. In the south, among such sites are Almuñécar, Morro de Mezquitilla, Toscanos, Chorreras and Cerro del Villar.[91] Along the Atlantic coast, the sites located well beyond Gadir at the mouths of the Sado, Tagus and Mondego rivers revealed Phoenician foundations. Finally, the modern cities of Cádiz, Málaga, Almuñécar and Adra (respectively the ancient sites of Gadir, Malaka, Seks and Abdera known from classical sources) exhibit abundant evidence of a Phoenician presence.

Classical sources situate the foundation of Gadir (from Punic *gdr*, for 'wall' or 'fortified citadel') to the same time when Utica and Lixus in North Africa were founded in the twelfth century BCE, roughly three centuries before Carthage. Although archaeology has not been able to confirm these dates, the available evidence still suggests that permanent Phoenician settlements at a number of sites appeared as early as the tenth century BCE.[92] The Levantine/Tyrian character of those in the southwest has been suggested by a number of features. For example, several sites (such as El Carambolo and La Rebanadilla) revealed the use of mud-brick, stone foundations, clay or lime plaster and open-air patios – all traditional Levantine construction methods. The earliest Phoenician settlements were also arranged in the manner most beneficial for the trade in metals along Bronze Age commercial routes.

After the earliest wave of settlements, Gadir emerged as the most important outpost in the far west. Excavations in the Bay of Cádiz revealed complex urban structures dated to the late ninth or the beginning of the eighth century BCE.[93] The Temple of Melqart, a Tyrian marker, was located at Gadir as well (the cult of Melqart is also attested at Seks and Abdera). Zooarchaeology revealed that besides metalworking, luxury goods production and ceramics, the Phoenicians at Gadir ventured into agriculture, cultivating wheat and barley, olive trees and grapevines as well as numerous kinds of fruit. They also raised cattle, sheep and goats and, in smaller numbers, pigs, and they exploited marine resources. By the seventh century BCE, the existing settlements grew in size to accommodate the exploding population, and there are many signs that the western Phoenicians engaged in lively trade with the Iberian and Moroccan coasts, extending as far as the central Mediterranean. One of the most important exports was pottery, which was produced in the Levantine style. In turn, they were importing large quantities of Carthaginian, Etruscan, Ionian Greek, Attic Greek and Corinthian pottery, mostly amphorae.

Western Phoenician societies were cosmopolitan and diverse and were headed by Tyrian aristocracy. Burials reveal this, as set-apart chamber tombs were designated for ruling families using Levantine burial traditions. The western Phoenicians employed Egyptian or Egyptian-style alabaster vases for urns, some of which were royal gifts from the East.[94] Indigenous people were employed in the labour force and there are indications that mixed marriages occurred with the local population, as archaeology has revealed the use of local ceramics in everyday cooking. However, since the locals appear to have been excluded from burial rituals, complete integration did not take place.[95]

The former Tyrian domination of the southwest region of the Iberian Peninsula likely weakened in the wake of Tyre's fall to the Babylonians in 573 BCE. The settlements underwent a number of threats, including a fortifying stage to protect economic interests from Etruscans, Phocaeans and Iberian rulers who were eyeing the rich resources available to the western Phoenicians. Eventually, Gadir and other settlements aligned themselves with Carthage, and by 237 BCE they were firmly incorporated into the Punic cultural realm.[96]

Portugal

The western Phoenicians, eager to explore and exploit the Iberian Peninsula, ventured further north into what is now Portugal in the ninth or eighth centuries BCE. Undertaken by the inhabitants of Huelva with the collaboration of indigenous people, such exploration left behind numerous Levantine artefacts, including traces of 'domestic and defensive architecture, building techniques, archaeological remains, language and texts'.[97] Although mostly within coastal areas, the Phoenician presence left a deep social and cultural impact on the inland territories as well. Metals were the focus, although the region was also part of ancient commercial routes that the Phoenicians used for their own trade. Quite a few sites in Portugal are associated with Phoenicians, mostly in the river estuaries, along with two significant necropolises in the Beja and Ourique regions. The Phoenician occupation only stretches to the north of Iberia, which suggests a planned exploration intended to reach only certain regions and in line with existing trade networks.

Among the Phoenician markers found at the sites in Portugal are red slip pottery, including trefoil-rim jugs, red-and-black pithoi, metalworking paraphernalia, glass production, and architecture dominated by Levantine types (rectangular buildings). Also, a pair of inscriptions in Phoenician discovered in Lisbon point to a Phoenician presence. The adoption of the Phoenician language by the indigenous population suggests a close relation between the native and Phoenician cultures.

Overall, it appears that the Phoenician colonization of Portugal was undertaken by western settlers of Huelva, although the data is not as rich as one can find in the Gadir region of the Iberian Peninsula. This can be explained both by the fervour of archaeologists working in Spain and the peripheral importance of the settlements in Portugal.

Northern Africa

Although there have been great strides in the archaeology of northern Africa since the beginning of this millennium, the scope of excavations is still comparatively narrow, hampered by a lack of resources and the geopolitical situation in the region. International teams from Spain, France, Italy and Germany, assisted by local researchers, have been able to conduct archaeological work mostly in Morocco, where the political situation has been much quieter than in Algeria.[98]

Moving from west to east, we first encounter the island of Mogador, which around 700 BCE was connected to the mainland by an isthmus.[99] The island was known in antiquity by the name Amogdoul or Amegdoul (Hebrew *migdol*; Punic *mogdul*), which means 'tower'; the name conceivably refers to a watchtower on the island from which a spotter looked for schools of tuna.[100] Excavations revealed that Mogador was occupied since

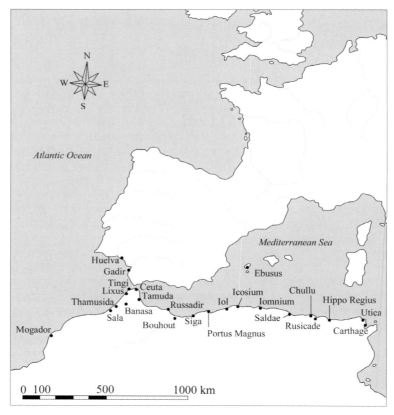

Phoenician and Punic sites in northern Africa.

at least the last quarter of the seventh century BCE, with the more intense occupation taking place a few decades later. Besides Cypriot amphorae of unknown provenance and toponyms hinting at Phoenician or Punic origins, there is not much in the way of concrete evidence that would clearly connect the area with Phoenicia.

The city of Lixus, located to the southwest of the Strait of Gibraltar, was mentioned in classical sources (for example, Pliny's *Natural History*) as one of the oldest Phoenician settlements, but archaeology does not support this, the excavated settlements dating to no earlier than the eighth century BCE.[101] Pliny also mentions a temple of Melqart at the mouth of the Lixo river, but archaeologists have not been able to locate it.

Another site that is frequently mentioned by classical authors is Utica, on the coast of Tunis about 40 kilometres to the southeast of Carthage. Most sources date its foundation (rather precisely) to 1101 BCE, which raises the question of whether numerous authors, including Pliny, Silius Italicus and the Pseudo-Aristotle, all used the same ur-source, now lost. Recent Tunisian-Spanish excavations point to a later date, the ninth century BCE, that would pre-date the founding of Carthage.[102] Archaeology has yet to provide much concrete information about the Phoenician-Punic history of the site.

Finally, we come to Carthage. If we believe the classical sources (such as Justin's *Philippic Histories*), the city was founded in 814 BCE by Elissa (Dido), the sister of the king of Tyre, Pygmalion (or Pumayyaton). Elissa is said to have fled her native Tyre because her brother had murdered her husband Acerbas. Having arrived at the location of the new city ('Carthage' is derived from *qarthadasht*, 'a new city'), Elissa and her entourage were assisted by the people of Utica, who had mercantile interests in the matter, welcoming an 'opportunity of bartering commodities with them'. Archaeology has not been able to support the date conclusively, although a consensus is emerging that dates the foundation of the city to the second half or, more specifically, the last quarter of the ninth century BCE.[103]

The connections between Tyre and Carthage are numerous and convincing. Although the chief god of Carthage was Baal

Hammon rather than the expected Melqart, the chief god of Tyre, the relations between Tyre and Carthage lasted for many centuries, judging by literary sources. Herodotus relates a story about Cambyses II, who gave orders to the Phoenicians to set sail against Carthage, but the Phoenicians refused because of the close ties between Phoenicia and Carthage and the abomination that it was to wage war against their own 'children'.[104]

Throughout its history, Carthage reportedly sent gifts to Tyre. One example is listed in Diodorus Siculus' *Library of History*, which mentions the Carthaginians sending a colossal statue of Apollo to Tyre.[105] Manuel Álvarez Martí-Aguilar summarizes the ebb and flow of the Tyre–Carthage relationship by stating that 'after an initial period of dependency, the colonies break their bonds of subordination with the metropolis in the political and economic sphere, but even so they do not lose the extremely strong religious and ethnic bond.'[106]

Shortly after it was founded, Carthage was able to forge ties with Greek and Phoenician centres in the Mediterranean.[107] By the sixth century, the Carthaginians were all over Africa, Sardinia, Sicily and the Tyrrhenian Basin, engaging in trade and founding new outposts. Since Carthage and the Punic world it established lie outside the scope of this book, we have largely focused on the Phoenician – that is, Levantine – expansion. Having said this, Glenn Markoe's observation regarding the Phoenician penetration into northern Africa and the Mediterranean is invaluable, especially in regard to currents and winds:

> The strong west–east current that runs along the North African littoral from the Straits of Gibraltar to Port Said made a westerly coastal advance toward Carthage from Egypt extremely problematic. So, too, did the buffering winds, hazardous shoals, and poor visibility encountered along the barren 480-kilometre . . . coastal stretch of central Libya . . . In the face of such difficulties, Phoenician sailors from the eastern mainland heading for Carthage and points beyond would have opted for a more direct westerly route via open seas.[108]

In the case of Carthage, once the Tyrians made it there, they never left, always remembering their roots but evolving into their own identity that resembled less and less the Tyrian identity of the homeland.

Phoenician trade in the Mediterranean

Classical authors' testimony regarding the date when Phoenician settlements were founded in the Mediterranean differs sharply from the dates provided by the archaeological record (the examples include Gadir, Utica and Lixus). The three-hundred-year gap has to be explained somehow, and one suggestion is to distinguish between 'pre-colonial' and properly 'colonial' phases.[109] In the pre-colonial phase, Levantine merchants would have prospected areas for their resources, to gauge the indigenous population's tolerance of newcomers, and to determine the viability of colonization. Such prospecting would be done by small groups of merchants, who would prepare trading posts and landing stages (*emporia*, singular *emporium*) in anticipation of the large-scale colonizing effort. Proposals such as this are deeply rooted in core–periphery theories, which in turn are based on the Marxist understanding of trade as a solely exploitative quest for resources.[110]

Newer interpretations downplay the importance of searching for resources, mostly metals,[111] in the Phoenician expansion, focusing more on social interactions. Phoenicians, unlike Greeks and Euboeans with whom they may have occasionally cooperated in commerce, were interested in engaging in trade relations with more complex societies, with elaborate systems of norms and values.[112] Some have pointed out that Levantine traders conducted their business on two levels: trade with important elites (of goods including ivory, silver or bronze bowls, more substantial vessels such as cauldrons, and so forth) and 'tramp' trading in small trinkets ubiquitous in the Mediterranean.[113] Having first earned the respect of the elites through gift-giving of more expensive objects, ensuring their support and patronage, the Levantines would proceed to conduct their trade in more plentiful domestic objects, satisfying the needs of both elites and commoners.

The way the Levantine Phoenicians conducted their trade has been viewed as a three-stage process, involving a seafaring phase, a settlement phase and an impact phase (when Phoenician influence became apparent in the archaeological record).[114] Richard Fletcher, a specialist in Mediterranean archaeology, suggests that in situations where the Levantines did not establish settlements, the three phases can be distinguished as 'reconnaissance', 'gift-giving' and 'focused-trade' phases.[115] In such cases, when interacting with native peoples, the Levantines were not interested in establishing and maintaining involved connections with indigenous cultures. Although relationships did exist, we cannot convincingly speak of cultural exchange, something that the Greeks excelled at.

Levantine trade in the Mediterranean spanned several centuries, with more intense explorations starting in the ninth and eighth centuries BCE.[116] Material remains suggest that Levantine involvement in the Mediterranean fluctuated over time. In Italy, for example, Phoenician exports declined in volume after the middle of the seventh century BCE, only to increase somewhat around the middle of the sixth century BCE.[117] Conceivably, the same pattern existed in other regions of the Mediterranean as well, following geopolitical, economic and cultural processes not only in the west but in the east, in the Phoenician homeland. The fall of Tyre in 573 BCE to the Babylonians undoubtedly affected trade, but other factors played a role as well, including the collapse in demand for silver in the Levant, increasing east Greek and Phocaean trade in the Tyrrhenian Basin and on the Iberian coast, and the devastation caused by Babylonian military actions in the broader Levant.[118]

Finally, we can also comment on the identity of Phoenician traders. Although most settlements are called simply 'Phoenician' or 'Levantine' in the existing literature, without differentiating between the city-states of the Levantine coast, the evidence points to Tyre as the main trader and colonizer in the Mediterranean before the sixth century BCE. Most of the evidence comes from classical sources, and often archaeology does not support their testimony. However, the oldest settlements of Huelva and Gadir and other locations unmistakably show strong connections with Tyre. Therefore, when speaking of the Phoenician expansion in the Mediterranean and the Atlantic coast in the ninth to sixth centuries BCE, we need to keep in mind the near certainty that it was Tyre that initiated and maintained these, although archaeological finds, especially from Ibiza, suggest that Sidon participated to some extent in the western expansion as well.

EPILOGUE

Herodotus began his *Histories* by pointing out that the main goal of his work was to ensure that 'human achievement may not be forgotten in time, and great and marvellous deeds . . . may not be without their glory'.[1] In a way, that was the inspiration behind this book – to acknowledge the contribution of the Phoenicians to human civilization. The Phoenicians of old might not have survived the turmoil of antiquity, and we rarely hear their clear and distinguishable voice, but their legacy continues to enrich us today. Their literary achievements, if not the outright invention of the alphabet, have made writing, reading and learning the quintessential characteristics of humanity. Phoenician maritime exploits have inspired numerous adventures in the quest to discover unknown places. Others have wanted to be like them, even centuries after their peak had passed. And their cultural fluidity, tolerance, ability to navigate political and cultural landscapes and to compromise serve as examples of how to survive, to persevere and to adjust.

On a certain level, we have only scratched the surface of who the Phoenicians really were. We mostly hear about them from the writings of other peoples. In attempting to reconstruct their cultures and societies, we can look only at the objects that have withstood time: artworks, the remains of their ancient cities and cemeteries, occasional inscriptions that fortunately survived and their coinage.

In recent years, the advent of DNA studies has provided much invaluable information not available from any other source, and

Reconstruction of the 'Young Man of Byrsa' at the Carthage National Museum.

we hope that, with the development of informed and sensible methodologies, new complex relations and networks of connections will be revealed. The first complete mitochondrial genome of a Phoenician man in Tunisia was sequenced by a team from the University of Otago, New Zealand, in 2016.[2] The remains were discovered on the Byrsa Hill, in the vicinity of the National Museum of Carthage in Tunisia, and the individual is now known as the

Young Man of Byrsa or as Ariche, 'the beloved one', as indicated by the funerary inscription accompanying the remains. The DNA evidence, in conjunction with the analysis of skeletal remains, even allowed the scholars to reconstruct how Ariche may have looked. Ariche was about 1.7 metres tall and aged between 19 and 24 years at the time of his death about 2,500 years ago (as burial goods suggest). What is surprising is that the Young Man of Byrsa belonged to a rare European haplogroup (a group of people with a common ancestor), 'likely linking his maternal ancestry to Phoenician influenced locations somewhere on the North Mediterranean coast, the islands in the Mediterranean or the Iberian Peninsula, rather than a North African or Asian ancestry'.[3] The co-leader of the study, Lisa Matisoo-Smith, noted that the findings establish the earliest evidence of European ancestry in North Africa as dating to at least the sixth century BCE.[4] Subsequent studies have added promising information about the Phoenicians as well.[5]

Much of the Phoenician heritage is hidden and buried underneath modern cities and infrastructure. The fascinating site of Khalde (modern Khaldah) lies beneath Beirut International Airport and a Lebanese Air Force Base. Additionally, the political situation in the Middle East is not conducive to carrying out excavations on any reasonable scale. Although it is doubtful that the archaeology of Phoenician cities will make many strides in the immediate years to come, one discipline to keep an eye on is marine archaeology. With proper investment and enthusiasm, it may yield unimaginable archaeological treasures. Given the extent of Phoenician maritime achievements, one can only guess at what the seas might yield.

The Phoenicians have fascinated humanity for thousands of years. In a way, the Phoenicians never left our human imagination. Some hated them, some admired them, but they rarely left anyone familiar with them without curiosity. My hope is that this book has served to kindle yours.

1 The Phoenician Homeland: History and Archaeology

1 Pomponius Mela, 'De situ orbis', 1.65, in Frank E. Romer, *Pomponius Mela's 'Description of the World'* (Ann Arbor, MI, 1998), p. 53.

2 Mark Woolmer, 'Introduction', in *A Short History of the Phoenicians* (I. B. Tauris Short Histories, Kindle Edition, 2017).

3 Ibid.

4 'Climate', www.britannica.com, accessed 31 July 2019.

5 Josette Elayi, *The History of Phoenicia* (Atlanta, GA, 2018), p. 27.

6 Ibid.

7 Gassia Artin, 'The Northern Levant during the Chalcolithic Period: The Lebanese–Syrian Coast', in *The Oxford Handbook of the Archaeology of the Levant, c. 8000–332 BCE*, ed. Ann E. Killebrew and Margreet Steiner (Oxford, 2013), p. 213.

8 Ibid., p. 215.

9 Ibid., p. 217.

10 Hermann Genz, 'The Northern Levant (Lebanon) during the Early Bronze Age', in *Oxford Handbook of the Archaeology of the Levant*, ed. Killebrew and Steiner, p. 292.

11 Ibid., p. 296.

12 Maurice Dunand, *Fouilles de Byblos*, vol. V: *l'architecture, les tombes, le matériel domestique des origines néolithiques à l'avènement urbain* (Paris, 1973), pp. 328–9.

13 Genz, 'The Northern Levant (Lebanon) during the Early Bronze Age', p. 300.

14 Ibid., p. 302.

15 Ibid., p. 303.

16 Elayi, *History of Phoenicia*, p. 48.

17 Genz, 'The Northern Levant (Lebanon) during the Early Bronze Age', p. 304.

18 Hanan Charaf, 'The Northern Levant (Lebanon) during the Middle Bronze Age', in *Oxford Handbook of the Archaeology of the Levant*, ed. Killebrew and Steiner, p. 434.

19 All dates for Egyptian history are from 'List of Rulers of Ancient Egypt and Nubia', in *Heilbrunn Timeline of Art History* (New York, 2000), www.metmuseum.org, accessed 10 December 2020.

20 Hermann Genz and Hélène Sader, 'Bronze Age Funerary Practices in Lebanon', *Archaeology and History in Lebanon*, 26–27 (Autumn 2007–Spring 2009), pp. 258–83.

21 Jean-Paul Thalmann, *Tell Arqa-1: les niveaux de l'âge du Bronze* (Beirut, 2006), p. 67.

22 Claude Doumet-Serhal, 'Sidon during the Bronze Age: Burials, Rituals and Feasting Grounds at the College Site', *Near Eastern Archaeology*, LXXII/2–3 (2010), pp. 114–29.

23 Charaf, 'The Northern Levant (Lebanon) during the Middle Bronze Age', pp. 443–4.

24 Ibid., p. 525.

25 Thalmann, *Tell Arqa-1*, p. 190.

26 William P. Anderson, 'The Kilns and Workshops of Sarepta (Sarafand, Lebanon): Remnants of a Phoenician Ceramic Industry', *Berytus*, XXXV (1988), pp. 41–66; Issam A. Khalifeh, *Sarepta II: The Late Bronze and Iron Age Periods of Area II, X* (Beirut, 1988).

27 Ellen Fowles Morris, *The Architecture of Imperialism: Military Bases and the Evolution of Foreign Policy in Egypt's New Kingdom* (Leiden, 2005), p. 120.

28 Roger Saidah, 'Beirut in the Bronze Age: The Khariji Tombs', *Berytus*, XLI (1993), pp. 137–210.

29 Elayi, *History of Phoenicia*, pp. 89–90.

30 Heinz and Kulemann-Ossen, 'The Northern Levant (Lebanon) during the Late Bronze Age', p. 535.

31 Susan Sherratt, '"Sea Peoples" and the Economic Structure of the Late Second Millennium in the Eastern Mediterranean', in *Mediterranean Peoples in Transition: Thirteenth to Early Tenth Centuries BCE*, ed. Seymour Gitin, Amihai Mazar and Ephraim Stern (Jerusalem, 1998), p. 307.

32 See an overview in Robert A. Mullins, 'The Emergence of Israel in Retrospect', in *Israel's Exodus in Transdisciplinary Perspective*, ed. Thomas E. Levy, Thomas Schneider and William H. C. Propp (New York, 2015), pp. 517–26.

33 Ann E. Killebrew, 'Canaanite Roots, Proto-Phoenician and the Early Phoenician Period: *c.* 1300–1000 BCE', in *The Oxford Handbook of the Phoenician and Punic Mediterranean*, ed. Carolina López-Ruiz and Brian R. Doak (Oxford, 2019), p. 42.

34 James Bennett Pritchard, *The Ancient Near East: An Anthology of Texts and Pictures*, vol. I (Princeton, NJ, 1973), pp. 16–24.

35 Killebrew, 'Canaanite Roots', pp. 48–52.

36 For more on the concept of 'kingship' in Phoenicia, see Elayi, *History of Phoenicia*, pp. 97–8.

37 For the concept of 'divine kingship' and its various manifestations, see Margaret Cool Root, *The King and Kingship in Achaemenid Art: Essays*

on the Creation of an Iconography of Empire (Leiden, 1979); Nicole Maria Brisch, ed., *Religion and Power: Divine Kingship in the Ancient World and Beyond* (Chicago, IL, 2008).

38 Carol Bell, 'The Influence of Economic Factors on Settlement Continuity across the LBA/Iron Age Transition on the Northern Levantine Littoral', PhD thesis, University of London (2005).

39 Killebrew, 'Canaanite Roots', p. 40.

40 Guy Bunnens, 'Phoenicia in the Later Iron Age: Tenth Century BCE to the Assyrian and Babylonian Periods', in *Oxford Handbook of the Phoenician and Punic Mediterranean*, ed. López-Ruiz and Doak, p. 58.

41 H. Jacob Katzenstein, *The History of Tyre, from the Beginning of the Second Millennium BCE until the Fall of the Neo-Babylonian Empire in 538 BCE* (Jerusalem, 1973), pp. 130–35; Bunnens, 'Phoenicia in the Later Iron Age', p. 58.

42 For an overview of Assyrian sources on Phoenicia, see Frederick Mario Fales, 'Phoenicia in the Neo-Assyrian Period: An Updated Overview', *State Archives of Assyria Bulletin*, XXIII (2017), pp. 181–295.

43 James Bennett Pritchard, *Ancient Near Eastern Texts Relating to the Old Testament* (Princeton, NJ, 1969), p. 275.

44 Elayi, *History of Phoenicia*, p. 106.

45 Pritchard, *Ancient Near Eastern Texts*, p. 276.

46 Bunnens, 'Phoenicia in the Later Iron Age', p. 66.

47 Pritchard, *Ancient Near Eastern Texts*, p. 287.

48 Ibid.

49 Ibid., p. 290.

50 Elayi, *History of Phoenicia*, p. 170.

51 Bunnens, 'Phoenicia in the Later Iron Age', p. 68.

52 Elayi, *History of Phoenicia*, p. 176.

53 Pritchard, *Ancient Near Eastern Texts*, pp. 295–6.

54 Flavius Josephus, *The Antiquities of the Jews*, X.11.222–223, in *The Works of Josephus*, updated edn, trans. William Whiston (Peabody, MA, 1987), p. 281.

55 Bunnens, 'Phoenicia in the Later Iron Age', p. 69.

56 María Eugenia Aubet, 'Phoenicia during the Iron Age II Period', in *Oxford Handbook of the Archaeology of the Levant*, ed. Killebrew and Steiner, p. 706.

57 Susan Frankenstein, 'The Phoenicians in the Far West: A Function of Neo-Assyrian Imperialism', in *Power and Propaganda: A Symposium on Ancient Empires*, ed. Mogens T. Larsen (Copenhagen, 1979), pp. 263–94; Joseph W. Shaw, 'Phoenicians in Southern Crete', *American Journal of Archaeology*, XCIII/2 (1989), pp. 165–83; Amélie Kuhrt, *The Ancient Near East, c. 3000–330 BC* (London and New York, 1995), pp. 403–10; J. Nicolas Coldstream, *Geometric Greece, 900–700 BC* (London and New York, 2004), pp. 240–41; Alexander Fantalkin, 'Identity in the Making: Greeks in the Eastern Mediterranean During the Iron Age', in *Naukratis: Greek Diversity in Egypt: Studies on East Greek Pottery and Exchange in*

the Eastern Mediterranean, ed. Alexandra Villing and Udo Schlotzhauer (London, 2006), pp. 199–235.

58 Richard N. Fletcher, 'Opening the Mediterranean: Assyria, the Levant and the Transformation of Early Iron Age Trade', *Antiquity*, LXXXVI/331 (2012), pp. 211–20.

59 Hélène Sader, 'The Northern Levant during the Iron Age I Period', in *Oxford Handbook of the Archaeology of the Levant*, ed. Killebrew and Steiner, p. 610.

60 Aubet, 'Phoenicia during the Iron Age II Period', pp. 707–8.

61 William P. Anderson, *Sarepta I: The Late Bronze and Iron Age Strata of Area II, Y* (Beirut, 1988), p. 387.

62 Patricia M. Bikai, *The Pottery of Tyre* (Warminster, Wilts, 1978).

63 Aubet, 'Phoenicia during the Iron Age II Period', p. 712.

64 María Eugenia Aubet, 'The Phoenician Cemetery of Tyre', *Near Eastern Archaeology*, LXXII/2–3 (2010), p. 144.

65 S. Vibert Chapman, 'A Catalogue of Iron Age Pottery from the Cemeteries of Khirbet Silm, Joya, Qrayé and Qasmieh of South Lebanon', *Berytus*, XXI (1972), p. 179.

66 Aubet, 'The Phoenician Cemetery of Tyre', p. 145.

67 Ibid., p. 146.

68 Ibid., p. 148.

69 I discuss Achaemenid Phoenicia in detail in Vadim S. Jigoulov, *The Social History of Achaemenid Phoenicia: Being a Phoenician, Negotiating Empires* (London and Oakville, CT, 2010). The following has been adapted with a general informed readership in mind. The Achaemenid period has enjoyed an acute interest in recent years, and a good start is the seminal work by Pierre Briant: Pierre Briant, *From Cyrus to Alexander: A History of the Persian Empire*, trans. Peter T. Daniels (Winona Lake, IN, 2002). Briant also maintains an ongoing *Persika* series, which can be found online at www.college-de-france.fr/site/pierre-briant/collection_persika.htm.

70 Diodorus Siculus, *Library of History*, XVI.41.

71 For example see Root, *The King and Kingship in Achaemenid Art*; Margaret Cool Root, 'Circles of Artistic Programming: Strategies for Studying Creative Process at Persepolis', in *Investigating Artistic Environments in the Ancient Near East*, ed. Ann C. Gunter (Washington, DC, 1990), pp. 115–39; Margaret Cool Root, 'Imperial Ideology in Achaemenid Persian Art: Transforming the Mesopotamian Legacy', *Bulletin of the Canadian Society for Mesopotamian Studies*, 35 (2000), pp. 19–27; Mark B. Garrison and Margaret Cool Root, *Seals on the Persepolis Fortification Tablets*, vol. I: *Images of the Heroic Encounter* (Chicago, IL, 2001).

72 For more on Tripolis, see Elayi, *History of Phoenicia*, pp. 268–70.

73 Jigoulov, *The Social History of Achaemenid Phoenicia*, p. 111.

74 Hélène Sader, 'The Archaeology of Phoenician Cities', in *Oxford Handbook of the Phoenician and Punic Mediterranean*, ed. López-Ruiz and Doak, p. 125.

75 Ibid., pp. 125–6.

76 William A. Ward, 'Phoenicia', in *The Oxford Encyclopedia of Archaeology in the Near East*, vol. IV, ed. Eric M. Meyers (Oxford, 1997), p. 316; Sader, 'The Archaeology of Phoenician Cities', p. 134.

77 Robert Fleischer and Wolf Schiele, *Der Klagefrauensarkophag aus Sidon* (Tübingen, 1983).

78 Diana Edelman, 'Tyrian Trade in Yehud under Artaxerxes I: Real or Fictional? Independent or Crown Endorsed?', in *Judah and the Judeans in the Persian Period*, ed. Oded Lipschits and Manfred Oeming (Winona Lake, IN, 2006), pp. 207–46.

79 Jigoulov, *The Social History of Achaemenid Phoenicia*, p. 127.

80 Sader, 'The Archaeology of Phoenician Cities', p. 125. The following two works are essential for the history of Hellenistic Phoenicia: Maurice Sartre, *D'Alexandre à Zénobie, histoire du Levant antique: IVe siècle avant J.-C.–IIIe siècle après J.-C*, 2nd edn (Paris, 2003); Corinne Bonnet, *Les Enfants de Cadmos: le paysage religieux de la Phénicie hellénistique* (Paris, 2015).

81 For a critique of 'Hellenization', see Irad Malkin, *A Small Greek World: Networks in the Ancient Mediterranean* (Oxford, 2011); Corinne Bonnet, 'The Hellenistic Period and Hellenization in Phoenicia', in *Oxford Handbook of the Phoenician and Punic Mediterranean*, ed. López-Ruiz and Doak, pp. 99–101.

82 Bonnet, 'The Hellenistic Period', p. 101.

83 Arrian, *The Anabasis of Alexander*, II.20.1–3.

84 Quintus Curtius Rufus, *History of Alexander the Great of Macedonia*, IV.4.10–21.

85 Bonnet, 'The Hellenistic Period', pp. 103–4.

86 Corinne Bonnet, 'The Religious Life in Hellenistic Phoenicia: "Middle Ground" and New Agencies', in *The Individual in the Religions of the Ancient Mediterranean*, ed. Jörg Rüpke (Oxford, 2013), p. 41.

87 Corinne Bonnet refers to this process as 'hybridity': Bonnet, 'The Hellenistic Period', p. 107.

88 Ibid., p. 104.

89 Ibid.

90 Bonnet, 'The Religious Life in Hellenistic Phoenicia', p. 42.

91 Bonnet, 'The Hellenistic Period', p. 107.

92 For more on Phoenicia under the Roman rule, see Julien Aliquot, 'Phoenicia in the Roman Empire', in *Oxford Handbook of the Phoenician and Punic Mediterranean*, ed. López-Ruiz and Doak, pp. 111–24.

93 Jean-Paul Rey-Coquais, *Inscriptions grecques et latines de la Syrie VII: Arados et régions voisines* (Paris, 1970), pp. 25–7.

2 LOST IN TRANSLATION: PORTRAYALS OF PHOENICIANS IN GRAECO-ROMAN SOURCES

1 Homer, *Iliad*, 6:289–95; 23:740–45.

2 Homer, *Odyssey*, 14:287–97; 15:415–16. All translations are from Homer, *The Odyssey*, trans. Richmond A. Lattimore (New York, 1967).

3 Josephine Crawley Quinn, 'Phoenicians and Carthaginians in Greco-Roman Literature', in *The Oxford Handbook of the Phoenician and Punic Mediterranean*, ed. Carolina López-Ruiz and Brian R. Doak (Oxford, 2019), p. 672. See also Erich S. Gruen, *Rethinking the Other in Antiquity* (Princeton, NJ, 2011), p. 116.

4 Federico Mazza, 'The Phoenicians as Seen by the Ancient World', in *The Phoenicians*, ed. Sabatino Moscati (New York, 1999), p. 633.

5 Herodotus, *Histories*, 3.107, 111.

6 Ibid., 4.42.

7 Ibid., 6.14.

8 Gruen, *Rethinking the Other in Antiquity*, p. 118.

9 Herodotus, *Histories*, 3.19.

10 For example, Herodotus, *Histories*, 2.49, 4.147, 5.57–8.

11 Euripides, *Phoenician Women*, lines 193–290.

12 Quinn, 'Phoenicians and Carthaginians', p. 673.

13 Herodotus, *Histories*, 7.44 and 7.96.

14 Ibid., 8.67.

15 Vadim S. Jigoulov, *The Social History of Achaemenid Phoenicia: Being a Phoenician, Negotiating Empires* (London and Oakville, CT, 2010), p. 20.

16 Thucydides, *History of the Peloponnesian War*, 1.7–8; 6.2.

17 Jigoulov, *The Social History of Achaemenid Phoenicia*, p. 35.

18 Diodorus Siculus, *Library of History*, XVII.44.1–3.

19 Ibid.

20 Quinn, 'Phoenicians and Carthaginians', p. 676.

21 Jonathan Prag explains: '"Punic" is the modern term derived from the Latin *poenus*, usually, but not consistently, applied to all the originally Phoenician peoples in the western Mediterranean; "Phoenician", from the Greek *phoinix*, is used to refer to the eastern Phoenicians and frequently also to the original Phoenician diaspora in the West prior to approximately the sixth century BC (the century in which Carthage first rose to power in the West); "Carthaginian" properly only refers to those from the city-state of Carthage itself – Carthaginians are Punic, but not all those who are Punic (or western Phoenician) are Carthaginian. For clarity, in modern usage "eastern" and "western Phoenician" are increasingly the preferred terms, with "Punic" best avoided except in the realm of linguistics. Note that Greek lacks an equivalent to *poenus*, using *phoinix* universally, while, vice versa, early Latin seems to have lacked the distinct term *phoenix*, using *poenus* universally.' Jonathan Prag, 'Tyrannizing Sicily: The Despots Who Cried "Carthage!"', in *Private and Public Lies: The Discourse of Despotism and Deceit in the Graeco-Roman World*, ed. Andrew J. Turner, Kim On Chong-Gossard and Frederik Juliaan Vervaet (Leiden, 2010), p. 51, n. 1.

22 Diodorus Siculus, *Library of History*, XIII.57.1–3.

23 Ibid., 20.14.1–2, 5.

24 Quinn, 'Phoenicians and Carthaginians', p. 675.

25 Mazza, 'The Phoenicians as Seen by the Ancient World', p. 643.

26 Plato, *Republic*, 3.414B–C, quoted from Plato, *The Republic*, trans. Richard W. Sterling and William C. Scott (New York and London, 1996).

27 For example, see Gruen, *Rethinking the Other in Antiquity*, p. 121.

28 Quinn, 'Phoenicians and Carthaginians', pp. 674–5.

29 Ibid.

30 Ibid., p. 675.

31 Strabo, *Geography*, XVI.2.24.

32 Gruen, *Rethinking the Other in Antiquity*, p. 119.

33 Ibid., p. 120. Gruen cites Aristotle's *Politics*, 1272.b, 1273.b.

34 Gruen, *Rethinking the Other in Antiquity*, p. 120.

35 Ibid., p. 123. Gruen gives an extensive overview of 'Punica fides' ibid., pp. 122–40.

36 Quinn, 'Phoenicians and Carthaginians', p. 677. Quinn quotes from Diodorus Siculus, *Library of History*, XXX.7.

37 Ibid. Quinn quotes from Plautus, *Poenulus*, 112–13.

38 Marcus Tullius Cicero, *For Aemilius Scaurus*, 42, in *The Orations of Marcus Tullius Cicero: Orations for Quintius, Sextus Roscius, Quintus Roscius, Against Quintus Cæcilius, and Against Verres*, trans. Charles Duke Yonge (London, 1856).

39 Quinn, 'Phoenicians and Carthaginians', p. 678.

3 AT THE SERVICE OF THE KINGS: PHOENICIANS IN THE BIBLE

1 For example David M. Carr, 'Criteria and Periodization in Dating Biblical Texts to Parts of the Persian Period', in *On Dating Biblical Texts to the Persian Period*, ed. Richard J. Bautch and Mark Lackowski (Heidelberg, 2019), pp. 11–18.

2 Vadim S. Jigoulov, *The Social History of Achaemenid Phoenicia: Being a Phoenician, Negotiating Empires* (London and Oakville, CT, 2010), p. 145.

3 Translation is from Lancelot C. Brenton, *The Septuagint with Apocrypha: Greek and English* (Peabody, MA, 1986), p. 459, emphasis added.

4 Translation ibid., pp. 577–8, emphasis added.

5 Brian R. Doak, 'Phoenicians in the Hebrew Bible', in *The Oxford Handbook of the Phoenician and Punic Mediterranean*, ed. Carolina López-Ruiz and Brian R. Doak (Oxford, 2019), p. 659.

6 Carolina López-Ruiz, 'Tarshish and Tartessos Revisited: Textual Problems and Historical Implications', in *Colonial Encounters in Ancient Iberia: Phoenician, Greek, and Indigenous Relations*, ed. Michael Dietler and Carolina López-Ruiz (Chicago, IL, 2009), pp. 255–80.

7 For more on Jezebel, see Doak, 'Phoenicians in the Hebrew Bible', pp. 663–4.

8 'KAI' stands for 'Kanaanäische und Aramäische Inschriften' (in English, 'Canaanite and Aramaic Inscriptions') published in three volumes by Herbert Donner and Wolfgang Röllig in the 1960s. KAI numbers are the standard way to refer to non-biblical Canaanite and Aramaic inscriptions from the Ancient Near East.

9 Gunnar Lehmann, 'Phoenicians in Western Galilee: First Results of an Archaeological Survey in the Hinterland of Akko', in *Studies in the Archaeology of the Iron Age in Israel and Jordan*, ed. Amihai Mazar and Ginny Mathias (Sheffield, 2001), pp. 65–112; Jigoulov, *The Social History of Achaemenid Phoenicia*, p. 153.

10 Ephraim Stern, *The Archaeology of the Land of the Bible: The Assyrian, Babylonian, and Persian Periods (732–332 BCE)* (New York, 2001), pp. 373–85.

11 David Ussishkin, 'Lachish', in *The New Encyclopedia of Archaeological Excavations in the Holy Land*, vol. III, ed. Ephraim Stern (New York, 1993), pp. 897–911; Edward Lipiński, *Itineraria Phoenicia*, Studia Phoenicia XVIII; Orientalia Lovaniensia Analecta 127 (Leuven, 2004), p. 508.

12 Herodotus, *Histories*, 2:112.

13 Doak, 'Phoenicians in the Hebrew Bible', p. 662. Dius's name is also spelled as 'Dios'. The spelling 'Dius' is from Flavius Josephus, *The Works of Josephus*, updated edn, trans. William Whiston (Peabody, MA, 1987).

14 Josephus, *Against Apion*, 1.17–20; Josephus, *The Antiquities of the Jews*, VIII.5.146–8.

15 John M. G. Barclay, *Flavius Josephus: Translation and Commentary*, vol. X: *Against Apion*, ed. Steven Mason (Leiden and Boston, 2007), p. 67.

16 Doak, 'Phoenicians in the Hebrew Bible', pp. 665–6. Doak echoes arguments made by Shalom M. Paul, *Amos: A Commentary on the Book of Amos*, ed. Frank Moore Cross (Minneapolis, MN, 1991), pp. 59–63.

17 Stern, *Archaeology of the Land of the Bible*, p. 407.

18 Glenn E. Markoe, *Phoenicians* (London, 2000), pp. 170–89; María Eugenia Aubet, *The Phoenicians and the West: Politics, Colonies and Trade*, trans. Mary Turton, 2nd edn (Cambridge, 2001), pp. 212–304.

19 Daniel I. Block, *The Book of Ezekiel: Chapters 25–48*, The New International Commentary on the Old Testament (Grand Rapids, MI, 1998), pp. 121–22; Martin Alonso Corral, *Ezekiel's Oracles against Tyre: Historical Reality and Motivations*, Biblica et Orientalia 46 (Rome, 2002), pp. 57, 170.

20 Doak, 'Phoenicians in the Hebrew Bible', p. 657.

4 Rare Voices: Phoenician Writings

1 Barbara W. Tuchman, 'The Book', *Bulletin of the American Academy of Arts and Sciences*, XXXIV/2 (1980), pp. 16–32.

2 Daniel Stone, 'Discovery May Help Decipher Ancient Inca String Code', https://news.nationalgeographic.com, 19 April 2017.

3 Carolina López-Ruiz, 'Phoenician Literature', in *The Oxford Handbook of the Phoenician and Punic Mediterranean*, ed. Carolina López-Ruiz and Brian R. Doak (Oxford, 2019), p. 258.

4 Ibid., pp. 259–67.

5 Herodotus, *Histories*, 5.58. Translation from Andrea L. Purvis and Robert B. Strassler, *The Landmark Herodotus: The Histories* (New York, 2009), p. 514.

6 Benjamin Sass, *The Genesis of the Alphabet and Its Development in the Second Millennium BC* (Wiesbaden, 1988), pp. 151–6.

7 Maria Giulia Amadasi Guzzo, 'The Language', in *Oxford Handbook of the Phoenician and Punic Mediterranean*, ed. López-Ruiz and Doak, p. 201.

8 For an extended overview of the emergence of the writing system in the Phoenician city-states, see Holger Gzella, 'Phoenician', in *Languages from the World of the Bible*, ed. Holger Gzella (Berlin, 2011), pp. 55–75. For the exhaustive overview of the Phoenician and Punic languages, see Jo Ann Hackett, 'Phoenician and Punic', in *The Ancient Languages of Syria-Palestine and Arabia*, ed. Roger D. Woodard (Cambridge, 2008), pp. 82–102.

9 Amadasi Guzzo, 'The Language', p. 203.

10 Benjamin Sass, 'The Pseudo-Hieroglyphic Inscriptions from Byblos, their Elusive Dating, and their Affinities with the Early Phoenician Inscriptions', in *Cultures et sociétés syro-mésopotamiennes: mélanges offerts à Olivier Rouault*, ed. Philippe Abrahami and Laura Battini (Oxford, 2019), pp. 157–80.

11 Amadasi Guzzo, 'The Language', p. 201.

12 For the earliest date (*c.* 1000 BCE), see Joseph Naveh, 'Some Semitic Epigraphical Considerations on the Antiquity of the Greek Alphabet', *American Journal of Archaeology*, LXXVII/1 (1973), pp. 1–8. For the later date, see Benjamin Sass, *The Alphabet at the Turn of the Millennium: The West Semitic Alphabet, c. 1150–850 BCE* (Tel Aviv, 2005), pp. 133–46.

13 For more on the adoption of the alphabet by the Greeks, see Madadh Richey, 'The Alphabet and its Legacy', in *Oxford Handbook of the Phoenician and Punic Mediterranean*, ed. López-Ruiz and Doak, pp. 245–50.

14 Paolo Xella and José Á. Zamora, 'Phoenician Digital Epigraphy: CIP Project, the State of the Art', in *Crossing Experiences in Digital Epigraphy: From Practice to Discipline*, ed. Irene Rossi and Annamaria De Santis (Warsaw, 2018), pp. 93–101; Madadh Richey, 'Inscriptions', in *Oxford Handbook of the Phoenician and Punic Mediterranean*, ed. López-Ruiz and Doak, p. 224.

15 Richey, 'Inscriptions', p. 226.

16 Throughout this overview, one may notice variant spellings of personal and geographic names. Quite often, the English spelling will depend on one's individual preference. I will try to use the most widely accepted spellings.

17 Glenn E. Markoe, *Phoenicians* (London, 2000), pp. 137–8. Also see Helen M. Dixon, 'Phoenician Mortuary Practice in the Iron Age I–III (*c.* 1200–*c.* 300 BCE) Levantine "Homeland"', PhD dissertation, University of Michigan (2013), p. 40.

18 David Silverman, 'The Curse of the Curse of the Pharaohs', *Expedition*, XXIX/2 (1987), p. 56.

19 Herodotus, *Histories*, 1.187, in John Dillery, 'Darius and the Tomb of Nitocris (Hdt. 1.187)', *Classical Philology Classical Philology*, LXXXVII/1 (1992), p. 30.

20 E. Theodore Mullen Jr, 'Baalat', in *Dictionary of Deities and Demons in the Bible*, ed. Karel van der Toorn, Bob Becking and Peter W. van der Horst (Grand Rapids, MI, 1999), p. 139.

21 Ibid.

22 Translation adapted from George Albert Cooke, *A Text-book of North-Semitic Inscriptions: Moabite, Hebrew, Phoenician, Aramaic, Nabataean, Palmyrene, Jewish* (Oxford, 1903), pp. 18–19.

23 John C. L. Gibson, *Textbook of Syrian Semitic Inscriptions*, vol. III: *Phoenician Inscriptions, Including Inscriptions in the Mixed Dialect of Arslan Tash* (Oxford, 1982), p. 100.

24 Cooke, *A Text-book of North-Semitic Inscriptions*, pp. 26–7.

25 Ibid., pp. 31–2.

26 Translation adapted from Cooke, *A Text-book of North-Semitic Inscriptions*, pp. 31–2.

27 Diodorus Siculus, *Library of History*, XVI.41.

28 Alan Ralph Millard, 'The Uses of the Early Alphabets: Phoenician', in *Phoinikeia grammata: lire et écrire en Méditerranée*, ed. Claude Baurain (Namur, 1991), p. 105.

29 Josette Elayi and Jean Sapin, *Beyond the River: New Perspectives on Transeuphratene*, trans. J. Edward Crowley (Sheffield, 1998), pp. 93–4.

5 MONEY MATTERS: PHOENICIAN COINAGE

1 Herodotus, *Histories*, 1.94. Translation from *Herodotus: The Histories*, trans. Aubrey de Selincourt (New York, 1996), p. 40.

2 David Schaps, *The Invention of Coinage and the Monetization of Ancient Greece* (Ann Arbor, MI, 2010), pp. 102, 105.

3 John W. Betlyon, 'Coinage', in *The Anchor Bible Dictionary*, ed. David Noel Freedman (New York, 1992), pp. 1076–89.

4 John H. Kroll and Nancy M. Waggoner, 'Dating the Earliest Coins of Athens, Corinth and Aegina', *American Journal of Archaeology*, LXXXVIII/3 (1984), pp. 325–40.

5 Robert Manuel Cook, 'Speculations on the Origins of Coinage', *Historia: Zeitschrift für Alte Geschichte*, VII/3 (1958), pp. 257–62; Colin M. Kraay, 'Hoards, Small Change and the Origin of Coinage', *Journal of Hellenic Studies*, LXXXIV (1964), pp. 76–91.

6 Schaps, *Invention of Coinage*, pp. 108–10.

7 Kraay, 'Hoards, Small Change and the Origin of Coinage', pp. 80–82.

8 William E. Metcalf, *The Oxford Handbook of Greek and Roman Coinage* (Oxford, 2016), p. 64.

9 Stephen Album, Michael Bates and Willem Floor, 'Coins and Coinage', in *Encyclopaedia Iranica*, VI/1, ed. Ehsan Yarshater (Costa Mesa, CA, 1993), pp. 36–40.

10 Ibid.

11 Josette Elayi, *The History of Phoenicia* (Atlanta, GA, 2018), p. 241.

12 María Eugenia Aubet, *The Phoenicians and the West: Politics, Colonies and Trade*, trans. Mary Turton, 2nd edn (Cambridge, 2001), pp. 141–2.

13 Herman T. Wallinga, 'The Ancient Persian Navy and its Predecessors', in *Achaemenid History I: Sources, Structures and Synthesis*, ed. Heleen Sancisi-Weerdenburg (Leiden, 1987), pp. 47–77. For a recent critique, see Philippe Guillaume, 'Phoenician Coins for Persian Wars: Mercenaries, Anonymity and the First Phoenician Coinage', in *Phéniciens d'Orient et d'Occident: mélanges Josette Elayi*, ed. André Lemaire (Paris, 2014), pp. 226–9.

14 Elayi, *History of Phoenicia*, pp. 228, 234–6.

15 Betlyon, 'Coins', p. 386.

16 Josette Elayi and Alain G. Elayi, *A Monetary and Political History of the Phoenician City of Byblos* (Winona Lake, IN, 2014), p. 3; Elayi, *History of Phoenicia*, pp. 228, 266.

17 Elayi, *History of Phoenicia*, p. 241.

18 John W. Betlyon, *The Coinage and Mints of Phoenicia: The Pre-Alexandrine Period* (Atlanta, GA, 1982), p. 113; Betlyon, 'Coins', p. 394.

19 Betlyon, *Coinage and Mints of Phoenicia*, p. 112.

20 Betlyon, 'Coins', p. 395.

21 J. Elayi and A. Elayi, *Monetary and Political History*, pp. 94–5.

22 Betlyon, *Coinage and Mints of Phoenicia*, p. 118.

23 Margaret Cool Root, 'Animals in the Art of Ancient Iran', in *A History of the Animal World in the Ancient Near East*, ed. Billie Jean Collins (Leiden, 2002), pp. 201–3.

24 Elayi, *History of Phoenicia*, p. 96.

25 Betlyon, 'Coins', p. 391.

26 Elayi, *History of Phoenicia*, p. 96.

27 Paulo Naster et al., 'Numismatique', in *Dictionnaire de la civilisation phénicienne et punique*, ed. Edward Lipiński (Turnhout, 1992), p. 320.

28 Margaret Cool Root, 'Circles of Artistic Programming: Strategies for Studying Creative Process at Persepolis', in *Investigating Artistic Environments in the Ancient Near East*, ed. Ann C. Gunter (Washington, DC, 1990), p. 115.

29 Ernest Babelon, *Traité des monnaies grecques et romaines* (Paris, 1910), vol. II, part 2, no. 889.

30 Mark B. Garrison, 'Achaemenid Iconography as Evidenced by Glyptic Art: Subject Matter, Social Function, Audience and Diffusion', in *Images as Media: Sources for the Cultural History of the Near East and the Eastern Mediterranean, 1st Millennium BCE*, ed. Christoph Uehlinger (Fribourg, 2000), pp. 115–63.

31 Xenophon, *Cyropaedia*, VIII.3.13–14, in *Xenophon in Seven Volumes*, trans. Walter Miller (Loeb Classical Library, vol. V, London, 1968).

32 Mark B. Garrison and Margaret Cool Root, *Seals on the Persepolis Fortification Tablets*, vol. I: *Images of the Heroic Encounter* (Chicago, IL, 2001), pp. 53–60.

33 Translation from Roland Grubb Kent, *Old Persian: Grammar, Texts, Lexicon*, 2nd edn (New Haven, CT, 1953), p. 140.

34 Georges Le Rider, 'Le Début du monnayage achéménide: continuation ou innovation', in *Light on Top of the Black Hill: Studies Presented to Halet Çambel*, ed. Guven Arrabük, Machteld J. Mellink and Wulf Schirmer (Istanbul, 1998), pp. 665–73.

35 Elspeth Rŏgers McIntosh Dusinberre, 'King or God? Imperial Iconography and the Tiarate Head Coins of Achaemenid Anatolia across the Anatolian Plateau: Readings in the Archaeology of Ancient Turkey', in *Across the Anatolian Plateau: Readings in the Archaeology of Ancient Turkey*, ed. David C. Hopkins (Boston, MA, 2002), p. 164.

36 Elayi, *History of Phoenicia*, p. 96.

37 Betlyon, *Coinage and Mints of Phoenicia*, p. 87.

38 Ibid., pp. 78–9; Betlyon, 'Coins', p. 394.

6 Cities of Gods: Phoenician Religions

1 Elizabeth Bloch-Smith, 'Archaeological and Inscriptional Evidence for Phoenician Astarte', in *Transformation of a Goddess: Ishtar – Astarte –Aphrodite*, ed. David T. Sugimoto (Fribourg, 2014), pp. 167–94.

2 Peter Barr Reid Forbes, 'Philon of Byblos', in *The Oxford Classical Dictionary*, ed. Nicholas Geoffrey Lemprière Hammond and Howard Hayes Scullard (New York, 1991), p. 823. Forbes mentions that the Ugaritic texts 'proved conclusively that Sanchuniathon is doubtless a verity in view of the many correspondences between him and these fresh texts'.

3 Eusibius, *Preparatio Evangelica*, 1.10.22–4. Translation from Eusebius of Caesarea, *Delphi Collected Works of Eusebius (Illustrated)*, trans. Andrew Smith et al. (Delphi Ancient Classics, Kindle Edition, 2019).

4 Wolfgang Herrmann, 'Baal', in *Dictionary of Deities and Demons in the Bible*, ed. Karel van der Toorn, Bob Becking and Peter W. van der Horst (Grand Rapids, MI, 1999), pp. 134–5.

5 See such Ugaritic texts as KTU 1.47:5–11; 1.118:4–10; 1.148:2–4.

6 After ANET 533–4.

7 For example Paolo Xella, 'Pantheon e culto a Biblo', in *Biblo: una città e la sua cultura*, ed. Enrico Acquaro et al. (Rome, 1994), pp. 191–214.

8 Paolo Xella, 'Eschmun von Sidon: Der phönizische Asklepios', in *Mesopotamica – Ugaritica – Biblica: Festschrift für Kurt Bergerhof*, ed. Manfried Dietrich and Oswald Loretz (Kevelaer and Neukirchen-Vluyn, 1993), pp. 481–98; Vadim S. Jigoulov, 'Eshmun', in *The Routledge Encyclopedia of Ancient Mediterranean Religions*, ed. Eric M. Orlin (New York and London, 2016), pp. 313–14.

9 For other possibilities, see Sergio Ribichini, 'Eshmun', in *Dictionary of Deities and Demons in the Bible*, ed. van der Toorn, Becking and van der Horst, pp. 306–9.

10 Bronwen Wickkiser, 'Asklepios', in *Routledge Encyclopedia*, ed. Orlin, pp. 98–9.

11 Alan M. Cooper, 'Phoenician Religion', in *Encyclopedia of Religion*, ed. Lindsay Jones (Detroit, MI, 2005), pp. 7128–33.

12 Paolo Xella, 'Religion', in *The Oxford Handbook of the Phoenician and Punic Mediterranean*, ed. Carolina López-Ruiz and Brian R. Doak (Oxford, 2019), p. 277.

13 Herodotus, *Histories*, 2:44.

14 Josephine Crawley Quinn, *In Search of the Phoenicians* (Princeton, NJ, 2017), pp. 121–6.

15 Xella, 'Religion', p. 278.

16 Josephus, *The Antiquities of the Jews*, VIII.5.3. Of note, the most widely used translation of the *Antiquities*, by William Whiston (*The Works of Josephus*, updated edn, Peabody, MA, 1987), mistranslates the passage by stating that 'He both built the temple of Hercules and that of Astarte; *and he first set up the temple of Hercules in the month of Peritius*' (the mistranslated portion is in italics).

17 For more on Adonis, see Sergio Ribichini, *Adonis: Aspetti 'orientali' di un mito greco* (Rome, 1981); Edward Lipiński, 'Adonis', in *Encyclopedia of Religion*, ed. Jones, pp. 34–6.

18 Lucian, *The Syrian Goddess*, 6.

19 Jigoulov, 'Melqart', in *Routledge Encyclopedia*, ed. Orlin, p. 591.

20 Xella, 'Religion', p. 282.

21 For more on tophets, see Paolo Xella, '"Tophet": An Overall Interpretation', in *The Tophet in the Phoenician Mediterranean*, ed. Paolo Xella (Verona, 2013), pp. 259–81; Valentina Melchiorri, 'Child Cremation Sanctuaries ("Tophets") and Early Phoenician Colonisation: Markers of Identity?', in *Conceptualising Early Colonisation*, Proceedings of the International Congress, Rome, 21–23 June 2012, ed. Gert Jan Burgers, Lieve Donnellan and Valentino Nizzo (Brussels, 2016), p. 246; Adriano Orsingher, 'Understanding Tophets: A Short Introduction', *The Ancient Near East Today: Current News about the Ancient Past*, VI (2018), www.asor.org. For tophets in the Punic world, see Josephine Crawley Quinn, 'Tophets in the "Punic World"', *Studi Epigrafici e Linguistici*, 29–30 (2012), pp. 23–48.

22 See for example Matthew M. McCarty, 'The Tophet and Infant Sacrifice', in *Oxford Handbook of the Phoenician and Punic Mediterranean*, ed. López-Ruiz and Doak, pp. 311–28; Xella, 'Religion', pp. 287–8.

23 Jeffrey H. Schwartz et al., 'Skeletal Remains from Punic Carthage Do Not Support Systematic Sacrifice of Infants', *PLoS ONE*, V/2 (2010), e9177.

24 For an alternative take, see Paolo Xella et al., 'Phoenician Bones of Contention', *Antiquity*, LXXXVII/338 (2013), pp. 1199–207.

25 Tawny L. Holm, 'Phoenician Religion [Further Considerations]', in *Encyclopedia of Religion*, ed. Jones, p. 7134.

26 Aaron J. Brody, 'Further Evidence of the Specialized Religion of Phoenician Seafarers', in *Terra Marique: Studies in Art History and Marine Archaeology in Honor of Anna Marguerite McCann*, ed. John Pollini (Oxford, 2005), p. 181.

27 Sara A. Rich, '"She Who Treads on Water": Religious Metaphor in Seafaring Phoenicia', *Journal of Ancient West and East*, XI (2012), p. 19.

28 Aaron J. Brody, *'Each Man Cried Out to His God': The Specialized Religion of Canaanite and Phoenician Seafarers* (Atlanta, GA, 1998), p. 179. For a more recent take, see Mark A. Christian, 'Phoenician Maritime Religion: Sailors, Goddess Worship, and the Grotta Regina', *Die Welt des Orients*, XLIII/2 (2013), pp. 179–205.

29 Amy G. Remensnyder, 'Mary, Star of the Multi-confessional Mediterranean: Ships, Shrines and Sailors', in *Ein Meer und seine Heiligen*, ed. Nikolas Jaspert, Christian A. Neumann and Marco di Branco (2018), p. 303.

30 Lorenzo Nigro, 'Temples in Motya and their Levantine Prototypes: Phoenician Religious Architectural Tradition', in *Cult and Ritual on the Levantine Coast and its Impact on the Eastern Mediterranean Realm*, Proceedings of the International Symposium, Beirut, 2012, ed. Anne-Marie Maila-Afeiche (Beirut, 2015), p. 86.

31 For example, see a discussion in Ida Oggiano, 'Collecting Disiecta Membra: What Did the Cult Place of Kharayeb Look Like?', in *Cercando con zelo di conoscere la storia fenicia: atti della giornata di studio dedicata a Sergio Ribichini*, ed. Giuseppe Garbati (Roma, 2018), pp. 17–35.

32 Glenn E. Markoe, *Phoenicians* (London, 2000), p. 128.

33 For example, see 1 Kings 9:10–11.

34 For example, see an entry in the *Ancient History Encyclopedia*, an otherwise commendable source for the layperson's study of history: 'Phoenician Architecture', *Ancient History Encyclopedia*, www.ancient.eu, 23 May 2016.

35 See Joseph Azize, *The Phoenician Solar Theology: An Investigation into the Phoenician Opinion of the Sun Found in Julian's Hymn to King Helios* (Piscataway, NJ, 2005).

36 José Luis Escacena Carrasco, 'Orientation of Phoenician Temples', *Handbook of Archaeoastronomy and Ethnoastronomy* (New York, 2015), p. 1797.

37 Ibid., p. 1795.

38 Markoe, *Phoenicians*, p. 120.

39 Translation from Silius Italicus, *Punica*, vol. I, Books 1–8, trans. James D. Duff (Cambridge, MA, 1934), p. 115.

40 Herodotus, *Histories*, 1.199.

41 Markoe, *Phoenicians*, p. 120.

42 Maria Giulia Amadasi Guzzo and José Á. Zamora, 'The Phoenician *marzeaḥ*: New Evidence from Cyprus in the 4th Century BC', *Studia Eblaitica*, 4 (2018), pp. 187–214.

43 Nadav Na'aman, 'Four Notes on the Ancient Near Eastern Marzeah', in *Open-mindedness in the Bible and Beyond: A Volume of Studies in Honour of Bob Becking*, ed. Marjo Korpel and Lester L. Grabbe (London, 2015), pp. 219–21.

44 Translation from John C. L. Gibson, *Textbook of Syrian Semitic Inscriptions*, vol. III: *Phoenician Inscriptions, Including Inscriptions in the Mixed Dialect of Arslan Tash* (Oxford, 1982), p. 149.

45 Glenn E. Markoe, *Phoenician Bronze and Silver Bowls from Cyprus and the Mediterranean* (Berkeley, CA, 1985), pp. 56–9.

46 Markoe, *Phoenicians*, p. 121.

47 Ibid., p. 122.

48 For example, see Brian R. Doak, *Phoenician Aniconism in its Mediterranean and Ancient Near Eastern Contexts* (Atlanta, GA, 2015).

49 Markoe, *Phoenicians*, p. 125.

50 Mireia López-Bertrán, 'Funerary Ritual', in *Oxford Handbook of the Phoenician and Punic Mediterranean*, ed. López-Ruiz and Brian R. Doak, p. 293.

51 Quinn, *In Search of the Phoenicians*, p. 73.

52 Aubet, 'The Phoenician Cemetery of Tyre', p. 151.

53 Alan M. Cooper, 'Phoenician Religion', in *Encyclopedia of Religion*, ed. Jones, p. 7132.

54 Markoe, *Phoenicians*, p. 138.

7 MASTERS OF CRAFTSMANSHIP: PHOENICIAN ART AND TRADE

1 For an overview of the issues associated with studying Near Eastern art, see Margaret Cool Root, 'Style', in *A Companion to Ancient Near Eastern Art*, ed. Ann C. Gunter (Medford, MA, 2019), pp. 75–101.

2 James Whitley, 'Near Eastern Art in the Iron Age Mediterranean', in *Companion to Ancient Near Eastern Art*, ed. Gunter, pp. 589–90.

3 Mark Woolmer, 'Art and Material Culture', in *A Short History of the Phoenicians* (I. B. Tauris Short Histories, Kindle Edition, 2017). Woolmer draws on the ideas first expressed in Glenn E. Markoe, 'The Emergence of Phoenician Art', *Bulletin of the American Schools of Oriental Research*, 279 (1990), pp. 13–26.

4 Glenn E. Markoe, *Phoenicians* (London, 2000), p. 145.

5 Ibid., p. 160.

6 For an extensive overview of pottery and its function in the two contexts, see Francisco J. Núñez, 'Pottery and Trade', in *The Oxford Handbook of the*

Phoenician and Punic Mediterranean, ed. Carolina López-Ruiz and Brian R. Doak (Oxford, 2019), pp. 329–48.

7 Ibid., p. 332.

8 The following is adapted from ibid., pp. 332–5.

9 Ibid., pp. 335–6.

10 James Bennett Pritchard, *Recovering Sarepta, a Phoenician City: Excavations at Sarafand, Lebanon, 1969–1974, by the University Museum of the University of Pennsylvania* (Princeton, NJ, 1978), pp. 11–26; William P. Anderson, 'The Kilns and Workshops of Sarepta (Sarafand, Lebanon): Remnants of a Phoenician Ceramic Industry', *Berytus*, xxxv (1988), pp. 41–66; William P. Anderson, 'The Pottery Production Industry at Phoenician Sarepta (Sarafand, Lebanon) with Parallels to Kilns from Other East Mediterranean Sites', in *Cross-craft and Cross-cultural Interactions in Ceramics*, ed. Patrick E. McGovern and Michael D. Notis (Westerville, OH, 1989), pp. 197–216.

11 William P. Anderson, 'The Beginnings of Phoenician Pottery: Vessel Shape, Style, and Ceramic Technology in the Early Phases of the Phoenician Iron Age', *Bulletin of the American Schools of Oriental Research*, 279 (1990), p. 279.

12 Ayelet Gilboa and Ilan Sharon, 'An Archaeological Contribution to the Early Iron Age Chronological Debate: Alternative Chronologies for Phoenicia and their Effects on the Levant, Cyprus, and Greece', *Bulletin of the American Schools of Oriental Research*, 332 (2003), pp. 7–80. See also Ephraim Stern, *The Archaeology of the Land of the Bible: The Assyrian, Babylonian, and Persian Periods (732–332 BCE)* (New York, 2001), p. 101.

13 Vadim S. Jigoulov, *The Social History of Achaemenid Phoenicia: Being a Phoenician, Negotiating Empires* (London and Oakville, CT, 2010), p. 115.

14 Patricia M. Bikai, 'The Late Phoenician Pottery Complex and Chronology', *Bulletin of the American Schools of Oriental Research*, 229 (1978), pp. 47–56; Patricia M. Bikai, *The Pottery of Tyre* (Warminster, Wilts, 1978), p. 75. William Culican, 'Cesnola Bowl 4555 and Other Phoenician Bowls', *Rivista di Studi Fenici*, x (1982), pp. 13–32.

15 Josephine Crawley Quinn, *In Search of the Phoenicians* (Princeton, NJ, 2017), pp. 71–2.

16 Woolmer, 'Art and Material Culture', in *A Short History of the Phoenicians* (Kindle Edition).

17 Ibid.

18 Eric Gubel, 'Art and Iconography', in *Oxford Handbook of the Phoenician and Punic Mediterranean*, ed. López-Ruiz and Doak, p. 354.

19 Markoe, *Phoenicians*, p. 163. The original report is in Vronwy Hankey, 'Pottery-making at Beitshebab, Lebanon', *Palestine Exploration Quarterly*, C/1 (1968), pp. 27–32.

20 Pliny the Elder, *Natural History*, 36.65.

21 Woolmer, 'Art and Material Culture', in *A Short History of the Phoenicians* (Kindle Edition).

22 Josette Elayi, *The History of Phoenicia* (Atlanta, GA, 2018), p. 21.

23 Woolmer, 'Art and Material Culture', in *A Short History of the Phoenicians* (Kindle Edition).

24 Ibid.

25 Markoe, *Phoenicians*, p. 158.

26 Gubel, 'Art and Iconography', p. 359.

27 Markoe, *Phoenicians*, p. 146.

28 Ibid.; Gubel, 'Art and Iconography', p. 360.

29 Markoe, *Phoenicians*, p. 146.

30 Ibid.

31 Georgina Herrmann and Stuart Laidlaw, 'Assyrian Nimrud and the Phoenicians', *Archaeology International*, XVI (2013), pp. 84–95.

32 Markoe, *Phoenicians*, p. 147.

33 Gubel, 'Art and Iconography', p. 361.

34 Eric Gubel, 'Decoding Phoenician Art (I): Pharaoh Triumphant', *Rivista di Studi Fenici*, 40 (2012), pp. 21–38.

35 Homer, *Iliad*, 23:740–45.

36 Markoe, *Phoenicians*, p. 148.

37 The volume accompanying the exhibition contains a chapter on those bowls: Sabatino Moscati, 'Metal Bowls', in *The Phoenicians*, ed. Sabatino Moscati (New York, 1999), pp. 491–9.

38 Woolmer, 'Art and Material Culture', in *A Short History of the Phoenicians* (Kindle Edition).

39 Ibid.

40 The following is after Nicholas C. Vella, '"Phoenician" Metal Bowls: Boundary Objects in the Archaic Period', in *Proceedings of the XVIIth International Congress of Classical Archaeology*, ed. Martina Dalla Riva and Helga Di Giuseppe (Rome, 2010), pp. 24–5.

41 John Boardman, 'Copies of Pottery: By and for Whom?', in *Greek Identity in the Western Mediterranean: Papers in Honour of Brian Shefton*, ed. Kathryn Lomas (Leiden, 2004), pp. 149–62.

42 James D. Muhly, 'Comment to a Paper by Irene S. Lemos, "Craftsmen, Traders and Some Wives in Early Iron Age Greece"', in *PLOES: Sea Routes. Interconnections in the Mediterranean, 16th–6th C. BC*, Proceedings of the International Symposium Held at Rethymnon, Crete, 29 September–2 October 2002, ed. Nikolaos Chr. Stampolidēs and Vassos Karageorghis (Athens, 2003), p. 193.

43 Vella, '"Phoenician" Metal Bowls', p. 32.

44 Markoe, *Phoenicians*, p. 150.

45 Woolmer, 'Art and Material Culture', in *A Short History of the Phoenicians* (Kindle Edition).

46 Gubel, 'Art and Iconography', p. 361.

47 Markoe, *Phoenicians*, p. 154.

48 Gubel, 'Art and Iconography', p. 363. See also John Boardman, *Classical Phoenician Scarabs: A Catalogue and Study* (Oxford, 2003).

49 Markoe, *Phoenicians*, p. 159.

50 Gubel, 'Art and Iconography', p. 354.

51 Ibid., p. 355.

52 Adriano Orsingher, 'Phoenician and Punic Masks: What Are They and What Were They Good For?', *The Ancient Near East Today: Current News about the Ancient Past*, VII/4 (2019), www.asor.org.

53 Adriano Orsingher, 'Ritualized Faces: The Masks of the Phoenicians', in *The Physicality of the Other: Masks from the Ancient Near East and the Eastern Mediterranean*, ed. Angelika Berlejung and Judith E. Filitz (Tübingen, 2018), p. 264.

54 Markoe, *Phoenicians*, p. 151.

55 Hélène Sader, *Iron Age Funerary Stelae from Lebanon* (Barcelona, 2005), pp. 15–16.

56 Ibid., p. 16.

57 Ibid., pp. 15–16.

58 Woolmer, 'Art and Material Culture', in *A Short History of the Phoenicians* (Kindle Edition).

59 Eric Gubel, 'Bronze Work in the Phoenician Homeland: A Preliminary Survey', in *Phoenician Bronzes in Mediterranean*, ed. F. Javier Jiménez Ávila (Madrid, 2015), p. 241.

60 Markoe, *Phoenicians*, p. 152.

61 Ibid.

62 Ibid., p. 153.

63 Homer, *Iliad*, 6:289.

64 Salvatore Gaspa, 'Garments, Parts of Garments, and Textile Techniques in the Assyrian Terminology: The Neo-Assyrian Textile Lexicon in the 1st-Millennium BC Linguistic Context', in *Textile Terminologies from the Orient to the Mediterranean and Europe, 1000 BC to 1000 AD*, ed. Salvatore Gaspa, Cécile Michel and Marie-Louise Nosch (Lincoln, NE, 2017), pp. 47–8.

65 Lawrence Stager, 'Phoenician Shipwrecks in the Deep Sea', in *PLOES: Sea Routes*, ed. Stampolidēs and Karageorghis, pp. 222–47.

66 Woolmer, 'Art and Material Culture', in *A Short History of the Phoenicians* (Kindle Edition).

67 Julius Pollux, *Onomasticon*, 1:45–9.

68 Robert R. Stieglitz, 'The Minoan Origin of Tyrian Purple', *Biblical Archaeologist*, LVII/1 (1994), pp. 46–54; Dina Frangié-Joly, 'Perfumes, Aromatics, and Purple Dye: Phoenician Trade and Production in the Greco-Roman Period', *Journal of Eastern Mediterranean Archaeology and Heritage Studies*, IV/1 (2016), p. 54.

69 Pliny the Elder, *Natural History*, 9:60–65.

70 Strabo, *Geography*, XVI.2.23.

71 Frangié-Joly, 'Perfumes, Aromatics, and Purple Dye', p. 51.

72 Pliny, *Natural History*, 9:60–65.

73 David S. Reese, 'Shells from Sarepta (Lebanon) and East Mediterranean Purple-dye Production', *Mediterranean Archaeology and Archaeometry*, x/1 (2010), pp. 113–41; Frangié-Joly, 'Perfumes, Aromatics, and Purple Dye', p. 51.

74 David Jacoby, 'Silk Economics and Cross-cultural Artistic Interaction: Byzantium, the Muslim World, and the Christian West', *Dumbarton Oaks Papers*, 58 (2004), p. 210.

75 Eric Gubel, 'Un Dépôt votif phénicien d'œufs d'autruche', *Semitica et Classica*, VIII (2015), pp. 117–23.

76 Gubel, 'Art and Iconography', p. 363.

77 Ibid., pp. 363–4; Baruch Brandl, 'Two Engraved Tridacna Shells from Tel Miqne-Ekron', *Bulletin of the American Schools of Oriental Research*, CCCXXIII/1 (2001), pp. 49–62.

8 Travels and Trade: Phoenician Westward Expansion

1 Jeffrey P. Emanuel, 'Seafaring and Shipwreck Archaeology', in *The Oxford Handbook of the Phoenician and Punic Mediterranean*, ed. Carolina López-Ruiz and Brian R. Doak (Oxford, 2019), pp. 423–4. Emanuel also provides an overview of existing shipwrecks.

2 Jeffrey P. Emanuel, 'The Sea Peoples, Egypt, and the Aegean: Transference of Maritime Technology in the Late Bronze–Early Iron Transition (LH IIIB–C)', *Aegean Studies*, I (2014), pp. 21–56.

3 Sean McGrail, *Boats of the World: From the Stone Age to Medieval Times* (Oxford, 2004), pp. 129–34. For more on Phoenician ships, see María Eugenia Aubet, *The Phoenicians and the West: Politics, Colonies and Trade*, trans. Mary Turton, 2nd edn (Cambridge, 2001), pp. 172–8.

4 Homer, *Odyssey*, 15:415.

5 Herodotus, *The Histories*, 4:42

6 Duane W. Roller, 'Phoenician Exploration', in *The Oxford Handbook of the Phoenician and Punic Mediterranean*, ed. López-Ruiz and Doak, pp. 645–53.

7 Strabo, *Geography*, I.1.6. For more on Phoenician navigation, see Victoria Peña, Carlos G. Wagner and Alfredo Mederos, *La navegación fenicia: tecnología naval y derroteros* (Madrid, 2005).

8 Diodorus Siculus, *Library of History*, v.20.3.

9 Roller, 'Phoenician Exploration', p. 648.

10 Herodotus, *Histories*, 4.42.

11 Roller, 'Phoenician Exploration', p. 649.

12 Ronald Fritze has a thorough overview of several theories in Ronald H. Fritze, *Invented Knowledge: False History, Fake Science and Pseudo-Religions* (London, 2011), pp. 84–8.

13 Ibid., p. 86.

14 From Frank Moore Cross, 'The Phoenician Inscription from Brazil: A Nineteenth-century Forgery', *Orientalia*, XXXVII/4 (1968), pp. 437–60.

15 Fritze, *Invented Knowledge*, p. 86.

16 For example, see Thomas Crawford Johnston, *Did the Phoenicians Discover America?* (London, 1890).

17 Mark A. McMenamin, *Phoenicians, Fakes and Barry Fell* (South Hadley, MA, 2000).

18 Jim Wyss, 'Dismissed as Fakes for a Century, Enigmatic Puerto Rican Stones Could Rewrite History', www.miamiherald.com, 7 October 2019.

19 Josephine Crawley Quinn, *In Search of the Phoenicians* (Princeton, NJ, 2017), p. 206. The entirety of Chapter Nine of the book is a splendid exploration of how Phoenicianism flourished in Britain and other countries.

20 Thomas W. Thacker and Richard P. Wright, 'A New Interpretation of the Phoenician Graffito from Holt, Denbighshire', *Iraq*, XVII/1 (1955), pp. 90–91.

21 Quinn, *In Search of the Phoenicians*, p. 199.

22 Maria Iacovou, 'Cyprus during the Iron Age through the Persian Period', in *The Oxford Handbook of the Archaeology of the Levant, c. 8000–332 BCE*, ed. Ann E. Killebrew and Margreet Steiner (Oxford, 2013), p. 799; Anna Georgiadou, 'La Diffusion de la céramique chypriote d'époque géométrique en Méditerranée orientale', *Cahiers du Centre d'Etudes Chypriotes*, XLVI (2016), pp. 89–112.

23 Sabine Fourrier, 'The Iron Age City of Kition: The State of Research 85 Years after the Swedish Cyprus Expedition's Excavations', in *Ancient Cyprus Today: Museum Collections and New Research*, ed. Giorgos Bourogiannis and Christian Mühlenbock (Uppsala, 2016), p. 137.

24 Adriano Orsingher, 'A Stopover Along the Journey of Elissa: Kition between Tyre and Carthage', in *The Many Face(t)s of Cyprus*, 14th Meeting of Postgraduate Cypriot Archaeology, ed. Kim Kittig et al. (Bonn, 2019), pp. 123–35.

25 Sabine Fourrier, 'Cyprus', in *Oxford Handbook of the Phoenician and Punic Mediterranean*, ed. López-Ruiz and Doak, p. 484.

26 Josette Elayi, *The History of Phoenicia* (Atlanta, GA, 2018), p. 96.

27 Andrew T. Reyes, *Archaic Cyprus: A Study of the Textual and Archaeological Evidence* (Oxford, 1994), p. 125.

28 Vadim S. Jigoulov, *The Social History of Achaemenid Phoenicia: Being a Phoenician, Negotiating Empires* (London and Oakville, CT, 2010), p. 26.

29 Olivier Callot, 'Les Hangars du port de Kition (ve–ive s.av. J.C.)', in *Res maritimae: Cyprus and the Eastern Mediterranean from Prehistory to Late*

Antiquity, ed. Stuart Swiny, Robert L. Hohlfelder and Helena Wylde Swiny (Atlanta, GA, 1997), pp. 71–81.

30 Fourrier, 'Cyprus', p. 487.

31 Herodotus, *Histories*, 6.47.

32 J. Nicolas Coldstream, 'The Phoenicians of Ialysos', *Bulletin of the Institute of Classical Studies*, XVI (1969), pp. 1–18.

33 Diodorus Siculus, *Library of History*, v.58.2.

34 Herodotus, *Histories*, 1.1 (Argos); Homer, *Odyssey*, 15.403–84 (North Aegean).

35 Nikolaos Chr. Stampolidēs, 'The Aegean', in *Oxford Handbook of the Phoenician and Punic Mediterranean* ed. López-Ruiz and Doak, p. 494.

36 Ibid., pp. 494–5.

37 Ibid., p. 495.

38 Glenn E. Markoe, *Phoenicians* (London, 2000), p. 171.

39 Ibid.

40 Stampolidēs, 'The Aegean', p. 499.

41 Markoe, *Phoenicians*, p. 173.

42 Vassos Karageorghis, 'Phoenician Marble Anthropoid Sarcophagi and their Parian Connection', in *Paria lithos: Parian Quarries, Marble and Workshops of Sculpture* [in Greek], Proceedings of the First International Conference of the Archaeology of Paros and the Cyclades, Paros, 2–5 October 1997, ed. Demetrio Schilardi and Ḏora Katsōnopoulo (Athens, 2010), pp. 469–77.

43 Quinn, *In Search of the Phoenicians*, pp. 39–40.

44 Ibid., p. 40.

45 Markoe, *Phoenicians*, p. 172.

46 John Boardman, *The Greeks Overseas: Their Early Colonies and Trade* (London, 1999), pp. 56–7.

47 Nikolaos Chr. Stampolidēs and Antonis Kotsonas, 'Phoenicians in Crete', in *Ancient Greece: From the Mycenaean Palaces to the Age of Homer*, ed. Sigrid Deger-Jalkotzy and Irene S. Lemos (Edinburgh, 2006), pp. 337–60.

48 Stampolidēs, 'The Aegean', p. 497.

49 Thucydides, *History of the Peloponnesian War*, 6.2.

50 Markoe, *Phoenicians*, p. 176.

51 Ibid., p. 175.

52 Caterina Greco, 'La necropoli punica di Solunto', in *Actas del IV Congreso Internacional de Estudios Fenicios y Púnicos: Cádiz, 2 al 6 de octubre de 1995*, ed. Manuela Barthélemy and María Eugenia Aubet (Cádiz, 2000), pp. 1319–35.

53 Salvatore de Vincenzo, 'Sicily', in *Oxford Handbook of the Phoenician and Punic Mediterranean*, ed. López-Ruiz and Doak, p. 539.

54 Markoe, *Phoenicians*, p. 174.

55 De Vincenzo, 'Sicily', pp. 540–41.

56 Ibid., p. 542.
57 For an overview of the Punic history of Motya, see De Vincenzo, 'Sicily', pp. 543–7.
58 Jeremy Hayne, 'The Italian Peninsula', in *Oxford Handbook of the Phoenician and Punic Mediterranean*, ed. López-Ruiz and Doak (Oxford, 2019), p. 505.
59 Ian Morris, 'Mediterraneanization', *Mediterranean Historical Review*, XVIII/2 (2003), pp. 30–55.
60 Hayne, 'The Italian Peninsula', p. 506.
61 Richard N. Fletcher, *Patterns of Imports in Iron Age Italy* (Oxford, 2007), p. 104.
62 Hayne, 'The Italian Peninsula', p. 507.
63 Fletcher, *Patterns of Imports*, p. 105.
64 Ibid., p. 106.
65 Ibid.
66 Hayne, 'The Italian Peninsula', p. 508.
67 Ibid., pp. 508–15.
68 Olivia Kelley, 'Beyond Intermarriage: The Role of the Indigenous Italic Population at Pithekoussai', *Oxford Journal of Archaeology*, XXXI/1 (2012), pp. 245–60.
69 Markoe, *Phoenicians*, p. 177.
70 Ibid.
71 Emma Blake, 'Late Bronze Age Sardinia: Acephalous Cohesion', in *The Cambridge Prehistory of the Bronze and Iron Age Mediterranean*, ed. A. Bernard Knapp and Peter van Dommelen (Cambridge, 2014), pp. 96–108; Andrea Roppa, 'Sardinia', in *Oxford Handbook of the Phoenician and Punic Mediterranean*, ed. López-Ruiz and Doak (Oxford, 2019), p. 521.
72 Fletcher, for example, questions the dating based on epigraphy alone, stating, 'The Nora Stele, of which so much has been made, cannot be securely dated because it was found reused in the construction of a church some distance from Nora.' Fletcher, *Patterns of Imports in Iron Age Italy*, p. 12.
73 Markoe, *Phoenicians*, p. 177.
74 Roppa, 'Sardinia', p. 526.
75 Markoe, *Phoenicians*, p. 178.
76 Ibid., p. 180; Irad Malkin, *A Small Greek World: Networks in the Ancient Mediterranean* (Oxford, 2011), pp. 152–6.
77 Diodorus Siculus, *Library of History*, v.12.
78 Markoe, *Phoenicians*, p. 180.
79 Nicholas C. Vella and Maxine Anastasi, 'Malta and Gozo', in *Oxford Handbook of the Phoenician and Punic Mediterranean*, ed. López-Ruiz and Doak, pp. 561–5.
80 Ibid., p. 558.

81 Ibid.

82 Ibid., p. 553.

83 Ibid., pp. 553–6.

84 Benjamín Costa, 'Ibiza', in *Oxford Handbook of the Phoenician and Punic Mediterranean*, ed. López-Ruiz and Doak, p. 569.

85 Costa, 'Ibiza', p. 569.

86 Diodorus Siculus, *Library of History*, v.16.2–3.

87 Costa, 'Ibiza', pp. 570–71.

88 Maria Giulia Amadasi Guzzo and Paolo Xella, 'Eshmun-Melqart in una nuova iscrizione fenicia di Ibiza', *Studi Epigrafici e Linguistici sul Vicino Oriente Antico*, XXII (2005), pp. 47–57.

89 Costa, 'Ibiza', p. 574.

90 Manuel Álvarez Martí-Aguilar, 'The Gadir–Tyre Axis', in *Oxford Handbook of the Phoenician and Punic Mediterranean*, ed. López-Ruiz and Doak, pp. 617–26.

91 José Luis López Castro, 'The Iberian Peninsula', in *Oxford Handbook of the Phoenician and Punic Mediterranean*, ed. López-Ruiz and Doak, p. 585.

92 Ibid., pp. 587–8.

93 Aurora Higueras-Milena Castellano and Antonio M. Sáez Romero, 'The Phoenicians and the Ocean: Trade and Worship at La Caleta, Cadiz, Spain', *International Journal of Nautical Archaeology*, XLVII/1 (2018), pp. 81–102.

94 José Luis López Castro, 'Colonials, Merchants and Alabaster Vases: The Western Phoenician Aristocracy', *Antiquity*, LXXX/307 (2006), pp. 74–88.

95 Ana Delgado and Meritxell Ferrer, 'Cultural Contacts in Colonial Settings: The Construction of New Identities in Phoenician Settlements of the Western Mediterranean', *Stanford Journal of Archaeology*, V (2007), pp. 18–42; López Castro, 'The Iberian Peninsula', p. 592.

96 López Castro, 'The Iberian Peninsula', p. 596.

97 Ana Margarida Arruda, 'Phoenicians in Portugal', in *Oxford Handbook of the Phoenician and Punic Mediterranean*, ed. López-Ruiz and Doak, p. 603.

98 For the most recent update regarding archaeological research in northern Africa, see Alfredo Mederos Martín, 'North Africa: From the Atlantic to Algeria', in *Oxford Handbook of the Phoenician and Punic Mediterranean*, ed. López-Ruiz and Doak, pp. 627–8.

99 Helmut Brückner and Julius Lucas, 'Geoarchäologische studie zu Mogador, Essaouira und Umgebung', *Madrider Mitteilungen*, L (2009), pp. 102–13; Helmut Brückner and Julius Lucas, 'Landschaftswandel und Küstenveränderung im Gebiet von Mogador und Essaouira. Eine Studie die zur Paläogeographie und Geoarchäologie in Marokko', *Madrider Mitteilungen*, LI (2010), pp. 99–104.

100 Edward Lipiński, *Le Dictionnaire de la civilisation phénicienne et punique* (Turnhout, 1992), p. 296; Mederos Martín, 'North Africa', p. 629.

101 Mederos Martín, 'North Africa', p. 629. Aubet, who was using older
     reports, dates the earliest settlement to the seventh century BCE: Aubet,
     The Phoenicians and the West, p. 162.
102 José Luis López Castro et al., 'Proyecto Útica: Investigación en la ciudad
     fenicio-púnica', *Informes y Trabajos*, 11 (2014), pp. 204–20.
103 Hédi Dridi, 'Early Carthage: From Its Foundation to the Battle of Himera
     (*c.* 814–480 BCE)', in *Oxford Handbook of the Phoenician and Punic
     Mediterranean*, ed. López-Ruiz and Doak, p. 143.
104 Herodotus, *Histories*, 3.19.
105 Diodorus Siculus, *Library of History*, XIII.108.2–4.
106 Martí-Aguilar, 'The Gadir–Tyre Axis', p. 622.
107 Dridi, 'Early Carthage', p. 146.
108 Markoe, *Phoenicians*, pp. 181–2.
109 Hans Georg Niemeyer, 'The Phoenicians in the Mediterranean: A Non-
     Greek Model for Expansion and Settlement in Antiquity', in *Greek
     Colonists and Native Populations*, ed. Jean-Paul Descœudres (Oxford,
     1990), pp. 469–89.
110 Fletcher, *Patterns of Imports*, p. 129.
111 For example, see Philip A. Johnson, 'Toward a Systematic Approach to the
     Study of Phoenician Economic Activity in the Western Mediterranean',
     in *Identity and Connectivity: Proceedings of the 16th Symposium on
     Mediterranean Archaeology, Florence, Italy, 1–3 March 2012. Soma 2012*, ed.
     Luca Bombardieri et al. (Oxford, 2013), pp. 667–76; Giorgos Bourogiannis,
     'The Phoenician Presence in the Aegean during the Early Iron Age: Trade,
     Settlement and Cultural Interaction', *Rivista di Studi Fenici*, XLVI (2018),
     pp. 43–88; Tzilla Eshel et al., 'Lead Isotopes in Silver Reveal Earliest
     Phoenician Quest for Metals in the West Mediterranean', *Proceedings of
     the National Academy of Sciences*, CXVI/13 (2019), pp. 6007–12.
112 Fletcher, *Patterns of Imports*, p. 107.
113 Irene J. Winter, 'Homer's Phoenicians: History, Ethnography, or Literary
     Trope? (A Perspective on Early Orientalism)', in *The Ages of Homer: A
     Tribute to Emily Townsend Vermeule*, ed. Jane B. Carter and Sarah P.
     Morris (Austin, TX, 1995), p. 253.
114 Niemeyer, 'The Phoenicians in the Mediterranean', pp. 469–89.
115 Fletcher, *Patterns of Imports*, p. 106.
116 For the periodization of Phoenician colonizing activities, see Ida Oggiano,
     'The Mediterranean Dimension of Levantine Coast in the 1st Millennium
     BC: Ancient Sea Routes, New Explorations and "Colonial" Foundations', in
     Contexts of Early Colonization, I, ed. Lieve Donnellan, Valentin Nizzo and
     Gert-Jan Burgers (2016), pp. 89–103.
117 Fletcher, *Patterns of Imports*, p. 104.
118 María Eugenia Aubet, 'From Trading Post to Town in the Phoenician-
     Punic World', in *Social Complexity and the Development of Towns in*

Iberia: From the Copper Age to the Second Century AD, ed. Barry W. Cunliffe and Simon J. Keay (Oxford, 1995), pp. 52–5.

Epilogue

1 Herodotus, *Histories*, 1.1. Translation from Herodotus, *Herodotus: The Histories*, trans. Aubrey de Selincourt (New York, 1996), p. 3.
2 Elizabeth A. Matisoo-Smith et al., 'A European Mitochondrial Haplotype Identified in Ancient Phoenician Remains from Carthage, North Africa', *PLOS ONE*, XI/5 (2016), e0155046.
3 Ibid.
4 See 'Ancient DNA study finds Phoenician from Carthage had European Ancestry', https://phys.org, 25 May 2016.
5 M. Haber et al., 'Continuity and Admixture in the Last Five Millennia of Levantine History from Ancient Canaanite and Present-day Lebanese Genome Sequences', *American Journal of Human Genetics*, CI/1 (2017), pp. 274–82; Elizabeth A. Matisoo-Smith et al., 'Ancient Mitogenomes of Phoenicians from Sardinia and Lebanon: A Story of Settlement, Integration, and Female Mobility', *PLOS ONE*, XIII/1 (2018), e0190169; Pierre Zalloua et al., 'Ancient DNA of Phoenician Remains Indicates Discontinuity in the Settlement History of Ibiza', *Scientific Reports*, VIII/1 (2018), https://doi.org/10.1038/s41598-018-35667-y.

Anderson, William P., 'The Beginnings of Phoenician Pottery: Vessel Shape, Style, and Ceramic Technology in the Early Phases of the Phoenician Iron Age', *Bulletin of the American Schools of Oriental Research*, 279 (1990), pp. 35–54

Aubet, María Eugenia, 'From Trading Post to Town in the Phoenician-Punic World', in *Social Complexity and the Development of Towns in Iberia: From the Copper Age to the Second Century AD*, Barry W. Cunliffe and Simon J. Keay, Proceedings of the British Academy 86 (Oxford, 1995), pp. 47–65

—, 'The Phoenician Cemetery of Tyre', *Near Eastern Archaeology*, LXXIII/2–3 (2010), pp. 144–55

—, *The Phoenicians and the West: Politics, Colonies and Trade*, trans. Mary Turton, 2nd edn (Cambridge, 2001)

Azize, Joseph, *The Phoenician Solar Theology: An Investigation into the Phoenician Opinion of the Sun Found in Julian's Hymn to King Helios* (Piscataway, NJ, 2005)

Barrionuevo, Carmen Ana Pardo, and José Luis López Castro, *Economía y sociedad rural fenicia en el Mediterráneo Occidental* (Seville, 2015)

Betlyon, John W., *The Coinage and Mints of Phoenicia: The Pre-Alexandrine Period* (Atlanta, GA, 1982)

Bikai, Patricia M., *The Phoenician Pottery of Cyprus* (Nicosia, 1987)

—, *The Pottery of Tyre* (Warminster, Wilts, 1978)

Bloch-Smith, Elizabeth, 'Archaeological and Inscriptional Evidence for Phoenician Astarte', in *Transformation of a Goddess: Ishtar-Astarte-Aphrodite*, ed. David T. Sugimoto (Fribourg, 2014), pp. 167–94

Boardman, John, *Classical Phoenician Scarabs: A Catalogue and Study* (Oxford, 2003)

—, 'Copies of Pottery: By and for Whom?', in *Greek Identity in the Western Mediterranean: Papers in Honour of Brian Shefton*, ed. Kathryn Lomas (Leiden, 2004), pp. 149–62

—, *The Greeks Overseas: Their Early Colonies and Trade* (London, 1999)

Bondì, Sandro Filippo, Massimo Botto, Giuseppe Garbati and Ida Oggiano, *Fenici e cartaginesi: una civiltà mediterranea* (Rome, 2009)

Bonnet, Corinne, *Les Enfants de Cadmos: le paysage religieux de la Phénicie hellénistique* (Paris, 2015)

—, 'The Religious Life in Hellenistic Phoenicia: "Middle Ground" and New Agencies', in *The Individual in the Religions of the Ancient Mediterranean*, ed. Jörg Rüpke (Oxford, 2013), pp. 41–57

Bourogiannis, Giorgos, 'The Phoenician Presence in the Aegean During the Early Iron Age: Trade, Settlement and Cultural Interaction', *Rivista di Studi Fenici*, XLVI (2018), pp. 43–88

Briant, Pierre, *From Cyrus to Alexander: A History of the Persian Empire*, trans. Peter T. Daniels (Winona Lake, IN, 2002)

Brisch, Nicole Maria, ed., *Religion and Power: Divine Kingship in the Ancient World and Beyond* (Chicago, IL, 2008)

Brody, Aaron J., *'Each Man Cried Out to His God': The Specialized Religion of Canaanite and Phoenician Seafarers*, Harvard Semitic Monographs 58 (Atlanta, GA, 1998)

Bunnens, Guy, *L'Expansion phénicienne en Méditerranée: essai d'interprétation fondé sur une analyse des traditions littéraires* (Brussels and Rome, 1979)

Castellano, Aurora Higueras-Milena, and Antonio M. Sáez Romero, 'The Phoenicians and the Ocean: Trade and Worship at La Caleta, Cadiz, Spain', *International Journal of Nautical Archaeology*, XLVII/1 (2018), pp. 81–102

Christian, Mark A., 'Phoenician Maritime Religion: Sailors, Goddess Worship, and the Grotta Regina', *Die Welt des Orients*, XLIII/2 (2013), pp. 179–205

Costa, Benjamín, and Jordi H. Fernández, *Ibiza Fenicio-Púnica* (Palma de Mallorca, 2006)

Cross, Frank Moore, 'The Phoenician Inscription from Brazil: A Nineteenth-century Forgery', *Orientalia*, XXXVII/4 (1968), pp. 437–60

Culican, William, 'Cesnola Bowl 4555 and Other Phoenician Bowls', *Rivista di Studi Fenici*, X/1 (1982), pp. 13–32

Delgado, Ana, and Meritxell Ferrer, 'Cultural Contacts in Colonial Settings: The Construction of New Identities in Phoenician Settlements of the Western Mediterranean', *Stanford Journal of Archaeology*, V (2007), pp. 18–42

Dixon, Helen M., 'Phoenician Mortuary Practice in the Iron Age I–III (*c.* 1200–*c.* 300 BCE) Levantine "Homeland"', PhD dissertation, University of Michigan, 2013

Doak, Brian R., *Phoenician Aniconism in Its Mediterranean and Ancient Near Eastern Contexts*, Archaeology and Biblical Studies 21 (Atlanta, GA, 2015)

Dongen, Erik van, '"Phoenicia": Naming and Defining a Region in Syria-Palestine', in *Interkulturalität in der Alten Welt: Vorderasien, Hellas, Ägypten und die vielfältigen Ebenen des Kontakts*, ed. Robert Rollinger, Birgit Gufler, Martin Lang and Irene Madreiter (Wiesbaden, 2010), pp. 471–88

Doumet-Serhal, Claude, 'Sidon during the Bronze Age: Burials, Rituals and Feasting Grounds at the College Site', *Near Eastern Archaeology*, LXXIII/2–3 (2010), pp. 114–29

Dunand, Maurice, *Fouilles de Byblos* v: *l'architecture, les tombes, le matériel domestique des origines néolithiques à l'avènement urbain* (Paris, 1973)

—, and Nessib Saliby, *Le Temple d'Amrith dans la pérée d'Aradus* (Paris, 1985)

Elayi, Josette, *The History of Phoenicia* (Atlanta, GA, 2018)

—, and Alain G. Elayi, *A Monetary and Political History of the Phoenician City of Byblos* (Winona Lake, IN, 2014)

—, and Jean Sapin, *Beyond the River: New Perspectives on Transeuphratene*, trans. J. Edward Crowley, Journal for the Study of the Old Testament, Supplement Series 250 (Sheffield, 1998)

Fales, Frederick Mario, 'Phoenicia in the Neo-Assyrian Period: An Updated Overview', *State Archives of Assyria Bulletin*, XXIII (2017), pp. 181–295

Fleischer, Robert, and Wolf Schiele, *Der Klagefrauensarkophag aus Sidon* (Tübingen, 1983)

Fourrier, Sabine, 'The Iron Age City of Kition: The State of Research 85 Years after the Swedish Cyprus Expedition's Excavations', in *Ancient Cyprus Today: Museum Collections and New Research*, ed. Giorgos Bourogiannis and Christian Mühlenbock (Uppsala, 2016), pp. 129–39

Frangié-Joly, Dina, 'Perfumes, Aromatics, and Purple Dye: Phoenician Trade and Production in the Greco-Roman Period', *Journal of Eastern Mediterranean Archaeology and Heritage Studies*, IV/1 (2016), pp. 36–56

Frankenstein, Susan, 'The Phoenicians in the Far West: A Function of Neo-Assyrian Imperialism', in *Power and Propaganda: A Symposium on Ancient Empires*, ed. Mogens T. Larsen (Copenhagen, 1979), pp. 263–94

Fritze, Ronald H., *Invented Knowledge: False History, Fake Science and Pseudo-religions* (London, 2011)

Garbati, Giuseppe, 'Tyre, the Homeland: Carthage and Cadiz under the Gods' Eyes', in *Transformations and Crisis in the Mediterranean: 'Identity' and Interculturality in the Levant and Phoenician West during the 8th–5th Centuries BCE*, ed. Giuseppe Garbati and Tatiana Pedrazzi (Pisa and Rome, 2016), pp. 197–208

Genz, Hermann, and Hélène Sader, 'Bronze Age Funerary Practices in Lebanon', *Archaeology and History in Lebanon*, 26–27 (Autumn 2007–Spring 2009), pp. 258–83

Gruen, Erich S., *Rethinking the Other in Antiquity* (Princeton, NJ, 2011)

Gubel, Eric, 'Decoding Phoenician Art (I): Pharaoh Triumphant', *Rivista di Studi Fenici*, XL (2012), pp. 21–38

Guillaume, Philippe, 'Phoenician Coins for Persian Wars: Mercenaries, Anonymity and the First Phoenician Coinage', in *Phéniciens d'Orient et d'Occident: mélanges Josette Elayi*, ed. André Lemaire (Paris, 2014), pp. 225–32

Herrmann, Georgina, and Stuart Laidlaw, 'Assyrian Nimrud and the Phoenicians', *Archaeology International*, XVI (2013), pp. 84–95

Jigoulov, Vadim S., *The Social History of Achaemenid Phoenicia: Being a Phoenician, Negotiating Empires* (London and Oakville, CT, 2010)

Johnson, Philip A., 'Toward a Systematic Approach to the Study of Phoenician Economic Activity in the Western Mediterranean', in *Identity and Connectivity: Proceedings of the 16th Symposium on Mediterranean Archaeology, Florence, Italy, 1–3 March 2012. Soma 2012*, ed. Luca Bombardieri et al. (Oxford, 2013), pp. 667–76

Karageorghis, Vassos, *View from the Bronze Age: Mycenaean and Phoenician Discoveries at Kition* (New York, 1976)

Katzenstein, H. Jacob, *The History of Tyre, from the Beginning of the Second Millennium BCE until the Fall of the Neo-Babylonian Empire in 538 BCE* (Jerusalem, 1973)

Killebrew, Ann E., and Margreet Steiner, eds, *The Oxford Handbook of the Archaeology of the Levant, c. 8000–332 BCE* (Oxford, 2013)

Krahmalkov, Charles R., *A Phoenician-Punic Grammar* (Leiden, 2001)

Krings, Véronique, ed., *La Civilisation phénicienne et punique: manuel de recherche* (Leiden, 1994)

Kuhrt, Amélie, *The Ancient Near East, c. 3000–330 BC* (London and New York, 1995)

Lam, Joseph, 'The Invention and Development of the Alphabet', in *Visible Language: Inventions of Writing in the Ancient Middle East and Beyond*, ed. Christopher Woods, Geoff Emberling and Emily Teeter (Chicago, IL, 2015), pp. 189–201

Lincoln, Bruce, *Religion, Empire, and Torture: The Case of Achaemenian Persia, with a Postscript on Abu Ghraib* (Chicago, IL, 2007)

Lipiński, Edward, *Le Dictionnaire de la civilisation phénicienne et punique* (Turnhout, 1992)

—, *Itineraria Phoenicia*, Studia Phoenicia XVIII; Orientalia Lovaniensia Analecta 127 (Leuven, 2004)

López-Ruiz, Carolina, 'Tarshish and Tartessos Revisited: Textual Problems and Historical Implications', in *Colonial Encounters in Ancient Iberia: Phoenician, Greek, and Indigenous Relations*, ed. Michael Dietler and Carolina López-Ruiz (Chicago, IL, 2009), pp. 255–80

—, and Brian R. Doak, eds, *The Oxford Handbook of the Phoenician and Punic Mediterranean* (Oxford, 2019)

McMenamin, Mark A., *Phoenicians, Fakes and Barry Fell* (South Hadley, MA, 2000)

Markoe, Glenn E., 'The Emergence of Phoenician Art', *Bulletin of the American Schools of Oriental Research*, 279 (1990), pp. 13–26

—, *Phoenician Bronze and Silver Bowls from Cyprus and the Mediterranean*, Classical Studies 26 (Berkeley, CA, 1985)

—, *Phoenicians*, Peoples of the Past (London, 2000)

Melchiorri, Valentina, 'Child Cremation Sanctuaries ("Tophets") and Early Phoenician Colonisation: Markers of Identity?', in *Conceptualising Early Colonisation*, Proceedings of the International Congress, Rome, 21–23 June 2012, ed. Gert Jan Burgers, Lieve Donnellan and Valentino Nizzo (Brussels, 2016)

Moscati, Sabatino, ed., *The Phoenicians* (New York, 1999)

Niehr, Herbert, *Baʿalšamem* (Leuven and Paris, 2003)

Niemeyer, Hans Georg, 'The Phoenicians in the Mediterranean: A Non-Greek Model for Expansion and Settlement in Antiquity', in *Greek Colonists and Native Populations*, ed. Jean-Paul Descœudres (Oxford, 1990), pp. 469–89

Nigro, Lorenzo, 'Temples in Motya and their Levantine Prototypes: Phoenician Religious Architectural Tradition', in *Cult and Ritual on the Levantine Coast and its Impact on the Eastern Mediterranean Realm*, Proceedings of the International Symposium, Beirut, 2012, ed. Anne-Marie Maila-Afeiche (Beirut, 2015), pp. 83–108

Nunn, Astrid, *Der figürliche Motivschatz Phöniziens, Syriens und Transjordaniens vom 6. bis zum 4. Jahrhundert v. Chr*, Orbis Biblicus et Orientalis (Fribourg, 2000)

Oggiano, Ida, 'The Mediterranean Dimension of Levantine Coast in the 1st Millennium BC: Ancient Sea Routes, New Explorations and "Colonial" Foundations', in *Contexts of Early Colonization*, vol. I, ed. Lieve Donnellan, Valentino Nizzo and Gert-Jan Burgers (Rome, 2016), pp. 89–103

Orsingher, Adriano, 'Ritualized Faces: The Masks of the Phoenicians', in *The Physicality of the Other: Masks from the Ancient Near East and the Eastern Mediterranean*, ed. Angelika Berlejung and Judith E. Filitz (Tübingen, 2018), pp. 265–305

—, 'Phoenician and Punic Masks: What Are They and What Were They Good For?', *The Ancient Near East Today: Current News About the Ancient Past*, VII/4 (2019), accessible at www.asor.org

—, 'Understanding Tophets: A Short Introduction', *The Ancient Near East Today: Current News about the Ancient Past*, VI/2 (2018), accessible at www.asor.org

Peña, Victoria, Carlos G. Wagner and Alfredo Mederos, *La navegación fenicia: tecnología naval y derroteros* (Madrid, 2005)

Prag, Jonathan, 'Tyrannizing Sicily: The Despots Who Cried "Carthage!"', in *Private and Public Lies: The Discourse of Despotism and Deceit in the Graeco-Roman World*, ed. Andrew J. Turner, James H. Kim On Chong-Gossard and Frederik Juliaan Vervaet (Leiden, 2010), pp. 51–71

Pritchard, James Bennett, *Recovering Sarepta, a Phoenician City: Excavations at Sarafand, Lebanon, 1969–1974, by the University Museum of the University of Pennsylvania* (Princeton, NJ, 1978)

Quinn, Josephine Crawley, 'The Cultures of the Tophet: Identification and Identity in the Phoenician Diaspora', in *Cultural Identity in the Ancient Mediterranean*, ed. Eric Gruen (Los Angeles, CA, 2011), pp. 388–413

—, *In Search of the Phoenicians*, Miriam S. Balmuth Lectures in Ancient History and Archaeology (Princeton, NJ, 2017)

—, and Nicholas C. Vella, eds, *The Punic Mediterranean: Identities and Identification from Phoenician Settlement to Roman Rule* (Cambridge, 2014)

Reese, David S., 'Shells from Sarepta (Lebanon) and East Mediterranean Purple-dye Production', *Mediterranean Archaeology and Archaeometry*, X/1 (2010), pp. 113–41

Reyes, Andrew T., *Archaic Cyprus: A Study of the Textual and Archaeological Evidence* (Oxford, 1994)

Rich, Sara A., '"She Who Treads on Water": Religious Metaphor in Seafaring Phoenicia', *Journal of Ancient West and East*, XI (2012), pp. 19–34

Root, Margaret Cool, 'Circles of Artistic Programming: Strategies for Studying Creative Process at Persepolis', in *Investigating Artistic Environments in the Ancient Near East*, ed. Ann C. Gunter (Washington, DC, 1990), pp. 115–39

—, 'Imperial Ideology in Achaemenid Persian Art: Transforming the Mesopotamian Legacy', *Bulletin of the Canadian Society for Mesopotamian Studies*, 35 (2000), pp. 19–27

—, *The King and Kingship in Achaemenid Art: Essays on the Creation of an Iconography of Empire* (Leiden, 1979)

Sader, Hélène, *Iron Age Funerary Stelae from Lebanon*, Cuadernos de Arqueología Mediterránea 11 (Barcelona, 2005)

Sass, Benjamin, *The Alphabet at the Turn of the Millennium: The West Semitic Alphabet c. 1150–850 BCE* (Tel Aviv, 2005)

—, *The Genesis of the Alphabet and Its Development in the Second Millennium BC* (Wiesbaden, 1988)

Sommer, Michael, 'Shaping Mediterranean Economy and Trade: Phoenician Cultural Identities in the Iron Age', in *Material Culture and Social Identities in the Ancient World*, ed. Shelley Hales and Tamar Hodos (Cambridge, 2010), pp. 114–37

Stager, Lawrence, 'Phoenician Shipwrecks in the Deep Sea', in *PLOES: Sea Routes. Interconnections in the Mediterranean, 16th–6th C. BC*, Proceedings of the International Symposium Held at Rethymnon, Crete, 29 September–2 October 2002, ed. Nikolaos Chr. Stampolidēs and Vassos Karageorghis (Athens, 2003), pp. 222–47

Stampolidēs, Nikolaos Chr., *Sea routes: From Sidon to Huelva – Interconnections in the Mediterranean, 16th–6th C. BC* (Athens, 2003)

Winter, Irene J., 'Homer's Phoenicians: History, Ethnography, or Literary Trope? (a Perspective on Early Orientalism)', in *The Ages of Homer: A Tribute to Emily Townsend Vermeule*, ed. Jane B. Carter and Sarah P. Morris (Austin, TX, 1995), pp. 247–71

Woolmer, Mark, *Ancient Phoenicia: An Introduction* (Bristol, 2011)

—, *A Short History of the Phoenicians* (I. B. Tauris Short Histories, Kindle Edition, 2017)

Xella, Paolo, ed., *The Tophet in the Phoenician Mediterranean* (Verona, 2013)

Xella, Paolo, Josephine Crawley Quinn, Valentina Melchiorri and Peter Van Dommelen, 'Phoenician Bones of Contention', *Antiquity*, LXXXVII/338 (2013), pp. 1199–207

Yon, Marguerite, *Kition dans les textes: Testimonia littéraires et épigraphiques et Corpus des Inscriptions*, vol. V (Paris, 2004)

ACKNOWLEDGEMENTS

This book could not have been possible without the kind assistance, advice and direction of many individuals. I would like to express my deep gratitude to Todd Bolen, Daniel Brunson, Brian Doak, Anne Fisher, Jessica Garloff, Mark Garrison, Steve Lansdale, Carolina López-Ruiz, Ida Oggiano, Adriano Orsingher, Margaret Cool Root and Brian Schmidt. Many thanks also to Esther Rodríguez, who helped with the fabulous maps for this project. Reaktion Books has been immensely supportive and accommodating, and I would like to thank my editor David Watkins for his encouragement and direction. I would also like to acknowledge the financial support provided for this project by the Maryland Institute College of Art, Baltimore. Much gratitude goes to my family, Maria, Aleksandra and Anastasia, for their patience, love and support as I battled words and sentences. Thank you, Mum and Dad (1939–2021), for your love and encouragement. Dad, even though you did not get to see this book published, I cherished your support. I am grateful to Robert H. Greene (1975–2020), a dear friend and an outstanding historian who passed away too soon, for reading the chapters of this book. Robert's insights have made the prose smoother, and his patience was remarkable as he advised me in straightening out some of the more unwieldy sentences. Nevertheless, all errors are mine.

PHOTO ACKNOWLEDGEMENTS

The author and publishers wish to express their thanks to the below sources of illustrative material and/or permission to reproduce it. Every effort has been made to contact copyright holders; should there be any we have been unable to reach or to whom inaccurate acknowledgements have been made, please contact the publishers, and full adjustments will be made to subsequent printings.

Courtesy of the author: p. 33; Todd Bolen/BiblePlaces.com: pp. 35, 89, 117, 119, 120, 129, 135, 153, 159; CNG: pp. 98, 107 (top), 113; Diego Delso: p. 34; G. Eric and Edith Matson Photograph Collection: p. 85; Julian P. Guffog: p. 65; Heritage Auctions: p. 104; Jona Lendering: p. 160; I. Luca: p. 83; Oriental Institute of the University of Chicago: pp. 81, 82; M. Rais: p. 201; A. D. Riddle/BiblePlaces.com: pp. 41, 86, 90, 101, 125, 127, 131, 136, 137, 143, 156, 157; Esther Rodrigues: pp. 14, 15, 170, 175, 178, 187, 189, 194; M. C. Root: p. 105; Wolfgang Sauber: p. 133; Jerzy Strzelecki: p. 130; H. Zell: p. 166.

Page numbers in *italics* refer to illustrations